Seabury Place

Also by Daniel Wolfe

Cold Ground's Been My Bed: A Korean War Memoir

Seabury Place

A Bronx Memoir

Daniel Wolfe

iUniverse, Inc.
New York Lincoln Shanghai

Seabury Place
A Bronx Memoir

Copyright © 2007 by Daniel Wolfe

iUniverse books may be ordered through booksellers or by contacting:

iUniverse
2021 Pine Lake Road, Suite 100
Lincoln, NE 68512
www.iuniverse.com
1-800-Authors (1-800-288-4677)

Because of the dynamic nature of the Internet, any Web addresses or links contained in this book may have changed since publication and may no longer be valid.

The views expressed in this work are solely those of the author and do not necessarily reflect the views of the publisher, and the publisher hereby disclaims any responsibility for them.

The events in this memoir are true to the best of the author's recollection and research.

Cover photo: Dan and Harold Wolfe in company clothes, 1934
Cover design: Joan Olson, Petaluma, California

ISBN: 978-0-595-44043-6 (pbk)
ISBN: 978-0-595-88366-0 (ebk)

Printed in the United States of America

I am deeply indebted to my wife, Sheila, my daughter, Sharon, my son, Marc, and my late son, David, for the warm environment full of humor that they created throughout the years, as we evolved into a loving family. David was an extremely talented writer who would have grilled me on every sentence in this book. I look forward to having Marc, inquisitive from birth, drain all the details from my evaporating reservoir. I hope I haven't embarrassed Sharon with some of the gross events of my early life.

To them, I dedicate this memoir.

Contents

Preface

"If something is forgotten, it never happened."

—Michael Crichton

There are so many stories that were interred with the death of my parents. After they passed, so many questions about their unusual lives were left unanswered. There will never be another generation like them. In the anecdotes that follow, I have tried to cull from a fading memory some highlights of my life and theirs.

I want to thank Jerry Kaplan and Alvin Lakind, my friends since junior high school, who have filled in the gaps of our memorable childhood and adolescence. I also want to thank my writing teachers, Dr. Ruth Messinger and Maudy Benz at Duke University, Cathy Switzer at Sarah Lawrence College, and Joan Potter at the Hudson Valley Writers Center, along with all my classmates over the years, for their patience in hearing my stories and offering their suggestions for improving and clarifying my memoirs. I am indebted to my cousin Anna Shereff, her son Jesse Shereff, and his wife, Rochelle, for their substantial contribution toward publishing *Seabury Place*.

Finally, I want to thank Zipporah Collins, the editor of my first book, *Cold Ground's Been My Bed: A Korean War Memoir*. In spite of dodging flying shrapnel and bullets, she unsnapped her armored vest and flipped off her helmet to edit *Seabury Place: A Bronx Memoir*. Thank you, dear friend.

Childhood

My Carriage

My earliest memory of our Stebbins Avenue apartment in the Bronx is of our childless neighbor, Mrs. Levine. She was short and had a squeaky voice. She playfully chased after me when I was two, and I would hide under the kitchen table. Pretending I couldn't be found, she would leave the kitchen bewildered. After she was gone, I would holler "Finn, Finn," from under the table. She ran throughout our apartment in a frantic hunt, shouting "Where is that little devil?" With great joy, I would crawl out. Taken by surprise, she cried "Oh, there he is!" and then gave me a big hug. All the fun came to an end when my family moved five blocks east to Seabury Place.

Two-year-olds aren't very social animals. They eat, they entertain their parents and relatives, they soil their diapers, and they sleep. In a group, they usually busy themselves with their own activities, completely oblivious of their peers.

Seabury Place was not yet a friendly environment to me. The sidewalks were different. My apartment building, towering eighty feet over the sidewalk, was different. The fire escapes zigzagging down its front puzzled me, and a stoop leading to the entrance doors was a feature unknown on Stebbins Avenue. Adjacent to the building, was a large vacant lot with overgrown weeds and dragonflies buzzing over puddles. Their buzz terrified me. My father called them *schneiders* (tailors) because they sounded like an electric sewing machine. I hadn't met the neighbors, and where was "Finn"?

One sunny day I was toddling around the apartment, probably fingering anything that projected from the walls, when Ma said it was nap time. She took me down a flight of steps and placed me in my carriage on the sidewalk outside our apartment. The carriage had a black folding hood, and its thin plywood sides, painted dark green on the outside, were unpainted on the inside. Since the carriage was positioned right below our front window, Ma felt it was safe to leave me alone in it.

3

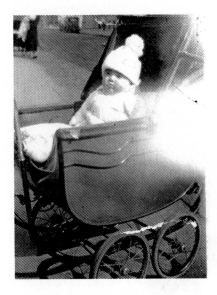

*My brother, Harold, in 1928, ensconced in
the carriage that terrified me five years later.*

When I awoke, I saw the raw plywood sides of the carriage walls
enveloping me, the blue sky, and part of the black hood above me. Where
was Ma? My screams were lubricated with tears. She came running to calm
me down, bearing in her hands the special-occasion navy blue pants and
matching jacket my aunt had knitted for me. The jacket's ruby red glass
buttons, like tiny stoplights, usually cheered me up, but this time they
were just red buttons. Soon, however, my sobs became whimpers, and the
whimpers ebbed. With her hand in mine, Ma and I walked to the empty
lot next to our building. Secure in her presence, I stooped among the
weeds to pick bright yellow dandelion flowers. Ma knotted them into a
bouquet. We walked to the end of the lot to admire the large, curving, colorful billboards.

Upon returning to our building, I saw the green-and-black carriage waiting near the wall. I gripped my mother's hand tightly, remembering my
recent trauma in that green box. Ma kept the carriage in the cellar. She
wisely asked me to help her bring it down the steps. Holding onto the bottom of its handlebar I cautiously renewed my friendship with the beast. The
carriage became no longer "a green box," but it took a while for me to regain
the comfort I once treasured and had lost within its raw plywood walls.

Pa and Me

I was sitting on the stoop waiting to be lifted to the next plateau: mature short pants and a buttoned cotton shirt. But with the heat and humidity of August in New York City, my childish navy blue sunsuit with a little white sailboat sewn onto its bib gave me a sparrow's freedom of movement. It was the summer uniform of the day for this four-year-old. So, I delayed passage to maturity in favor of comfort.

My brother, Harold, was seven, three years older. He played with the older boys in the neighborhood. No time for parents. Saturday was my time with Pa. We were going to Crotona Park, two blocks from my apartment house. Boston Road, whose surface was knobbed with cobblestones bisected by shiny steel trolley tracks, was a pedestrian's nightmare. Pa grasped my hand and did not let go until we reached the other side.

Upon arriving at the park, like a dog unleashed I ran ahead on a dirt path toward the playground. The route was cluttered with overgrown weeds and scattered with small rocks. Its edges were defined by a line of six-inch-high metal loops, many of which had fallen over—in spite of or because of maintenance by WPA (federal Works Progress Administration) employees. Finally, I arrived at the playground.

At the end of two thin linked chains each children's swing hung suspended like a wooden box. I lifted the retaining bar on its metal track and squiggled onto the swing seat. By the time I had lowered the bar and was secure in my chair, my father had arrived.

"Pa, could you give me a push?"

Where did his endless energy come from? This little man pushed and pushed in an unbroken cadence until *I* was fatigued. When the novelty of swinging wore off, I pulled up the bar, lowered my feet, and slid out of my seat.

As we left the playground, the seat of an errant swing glanced off the side of my father's head. I had never seen blood on him, except for the occasional shaving cut. Now, suddenly, blood was streaming down the side of his face. I was shocked. Would all the blood flow out of his body?

I stood helplessly as a passerby offered his handkerchief. It was a minor wound, but the incident made me realize that a parent could be injured.

When Pa regained his composure, we headed toward Crotona Lake. The lake was the stage for our usual musical interlude. We each picked a blade of grass and tucked it between the lengths of our two thumbs. With our hands in prayer, we blew into the space between the adjacent thumbs, producing a dissonant duet. No matter how much we practiced, we produced the same squeaks we had made the previous week, but it was fun.

With the concert over, I looked around and then stopped to pee near a tree. My sun suit had a small slit at the crotch with a little flap to keep the breezes out. I pulled out the flap, made a few short, strong squirts, and folded the flap back in. Pa continued his slow walk as if he were embarrassed. He probably was.

We walked around the four-acre lake to reach his friends, who, like Pa, were unemployed. In 1934, not many households were supported by a weekly paycheck. Men wanted to work, but where were the jobs? Home Relief was available, but these men had too much pride to accept the dole.

My uncle from Canada called Pa's friends the "Parliament." They discussed the virtues of socialism, condemned their landlords, analyzed current events, and spoke longingly of the tiny shtetls (villages) in Europe from which they had come.

While they debated these topics, I drifted off to the lake. With a black thread, a bobbing cork, and a worm pierced by a bent pin, the older boys were fishing for "sunnies." Most of these little fish they threw back, but some of the boys had jars proudly displaying their catch. When would I be able to do that? Maybe when I graduated from short pants to knickers?

Eventually, Parliament recessed, its agenda exhausted. Pa and I took the path toward home. Boston Road with its trolley cars and autos threatened. Pa took me by the hand and, when the light turned green, led me back across the cobblestones to our apartment house.

The Last Truck This Winter

It was a large metal baby crib painted dark brown to resemble oak. The gates on each side slid up and down, but as I grew older they remained permanently down. For my eighth birthday, Ma had promised I would get a folding bed. Any change is exciting for a seven-year-old but especially one that elevates his maturity status. Oh boy! From now on I would be sleeping in a folding bed just like my older brother. Was sleeping in a crib embarrassing to me? No, I didn't know the official age for graduating to a full-length bed. I never visited my friends' crowded apartments nor did they visit mine. Therefore I had no standard for an upgrade to an adult bed.

Our entire family slept in one bedroom. I slept near the window; my parents' bed was at the center of the room. Mrs. Gelernter, from the fourth floor, had given them the headboard, which stood against the wall facing my crib. Once, some ornament had been pasted at its center, but it had been removed before she gave the headboard to us. The remaining adhesive collected dust and pollutants in the air, leaving a grotesque form that resembled a scary human skull. I could have turned to face a blank wall but Ma had put the pillow against that wall, and that was where I left it. My brother's bed was near the left wall as we entered the room. He never mentioned the skull. My Uncle Shrolleh slept on a single bed in the living room.

My crib was adjacent to the window that faced the street in our ground floor apartment. Directly below my windowsill, a tan, five-foot-square wooden panel was set into the wall of our building. It had a small, dirty, opaque window in the center. What was behind this panel? Why was it there? Was it intended to be a window for the janitor's apartment? Was the wooden panel a temporary patch until new bricks filled the void?

The puzzle was solved one day when I was home from school with the flu. Not a molecule of air could pass through my nasal passages. My bladder was marinating in tea, lemon, honey, and a dissolved aspirin. I raised myself to adjust my damp, twisted union suit, which had coiled around my body from tossing all night. This union suit was my underwear during the day and pajamas at night. It was a one-piece, tightly woven, off-white cotton garment buttoning up to my neck in the front. A trap-door opening in the rear was highlighted by a button at the center. This button habitually sought warmth and comfort by burrowing into the crack of my rear end, so I had to constantly pull it out. Since the suit had no sleeves and the legs were only knee length, it was intended for summer, but for me it was an all-season garment. In summer I rolled up the legs so they wouldn't extend below my short pants.

How long can a recovering seven-year-old remain in bed, waterlogged and sweating? What was there to do? It was early in the morning. My third-grade class would be opening our blue-and-orange readers to join Peter and Peggy in a strange world of cars, dogs, and a wooden dining room table, in a home set behind a lawn and framed with bushes.

Let's see what's going on outside, I decided. I wrapped myself in my blanket and leaned on the sill below the cold window. Where is Mrs. Banner going with an empty milk bottle? Doesn't she know that Mr. Kosloff, the grocer, doesn't open until nine? There she goes, back to her apartment. Mr. Pinsky appeared, with his dirty white apron clinging to his overcoat; his wife behind him had just opened his barren fruit and vegetable store. Through the open door I could see Pinsky sitting on his wobbly oak chair examining heads of iceberg lettuce at the threshold of death. He tried to resuscitate them by peeling off their wilted brown leaves, while agonizing over discarding a bunch of rubbery carrots. His chipped white enamel pan was sitting on the cold cement floor. Would he fill it with heads of lettuce that had survived and lean them against the rear panel of the dreary wooden stand supported by the front window of his store?

Next door, Henry Lee was always spraying and ironing laundry under a lightbulb dangling from a chain. He wrapped the finished items in neat rectangles of tan paper with an identifying pink slip stamped with bold, black numbers. When did this man sleep? Who were his customers? The neighborhood residents finished their own laundry without that fancy tan wrapping and printed pink slip.

Adjacent to Henry Lee's laundry was Mr. Luboff's butcher store. It was not open yet. He would have had the same number of customers had he opened at 3:00 pm. Obviously it was not a thriving business.

Mr. Kosloff awakened Seabury Place by rolling his empty, battered, cylindrical metal milk cans out to the edge of the sidewalk. They would be picked up and replaced with full cans during a milk delivery. He would open soon.

It was a morning like any other. Wait, what was this? A big black chain-driven Mack coal truck pulled up alongside the curb directly in front of my window. In tall white block letters, BURNS was printed on the side panels of its overflowing container.

The driver removed two large, thick wooden blocks from his truck and pushed them against the curb in the gutter, so the truck could back up onto them and ease onto the sidewalk. To get a better view, I placed my nose against the cold window. The truck's container slowly rose to expose small, glistening pieces of coal. As it continued to climb I jumped back, fearing it would crash into my window. Then the container came to a halt.

The driver hopped out of the truck. His tan calf-high boots, covered with coal dust, added to the he-man appearance every seven-year-old boy longed for. He pulled out the mysterious wooden panel in the wall beneath my window, and directed a shiny steel chute from the truck into the cellar. Then, returning to the rear of the truck, he lifted a small door. The nuggets created a noisy, dusty, black haze as they crushed against the rear of the container, skidded through the door, and slid down the chute into the cellar. Aha! So the coal for the furnace was stored in a room directly below our apartment. Suddenly, our apartment became the most important apartment in the building. I had discovered a secret. None of the boys knew about this one.

The truck appeared to be empty. Apparently the driver was through. No, not yet. He climbed into the empty container with a corn broom and swept out the residue of coal, leaving an oily sheen on the shimmering steel interior of the container.

On rubbery legs I ran to my mother, who was talking to our neighbor, Mrs. Suslow.

"Ma, Ma! Did you see how the man sent a full truck of coal into our basement?"

"Go get your blanket. Who goes around with underwear when he has the flu? Look at him. He'll get pneumonia."

"But the coal ..."

"The coal? Coal? The way Tekula gives steam, it will be the last coal truck we'll see this winter."

Ma was probably right about the truck, but this memorable morning temporarily chased away all my discomfort from the flu.

Ma in the New World

In 1910, Ma had set off for Canada from Shtayotchisik. a tiny shtetl in Lithuania that she said was "as big as a yawn." All alone at the harbor in Antwerp, clutching her ticket in one hand and her single piece of cardboard luggage in the other, she boarded a ship to another world. Could there have been a more innocent seventeen-year-old? She had been reared in a cloistered micro-shtetl where religion blended with superstition, where her life was permeated by poverty and the neighbors' venomous anti-Semitism. It had to be better in the New World.

Who paid for her ticket? How did they get the money? Where was it purchased? I wish I had asked. How many times have we said, "I wish I had asked," after a parent or other loved one has passed away?

With her aunt's address in Montreal and a dream of a better life, she stepped off the gangplank in Halifax, Nova Scotia. While waiting at the station for a train to Montreal, she purchased an odd but beautiful red fruit. She stashed this novelty until pangs of hunger reminded her of it. On the train she took a bite. The tart, unfamiliar taste of the tomato disappointed her. Strange food in a strange country, she thought, wondering what other surprises were in store for her.

Her Aunt Dora greeted Ma at the Montreal station. Dora's husband had recently left her for a "perfumed fortune-teller" (Dora's words) working in his penny arcade. Although Dora had known Ma only as an infant, she was pleased to have a companion.

Upon leaving the station, Ma was surprised and overwhelmed at the sight of the awesome, huge office buildings and the bustle in the streets. She longed for her tiny shtetl with its straw roofs, muddy streets, green fields, and familiar faces. The cars startled her and led her to ask, "Where are the horses? Does everyone own a machine?"

Left: My maternal grandmother, Ada, and three of her children, Esther, Louis, and Dorothy, arrive in Canada from Ponovez, Lithuania, in 1924.

Below: The Waliak gang's all here! **Front row, left to right:** *Dorothy, Rose (Ma), Esther, and Louis.* **Back row:** *Ma's brothers Morris and Hymie, 1925.*

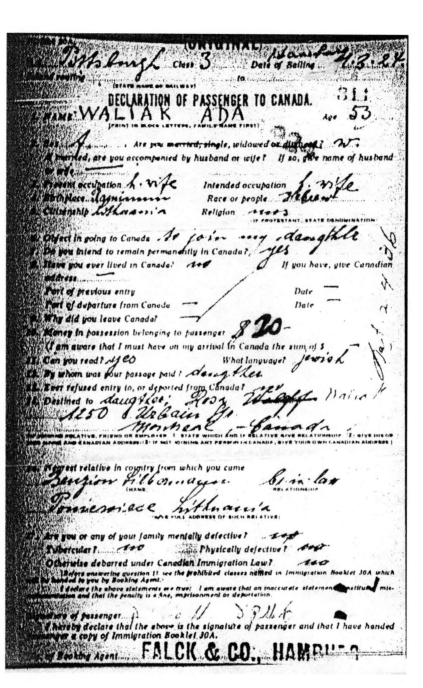

Document from Ada Waliak's passage to Canada.

Pa's first date with Ma in 1923. He shared the price for the tickets.

Let the horas begin! Ma and Pa's wedding, 1926. **Front row, left to right:** *Ma's sister Dorothy, the bride, Ma's sister Esther.* **Back row:** *Ma's brother Morris, the groom, Ma's brother Hymie.*

Pointing to a bank she quipped, "I think there are more people in that building than there are in all of Shtayotchisik."

Aunt Dora was happy to have a young and ebullient niece after a miserable life with her estranged husband. A friend of Dora's trained Ma to be a "bunchmaker" in a cigar factory. What was a bunchmaker? Maybe she cut and rolled tobacco leaves into bunches; maybe she rolled and cut cigars. I wish I had asked. Whatever she did, I'm sure it was done conscientiously and well.

She banked almost every cent she earned. Within three years, she had saved enough to send for her two younger brothers, Morris and Hymie. Their cousin Anna immediately found work for Morris at her brother-in-law's dress factory. Hymie was a free spirit who refused to be confined within a factory's walls. He sold newspapers, cigarettes, and candy on a commuter train between Montreal and the suburb of St. Jerome. Within a few years Ma, Morris, and Hymie had accumulated enough money to send for their mother, Ada, two sisters, Esther and Dorothy, and their youngest brother, Louis. Tutored by their cousin Anna, the two youngest completed elementary school. Esther went to work in a dress factory.

Ma learned that her shtetl boyfriend (and cousin), Morris Wolf, was living and working in New York City. Both of them had had the courage to leave their families and make the trip to the *goldeneh medina* (golden land). When I asked her how she discovered that Pa was living in New York City, she replied, "You ask God, and he answers."

After an exchange of letters, Pa visited Montreal to renew their shtetl romance. They were married in Montreal in 1924. With her mother, two sisters, and three brothers, and Pa's two sisters and brother present, along with their immigrant friends, it was like a jolly shtetl wedding.

Pa and His Father

As a boy, Pa had been an excellent student who qualified for intense religious instruction at the famous Ponovez Yeshiva in a city adjacent to his shtetl. However, his family had no money for this luxury, so his education ended at age thirteen when he became a bar mitzvah. Within a few months, he was sent to a starving tailor in another shtetl *tsu essen teg* (literally, to eat days; figuratively, to apprentice in return for three sparse meals a day and a straw bed in the tailor's house). My mother later claimed that all my father's digestive problems originated in this tailor's *shtibble* (tiny shack).

In 1912, at age seventeen, Pa packed his religious education and what he had learned from the tailor, along with his ragged clothing, and immigrated to the United States in the steerage section of a German liner. The passengers in steerage were not permitted on the deck or in the dining room, where they might mingle with the "legitimate" people. The steerage cuisine consisted of salted herring, onions, and potatoes, lowered in wooden barrels to be distributed among the crowd by a member of the crew. Pa said that the crewman addressed the passengers as *"verfluchte Juden"* (damned Jews). I could imagine the confidence this gave Pa when he stepped off the boat as an immigrant in the New World.

At first, Pa shared a room with two recent immigrants who lived on Allen Street on the Lower East Side of Manhattan. Occasionally he found work. He earned his combat ribbons with oak-leaf clusters in his own war on poverty. Pa worked as an operator (a freelance tailor) and a finisher of women's coats, carrying his own sewing machine (actually one he borrowed) around from job to job, with no steady employment. The factory employer would furnish him with a wooden table that had a cut-out space where Pa inserted the sewing machine. A leather strip around the wheel that moved the needle was connected to a treadle below. He rocked the treadle with his foot for ten hours a day, grateful that he was employed.

My father, just behind the man in the hat carrying the sign,
marching against sweatshop conditions in 1935 with the boys from his Parliament.

The International Ladies' Garment Workers' Union (ILGWU) was in its infancy, testing its first toddling steps. The tragic Triangle Factory fire boldly underlined employees' primitive working conditions, low pay, and mistreatment by the employers. Union-led protests, strikes, and lockouts were commonplace, further reducing Pa's earnings. He recalled the day there was a lockout in his shop. The employers refused to allow the employees to work unless they agreed to the bosses' terms. The union called a strike. Strikebreaking goons came, and violence ensued. Many of the strikers were beaten. Pa was arrested. The strikers were herded into police vans and incarcerated until a hearing the next day. The compassionate police sent out for coffee and ham sandwiches for the prisoners. Most had the coffee. Ham was not kosher, so the prisoners wouldn't touch it.

The ILGWU supported the workers' early battles, eventually winning more labor-friendly legislation; the struggle continues to this day.

Within a year, Pa sent his father a ticket to come to America. My grandfather arrived with empty pockets and no marketable skills. He had been a farmer. What does a farmer do in New York City? He found a menial job in a leather belt factory, but it required employees to work on Saturday. He left in the first week when he understood that he would have to work on

Just a couple of studs. Uncle Shrolleh is greeted by his brother, Morris (Pa), after arriving in New York from the continent.

the Jewish Sabbath. Within a month, without telling Pa, he bought a ticket to return to his shtetl. Pa arrived home one afternoon to find a note from his father saying he was leaving on a boat early that evening. Pa hurried to the dock and found his father preparing to board.

"Pa! What is it? Why are you leaving?"

"This is a godless country!" my grandfather replied.

With these words, he boarded the ship and returned to his shtetl, never to be seen or heard from again by his family in the United States.

Following this disturbing experience, Pa sent his brother, Shrolleh, a ticket to come to New York. Two years later, the brothers pooled their money and sent for their sisters, Rosie and Fannie. Both girls spent their entire careers behind sewing machines and never married. Shrolleh left my father to work in Botwinick's Diner in Bayonne, New Jersey, but he was to return to our fold.

A Family of Five

Ma was reluctant to leave her family in Montreal, but there was no work for Pa in that city, so, once they were married, she moved to New York. First the newlyweds lived in Pa's apartment on the Lower East Side, but soon they rented an apartment in the Bronx on Prospect Avenue, a broad, beautiful boulevard. Ma couldn't understand why the rent was so low ($15 per month) for such an attractive neighborhood. When summer rolled around, she learned the answer. Behind her apartment building was a stable inundated with flies enjoying the warm weather and feeding on the horses' droppings. Flies that couldn't find a seat on the dung spilled over to the kitchens in my parents' apartment building.

It was the worst of times. The Great Depression of the mid-1930s had everyone "tearing their pockets"—my father's expression for idle hands due to unemployment.

It was the best of times. My parents were young and healthy. To assist with the monthly rent, Ma and Pa took in Lilly and Moe Gerstenfeld as boarders for a monthly contribution of $5. Mr. Gerstenfeld eventually found a job that enabled him to rent his own apartment.

My parents left the flies and moved to Stebbins Avenue in the Bronx, where the rent was $18 a month. But who was going to fill the gap left by the Gerstenfelds? Pa's brother, Shrolleh, gave up working as a busboy at Botwinick's Diner in Bayonne, New Jersey, to move in with them and look for a job in the Bronx. The Loew's Spooner movie theater needed an employee at its lower-level candy stand, and, even though the stand was located indoors, Shrolleh, a fresh-air fanatic, took the job. Now, when asked what he did for a living, he replied, "kendy sailehsmen," with the dignity of a doctor identifying himself as a neurosurgeon. The salary was minimal, as was his contribution to our household, but every bit helped.

Shrolleh was there to taunt and amuse us until the day we left.

Left: Harold and me, ages four and one, 1931. Who would have thought that our hairlines would resemble furry horseshoes thirty years later?

Below: Our new apartment building, 1540 Seabury Place.

In June 1927, my brother, Harold, was added to the household. A further drain on my family's resources occurred when I was born three years later as the Great Depression took hold of the country.

In 1932, we moved five blocks east to 1540 Seabury Place, apartment 1. Three steps led into the building, and then a short flight of stairs brought us to our new apartment, which had one bedroom, a living room, a kitchen, and a bathroom. My brother slept on a folding bed on one side of my parents' bed, and I slept in a crib on the other side. Shrolleh slept in the living room on a single bed. Throughout those years I never heard my parents or my brother complain about our cramped space or their cramped finances.

The new address brought us closer to Crotona Park, where I could run freely and climb up and down the Indian Rock overlooking the lake, while my father participated in debates with the Parliament below.

Ma's Economic Acumen

My mother was a full-time housewife. Her economic savvy in the kitchen and at the market could not be matched by an employer's salary. Yesterday's bread at Maeger's Bakery was 3 cents a pound; fresh bread was 5 cents a pound. A five-pound rye bread disappeared in two days at our house. "Tomorrow, fresh bread will be yesterday's bread," she said.

Ma had the knack of making Pa feel as if he were the master of the house. Running the show very quietly, she ruled from her seat of power, the kitchen—although she never did take a seat there.

With five mouths to feed during the Great Depression, making maximum use of minimum income in running a household might have required a doctorate in economics, but Ma, unschooled, could have given graduate seminars to Alan Greenspan or Milton Friedman on money management.

Our garbage pail was a doubled brown paper bag sitting under the sink waiting for our leftovers. Sometimes it was a number 10 can, but where could that have come from? Canned food never crossed our threshold into the apartment.

The theme of most PTA meetings Ma attended was proper nutrition for a low-income household. Dr. Carlton Fredericks, a popular nutritionist, addressed the women at these meetings. Ma never cut his class and always arrived on time. Processing the data she had gleaned, she provided us with well-balanced, economical, wholesome meals never sullied by canned ingredients.

"Who knows what they put in those cans? Do the tomatoes inside the can look like the tomatoes I bring home from Jennings Street Market? Do they taste like the tomatoes from Jennings Street Market? Everything is red inside the can, maybe even a red worm. Cans are for fancy ladies who go to work. Here you get real tomatoes."

Ma waited for bargains in the perishables. The fruit and vegetable vendors at the Jennings Street Market lowered their prices toward Sunday evening, anticipating a fresh food delivery on Monday morning. As Ma hunted for produce bargains, Mrs. Miller, who owned the fruit stand, collected the soft yellow, orange, or red papers wrapped around the citrus fruits and gave them to Ma. They were recycled in our home as toilet tissue.

One of our frequent lunches was sour cream and bananas with rye bread and butter. When a small amount of sour cream was left in its container, Ma would slice up a banana, wipe the container clean with it, and transfer it to a bowl. The container was left as empty as the day it was manufactured.

She brought home a treat one day, a dozen cellophane-wrapped packages of Dugan's chocolate cupcakes. Before this, the only cookies and cakes in our kitchen were those that came out of her oven. They were neither iced nor filled with cream, just plain—but excellent. Honey cake with tea was our Friday night treat. But seeking a different taste she walked about two miles to Ward's Baking Company on Webster Avenue, where day-old returns sold for a fraction of their original price. We were enchanted with the cupcakes but soon were supersaturated by their sickly sweetness. Ma's delicious, wholesome, memorable, preservative-free masterpieces—honey cake, apple cake, and poppy seed cookies—returned to our table.

When I asked for her challah recipe, her finely calibrated measurements should have been inscribed in the annals of the Department of Weights and Measures.

"Three hoifenns [handfuls] of flour and some eggs, more if they're small."

"Yeast? How much?"

"You break it up and see. If you need more, put it in."

"Sugar?"

"If it's not sweet enough this time, use more the next time." The loaves she baked for the Sabbath have yet to be duplicated in any bakery in spite of her perpetual lament, "This time it didn't come out so good. Maybe next time it will be better."

Until her death, she presented Dr. Friedman with a challah at every office visit, along with the warning not to share it with his nurses.

The Kitchen Table

Ma served her meals on our metal-topped, white enamel table, a legacy from the previous tenant in the apartment. A pattern of linked blue diamonds ran along the outer edge and formed a large diamond shape in the center. A long wooden apron descended from the tabletop, preventing our legs from fitting under the table, so we had to sit a foot and a half away. After a meal, our pants resembled a Jackson Pollock abstract. Fortunately, we wore washable pants. Not a garment in our house ever went to the dry cleaner.

Ma didn't have a problem trying to get her knees under the table. She never sat at the table. Like a waitress in a diner, she served the meal and waited. Perhaps there might be an additional request. Whatever remained from the meal supplemented the small portion of the entrée she had left for herself. A glass of tea, made from yesterday's tea bag, along with a sugar cube lodged between her cheek and a molar, was her dessert.

The blue diamond design at the center of our table was the bull's-eye for Ma's cutlery blitz. She strafed the table with a pile of flatware before each meal. We selected our forks and knives from somewhere within the tangled mass.

One day a replacement table became a possibility at last! Mrs. Suslow, from apartment 3, burst into our apartment with the news, "Macy's has a sale on kitchen tables!"

But if we got a new table how would we get rid of the blue diamond monster? We could hardly budge it. The layers of paint caked on the legs and apron through the years weighed more than the table. Shlepping it downstairs would require the services of two world-class weight lifters. Nonetheless, a new table arrived, and my father, my uncle, my brother, and I somehow managed to slide our old one down the flights of stairs and onto the street, leaving a trail of enamel chips. Without knowing its pedigree, someone adopted it before the Department of Sanitation came the following day.

I knew that Ma's concept of setting the table didn't conform to Amy Vanderbilt's, but why disrupt the flow that had moved along so nicely for years? Sheila, my fiancée, was invited to dinner on a Friday night. She took me aside and asked why there was a mound of cutlery at the center of the table.

"So we can use them," I replied.

Her visit caused the knives, forks, and spoons to be shifted to their proper places on the table. It took a while for me to learn to reach for the cutlery at the side of my plate instead of in the center of the table.

Just as Ma learned from Sheila, Sheila learned from Ma. She learned never to go food shopping with her. On one early occasion, Sheila accompanied Ma and me to the supermarket. Ma's visit to the fruit or vegetable section was like a geologist's foray in search of ore. She had to find the mother lode or there was no sale. Ma was pushing the cart as we entered her turf. Sheila, fond of corn, selected five ears, without removing their husks to examine them, and threw them into the cart. Bagging the closest ten blue plums followed. Ma shot me a glance indicating that this would never do. As Sheila stopped to select some cherries, Ma stealthily removed an ear of corn. She lifted a husk, interrupting a green caterpillar feasting on the kernels. The soft plums and ears of corn were replaced by her choice selections. After this trauma, Sheila never again accompanied us to the supermarket.

When Ma visited, she would ask about the cost of peaches, plums, or apples at our supermarket. Sheila's stock reply was 69 cents a pound. I anticipated and received a questioning glare from Ma. To Sheila, this was amusement rather than criticism. Ma knew what was going on but was smart enough to keep quiet.

Pa's Bread and Wine

Pa was easy to please. Any meal served him was delicious. He never left a crumb. Without complaint, he took the same sandwich to work for twenty-five years: farmer cheese in a sliced bialy. Once I said to him, "Pa, there are other cheeses that fit inside a bialy besides farmer cheese."

"I know," he said, "but farmer cheese doesn't give me heartboining."

Heartburn was the bane of his existence. One day, Pa was eating his bialy with coffee at the Automat (a New York cafeteria) when heartburn attacked him. Maybe it was the onions in the pothole of the bialy. Always prepared, Pa ran to the bathroom with his new antacid, Bisodol. Without reading the instructions, he gulped a powdery tablespoonful of the remedy. Fortunately, another man was in the bathroom, because my father began to choke on the white powder, which should have been dissolved in a glass of water.

After he related this traumatic experience to us he shouted, "The Bisodol shtinkt" (stinks). He returned to his reliable milk of magnesia.

Ma and Pa never went to the movies; they felt it was an unnecessary luxury. Their entertainment was a weekly variety show presented by a large group of friends at nearby Crotona Park. Some were singers, one man played the balalaika, and another, the accordion. The master of ceremonies told humorous stories of life in the shtetl.

One of the singers was Fay, a very attractive friend of my parents'. She invested her husband's hard-earned dollars in voice training, but invested no time in cleaning her apartment. One evening, while she was singing, an admirer approached her husband and said, "Your wife sings beautifully."

"Yes," he replied. "*Mein veib zingt, und die* cockroaches *tahntzen*" (my wife sings and the cockroaches dance).

Fay pictured herself as an entertainer. Cleaning an apartment was not in the repertoire of a performing artist. Later in the year she went into a deep

Pa on Passover in 1940, with a Manischewitz-induced smile.
Left to right: Aunt Rosie, Aunt Fannie, Shrolleh, and Pa.

depression that her doctor called "a nervous breakdown." The alarm was sounded; Ma answered the call. One day a week she would go to Fay's apartment to clean and tidy up. Eventually, the family moved to another part of the Bronx, and that was the last we heard of them.

Did Pa drink? Did a Jew drink in those days? Only on Passover. In the early days he fermented Concord grapes in a tall gray crock, added sugar, and that was our Passover wine. As he aged, he discovered it was easier to buy Manischewitz than to make the wine at home. He supplemented the wine with a small glass of plum brandy, slivovitz, the precursor to the atom bomb.

Passover was a major event at my home. We borrowed a baby carriage from a neighbor and went to the Jennings Street Market to get "the order"—our food for Passover. I was given the privilege of pushing home the buggy laden with Passover goodies.

We didn't have a formal seder, but our dinner was as festive as any seder that followed the prescribed rituals. My two aunts, Fannie and Rosie, who lived in Brighton Beach, Brooklyn, always attended, and, of course, my brother, Harold, and Shrolleh were there. Shrolleh was always there when a meal was served.

My father began sipping wine as soon as the sun went down, which initiated his Passover. Slivovitz was the chaser. After many Passover meals, I was prepared for my father's lubricated performance just before the gefilte fish arrived. He began, under the influence of the fermented grape and atomic plums, by telling the same joke:

"In a shtetl, a bride, dressing for her wedding ceremony, stepped on a stool in order to see her dress in the mirror. She farted. Startled to see her calf behind her, she pleaded with the calf not to reveal to the groom what had just occurred."

In all the years and through all the Passovers, he never got beyond this point. The alcohol-induced story always evaporated, as contagious laughter erupted from him. It was immediately transmitted to his sisters, who passed it on to my mother, and then to Shrolleh, my brother, and myself. Unfortunately, the rest of the joke is buried with my father.

Shrolleh

Socially and intellectually my uncle had never left his tiny shtetl in Lithuania. With a change in garments he could have easily blended back into the thatched huts and muddy streets of Shtayotchisik in Lithuania.

Having minimum wage jobs—first as a busboy and then selling candy at a movie theater—Shrolleh was consumed with saving the pittance he earned.

In the 1930s, the razor was a three-piece metal instrument: a metal handle and two parts that sandwiched the blade. Screwing all the pieces together produced a double-edged razor. The lifespan of a blade was four, at most five, shaves. Not for Shrolleh. He would remove the dull blade from his razor, press it against the inside wall of a yahrtzeit glass (memorial candle glass), and rub it vigorously back and forth, using the glass as a strop, to resurrect a dead blade for three or four more shaves. He was a simple man of simple needs and used creative methods to satisfy them.

To avoid wearing out the soles of his shoes prematurely, he bought horseshoe metal taps at F. W. Woolworth's five-and-dime store. With spike-like nails, he affixed them to the tips of his soles and heels. Although they did prevent wear, they also pressed dents and gashes into the linoleum floors of our entire apartment. When my mother showed him the damage, he developed a peculiar stride resembling the glide of a speed skater, to prevent the guillotine action of his taps on the linoleum. After his shoes gave their last gasp, he removed the taps and laces, and the former shoes evolved into slippers. These slippers, as they matured, developed a fine network of cracks, giving the appearance of a fibrous entanglement of spiderwebs enveloping his feet as he shuffled around the apartment.

His shirts seemed to last forever. Actually, a reverse evolution was taking place. The shirt originally fashioned from cotton thread slowly retraced its steps. My father, a tailor, turned Shrolleh's shirt collars when they were worn. When the cuffs were frayed, he converted the shirts into short-sleeved ones for summer. When the turned collars became ragged, he removed them and—voila!—pajama tops! When Shrolleh was through with a shirt, the only clues to its existence were a few horizontal and vertical threads.

Everything my father bought or did was subject to close scrutiny and critique by Shrolleh. If it was a haircut, I made sure I was there for the show when Shrolleh first laid eyes on it.

He slowly promenaded around my father, then clapped a hand over his own nose and mouth, in an attempt to prevent an outburst of laughter. My father had four parallel creases running across the back of his neck. Frequently, the barber failed to completely trim the hair in these folds. This was the bull's-eye Shrolleh focused on. Finally, the laughter exploded through Shrolleh's squeezed nose and mouth.

"What's so funny?" my father asked.

Shrolleh's reply was a horizontal palm, making four swipes, depicting the four creases with the uncut hair.

We knew it was coming, we expected it, but it never failed to elicit a burst of laughter from all of us, including my father.

One day, it was undershirts that had us roaring. My father bought undershirts at a men's haberdashery store, Paley Brothers, that he called "the Druggist" because in his mind drugstores charged outrageously high prices. The salesmen, the two Paley brothers, he labeled "the Gengsters" (gangsters).

"The Druggist had a sale on undershirts," Pa said, "so I bought three from the Gengsters."

"The Druggist? A sale? The Paley Brothers? It can't be! Try them on. Let's see if they aren't seconds," replied Shrolleh.

My father removed his shirt and slipped into one of his new bargains. It seemed like a nice fit, but Shrolleh noticed an inordinate amount of material gathered around my father's waist.

"Is that how you're going to wear it?" asked Shrolleh.

"Why?"

"You have a bagel around your waist."

"So, I'll roll it down," my father replied.

"So, roll it down," replied Shrolleh.

Pa proceeded to unroll the undershirt past his knees. When it arrived at his ankles, he stood up. He resembled a white lumpy sausage with a head at one end and a little pair of black shoes at the other. We laughed so hard, we cried.

A suit never passed muster unless Shrolleh inspected it. When my father brought a suit home, it was hung from a dishtowel rack in the kitchen. Uninvited, Shrolleh stepped in to critique the garment.

"What kind of buttons are these?"

"Why?"

"They don't match the suit. It was probably from a job lot. Try it on, and let's see how it fits."

My father went into the bedroom to change. Heaven forbid we should see him in his undershorts.

My mother withdrew to the living room. She refused to participate in this nonsense.

When Pa strutted from his bedroom, Shrolleh circled the suit with a critical eye. His cheeks inflated; his face turned crimson.

"The cuffs, they're shorter in the back than in the front!"

"Rosie," called Pa, "do me a favor. Come here and check the cuffs."

Ma came in and looked them over.

"What's wrong with them?"

"Shrolleh said they're shorter in the back than in the front."

"Shrolleh is a *mishugener* [a crazy person]."

That slammed the door on Shrolleh's critique of the suit.

When we moved from apartment 1 to apartment 11, which had two bedrooms, I slept on a "high riser" in the living room. In the daytime, it was a couch. In the evening, its cover was removed, and it became a bed.

Shrolleh shared his bedroom with my brother, Harold. A camphorated lining in the closet masked a sinister aroma, the hallmark of Shrolleh's presence. In spite of his meticulous cleanliness, he manufactured a body odor that was as distinct as his fingerprints. Just as the walls and curtains of a smoker's room have nicotine impregnated into them, so did his essence permeate, envelop, and laminate every object in his room.

Deodorants were not part of a man's toilette in those days. Even if they existed, they would have failed to allay Shrolleh's fumes. In spite of his daily bath, the strength of his bouquet, permanently wedded to his clothing, would have changed any deodorant's scent to match his own.

He would proudly announce that he had never had a mosquito bite, while my nails were tearing at my skin where one of those parasites had feasted. Why would a mosquito want to stick its proboscis into that stench? I toyed with the idea of offering his beads of perspiration to a manufacturer of insect repellents. But it reminded me of the problem of the universal solvent—was there a container that could hold it?

Ma repeated her washing routine twice a week. She would pull out a corrugated metal washboard from under our footed cast-iron bathtub, bend to her knees, and then proceed to rub the soiled areas of the clothing in soapy water in the tub. When she was through, she pulled the stopper and rinsed the clothes with fresh water. Next, she filled the tub again and dissolved a ball of laundry bluing into the water. All the white garments were immersed in this sky blue solution. The final products, including Shrolleh's, sparkled with a blue-white glow.

He fondled his red-and-yellow-banded black Thermos bottle with the care accorded to an antique at Sotheby's. The cork was washed and cleansed under the hot water tap. He vigorously scoured the aluminum cup with a steel wool pad until it sparkled like a gem at Tiffany's. Finally, after a number of soapy hot water rinses, the Thermos bottle could not have been cleaner had it emerged from an autoclave. Thus the process ended, and the Thermos was fully prepared for the following day.

Next came the construction of his sandwich. Two slices of white bread were placed upon the collapsible wires of our top-of-the-stove toaster (a device later replaced by an automatic Toastmaster). As the gas flames toasted the bread, Shrolleh would select his cheese, usually cottage cheese. To observe his application of the cheese was like observing a master mason applying stucco to the walls of a house. Every square micromillimeter of bread was amply coated.

Shrolleh cleaning up in our state-of-the-art kitchen, 1940.

All of his meals came from our apartment. Shrolleh never missed a meal at home. On Yom Kippur, being nonobservant, he mysteriously disappeared for the day of fasting. But he continued his perfect attendance record by joining us in the evening to break the fast.

His shaving habits were as intense as the cleansing of his Thermos bottle. Standing erect at the bathroom sink like a preacher at his pulpit, he attacked his beard from every conceivable angle, pulling his skin along with the blade to get to the lowest point of the bristles. His face emerged with a flamingo pink glow and as smooth as Jell-O.

In the summer, he would lie uncovered at the beach, exposing his milk-white skin to the sun's rays. When he returned home from the barbecue, his pearlescent, naturally pink skin was an angry red. My mother would say that he looked like a boiled lobster. In the winter, and in the summer if he wasn't at the beach, he could be seen on the street corner, his head tilted up so that his sun-deprived neck could get its share of the rays.

Aside from braising in the sun, Shrolleh's favorite activity was returning merchandise after reflecting upon its true value. At the age of eleven I accompanied him to return a pair of woolen, trap-door long johns he had purchased at Macy's. The salesgirl at the department where he had purchased the underwear asked the reason for the return.

"Dey shrunk end I kent vehr dem ennymore."

He cheerfully received a refund, but that did not bring the curtain down on this nervy performance. He proceeded to ask the clerk if he could now purchase the long johns for half the price, since they were worn.

"Didn't you say they were too small?" she asked.

"I, uh, yeah, uh ..." He stood frozen and mute. Then he grabbed me by the hand and quickly led me to the subway station.

Shrolleh never married. He had a group of socialist single friends who met at Crotona Park Lake on weekends. Two of these "revolutionaries" were brothers. He called them *"Die Tepp"* (the Pots), because they cooked for themselves. He would have been a Pot himself had not my mother cooked for him. When it rained, Shrolleh's friends met in a doorway of Paley Brothers' haberdashery store on Boston Road. Shrolleh's pals were specialists in the nutritional value of foods and the best places to find unpolluted air. Where and at which lab they researched their data I do not know. But their primitive investigations arrived at conclusions that have been confirmed today by the most sophisticated technology.

My future wife, Sheila, was quite slim. After the first time Shrolleh met her, I asked him what he thought of her. His reply was, "Not bad, but if she wore a black raincoat she'd look like an umbrella."

In spite of some infirmities, Shrolleh was quite hearty as he entered his eighties. A major event in his life and a great source of pleasure was meeting and having brief encounters with my teaching colleague Larry and his wife, Martha. Martha was a Catholic who had converted to Judaism before she married Larry. After her conversion, she was given the Hebrew name

Rochel (Rachel). This was the magnet that drew Shrolleh toward them. His reports to me were like incoming bulletins to a newsroom.

"I saw Rochel and Larry today. They said hello."

"Rochel was shopping in Pelham Parkway. She sends her regards."

"Larry and Rochel were visiting his parents; then they are going to a concert."

With the proper training, he might have been an anchorman for a Yiddish CNN.

He paid dearly for his obsession with the sun. His skin did not have a trace of melanin to protect him from the harmful ultraviolet rays. He was one layer of pigmentation above an albino. In his waning years, the damage to his skin manifested itself in weeping, precancerous keratosis. But this did not lead to his demise.

One day, Shrolleh stepped from the sidewalk between two cars and onto the road. A passing taxicab hit him. An ambulance took him to Jacobi Hospital in the Bronx. I received a phone call at Jane Addams High School asking me to come to the hospital to provide information about Shrolleh.

The emergency area was overcrowded. Sick people were on the floor, lying on stretchers, waiting to be assigned to a room. The scene reminded me of the vast field of wounded soldiers being tended to by Vivien Leigh in *Gone with the Wind*.

I found Shrolleh waiting for a second X-ray to be taken, because in the first X-ray a pin in one of his bandages had interfered with diagnosing his injury. Finally, he was settled in a bed. The next day, I found him shivering under a blanket. I went to the nurse's station to get another blanket.

"We have only one blanket for each patient," the nurse replied.

I left the station, dismantled two empty beds, and covered Shrolleh with two more blankets. The nursing care was neither nursing nor caring.

Two days later the attending doctor told me that Shrolleh had developed pneumonia. I told the doctor I wanted Shrolleh transferred to a hospital near my home in Spring Valley, New York. The doctor strongly recommended it. Although Shrolleh received excellent care at the Spring Valley hospital, he never recovered from the pneumonia. He passed away within a week.

Addendum: Shrollehisms

Gestures

Nose Holding While Laughing

- If he wanted to mock an outfit worn by my father or a mispronunciation of a word by my mother, he would hold his nose, not say a word, and burst out laughing. Often this was followed by one of the other gestures described below.

- As my father aged, he developed an enlarged prostate. His bladder filled a few times each night. To avoid waking me on his trip to the bathroom, he kept an empty milk bottle near his bed and urinated into the bottle. In the morning, Pa would empty the bottle in the bathroom. If Shrolleh spotted Pa on his way to the bathroom, my uncle would look at me, extend his two index fingers to indicate the length of the bottle, and then hold his nose while laughing.

- When I began shaving, Shrolleh was there to witness the event. Whenever he saw me cleanly shaven, he would place the fingers of his right hand at his sideburn, make shaving gestures, and hold his nose while laughing.

- The growth of my beard accompanied the growth of hair under my arms. Whenever I lifted my arms, Shrolleh would lift his and rapidly point to his armpit while he laughed.

- When I was well into my teenage years, the hairs on my scalp began to thin. He would run his palm across his bald scalp and say, "I tink you're losing it!"

Mispronunciations

One day, my mother's aunt Dora visited us. She was explaining to Ma that, although her winter coat was relatively new, the lining was turning purple, a word that she pronounced "perrpl." Shrolleh quickly gathered this and filed it into his data bank. Holding his nose while laughing, he ran into Pa's bedroom to tell him of the mispronunciation. Whenever Ma mentioned Dora's name, Shrolleh would hold his nose, laugh, and burst out with "perrpl."

Third-Degree Grilling

* Whenever a new friend appeared in our apartment, Shrolleh would sit him down on one of our wooden chairs and exhaust him with personal questions. My friends were respectful but amused by his probing.

   One day Bob Jacobson made his appearance. After going through the usual interrogation, "Are you working? How much are you making an hour? Did you ask for a raise?" Shrolleh asked, "Are you going to school?"

   Bob answered in the affirmative.

   "So, what are you studying?"

   "I want to be an artist," Bob replied.

   Shrolleh responded, "*Vest shtarben drei mohl ah tugg foon* hunger!" (you will starve three times a day from hunger).

* One day, my friend Alvin visited to show me his new pair of pants. Shrolleh came in to investigate and said, "Let me check the cuffs," As Shrolleh bent down near a cuff, Alvin farted.

   "Aren't you ashamed of yourself?" responded Shrolleh.

   "Why?" replied Alvin.

   Ever since then, whenever Shrolleh saw Alvin, he would say, "I'd check your cuffs but ..."

Expressions

* *Krainehlach!* Whenever I dressed in a suit for the holidays or he saw a photo of my brother's children, he would shout, *"Krainehlach!"* a shtetl expression that meant jeweled crowns should be placed on our heads.

* *Ahy voonder* (wonder of wonders)! When he saw or heard of something that excited him, he would shout, *ahy voonder!* also a shtetl expression of amazement.

Giving People Names

Shrolleh's first language was Yiddish, which lends itself well to the craft of name-giving.

- *Der Kalb* (the Calf): Shrolleh always saw my friend Rock tagging alongside another friend, Muttle, just as a calf tags alongside its mother, so he dubbed Rock *Der Kalb.*

- *Der Shutten* (the Shadow): A depressed friend always had a dark, glum expression on his face, so he earned the name *Der Shutten.*

- *Der Hiltzener Mentsh* (the Wooden Man): My father had a friend who would visit us. He sat stiffly and spoke mechanically like a robot. He was *Der Hiltzener Mentsh.*

Just as the shtetl has disappeared and became a "toenote" in history, so has Shrolleh. He is gone, never to be replicated.

Brother, Can You Spare a Dime?

At the sound of the three o'clock bell at P.S. 61, I raced home and hopped up the short flight of stairs to apartment 1.

"Ma," I said between gasps, "Mrs. Hyman said I qualify for free lunch!"

"Kvallify?"

"Ma, the teacher said I could get lunch for nothing!"

"Feh! It's *treyf* [unkosher]," she said, and, without missing a stroke, continued peeling a carrot.

The finality of those three words ended my feeble attempt to relieve a household deeply entrenched in the Great Depression.

In the mid-1930s, my contribution toward our family's financial stability was to wear my older brother's hand-me-downs. I do not use hand-me-downs as a derogatory term. In my neighborhood, anyone with an older sibling knew that the garment wrapped around that brother or sister would be passed on as a legacy, once it became tight enough to stop the normal flow of blood.

One evening after dinner, Pa announced that winter was coming, and I didn't have a warm pair of pants. He escorted me to a tiny shop adjacent to the Loew's Boston Road movie theater. The repulsive tailor who measured me kept sucking his saliva through his misaligned, brown-stained teeth while a cigarette dangled from his lips. Only the expectation of a new pair of pants allowed me to endure the ordeal.

In three days I had a brand new pair of stiff, brown corduroy knickers. Their parallel naps rubbing against each other squeaked out a tune in cadence to my stride. After many washings, the knickers became softened and mute. With the passage of time, their undulating ridges disappeared at the points of wear. The end product was a limp pair of soft corduroys eroded at the seat, knees, and inner thighs, embellished with a frayed pair of stretched knit cuffs dangling from the knee ends like bell clappers.

My official first grade portrait, in 1935. I'm wearing a spread collar and Windsor knot, but you can tell from the baggy sleeves that this is my brother's old shirt.

New shoes were another story. Shoes were worn to school and at play. An active kid wore out soles quickly. Nick the Shoemaker was ready, willing, and able to replace worn leather heels and soles with rubber Cat's Paw ones. Although they gave better traction, they wore out as quickly as leather. Once that happened, we would return to Nick so that he could add a pair of taps at the worn ends of the soles and heels.

Only when the black leather uppers had lost their smooth finish and turned a rough gray was it time to replace the shoes. Coward Shoe Store on the street level of the Empire State Building was our destination. The salesman carried my worn shoes with his fingertips to the rear of the store and came out with a pair of new black shoes, the same style I'd been wearing since second grade. They had a shieldlike, grainy tip that could withstand the bite of a shark. Completely out of fashion, they bore no kinship to the dark brown, box-toed footwear the big guys bought at Adler's Shoe Store. The salesman brought me to a fluoroscope to show my parents that the fit was right.

As we left, Ma whispered to Pa, "Morris, in two weeks Nick will be waiting with his hammer to put heels and soles on them. Maybe we should ask him to nail on taps?"

"Leave Nick alone. He has to make a living," Pa replied.

The mystery of why we purchased a costly pair of new shoes on my father's pathetic income was cleared up when my mother related one of the many stories about her life in her Lithuanian shtetl.

As children, she and Morris (Pa) walked barefoot from late spring to early autumn. With the approach of winter, their feet were wrapped with heavy cotton strips like Ace bandages. In the evening, the wrappings were removed and dried. Children's feet grew, and shoes did not, so until their feet stopped growing, children coiled these flexible, expandable rags around their feet instead.

This background also influenced the costumes I wore above my ankles. On Seabury Place, we were not living in Dickensian poverty. Healthy boys and girls could be seen and heard playing in the streets. We did not know steaks, but we did not know hunger.

The Passing Parade

Although I lived on the ground floor facing the street, I rarely observed the parade from my apartment. Most of my free time was devoted to playing ball in the street, in the "eye" of the spectacle.

In the mid-1930s, the population density of our neighborhood was the magnet that brought itinerant entrepreneurs on their daily odyssey through our streets. The simple skills developed in the villages of Eastern Europe they honed and refined on the teeming streets of the East Bronx. Their given names were unknown to us. We identified them by their occupations.

The I Cash Clothes Man had a cart drawn by a plodding, stooped horse with an arched neck that brought its head so close to the asphalt that it appeared to be searching for a line to guide him from Anatevka (the tiny shtetl in *Fiddler on the Roof*) to Seabury Place. The ragman's scraggly beard matched the threads escaping from his worn collar. The bench upon which he sat was covered with an oily flannel blanket that had long ago surrendered its nap to the seat of his pants. He was the centerpiece of a rusty metal arch from which copper bells dangled. With reins in hand, he pleaded with a horse whose legs seemed to have forgotten the coordinated sequence to move him forward. His blasts of, "I Cash Clothes," accompanied by the clanging of his copper bells, let everyone in the neighborhood know he was there. The entire scene might have been featured in a film from the archives of the YIVO Institute, an organization that documents Jewish history.

"Ma, it's the I Cash Clothes Man."

"We send our old clothes to our relatives in Lithuania. They need them more than he does."

"Why don't they buy their own clothes?"

"They have no money for clothes."

"Why don't they work? Pa does."

"There is no work."

"Why don't they leave?"

"They're not allowed to leave."

"You left."

"Oy! You ask too many questions."

It puzzled me why the I Cash Clothes Man bothered to visit our neighborhood. Most of the residents wore what he collected as rags.

Without rising from his perch on the wagon, he belted out his familiar refrain as the windows on the street reverberated to his solo. If a housewife had accumulated enough *shmatehs* (rags), she would raise her window and call out her apartment number. The cart came to a halt. He strapped a feedbag to his horse's mouth and climbed the steps, hauling a large, empty, canvas bag.

The haggling began with the turn of the doorknob. The price for the pile of garments ranged between 25 and 50 cents. If a serviceable man's suit was included, the price could rocket to 75 cents or a dollar. With the booty in his sack, he returned to his wagon, removed the feedbag, and continued his pursuit of rejected rags.

Where did the I Cash Clothes Man come from? Where did he go?

Just as mysterious as the I Cash Clothes Man, who appeared to have driven off the stage of *Fiddler on the Roof*, was the Lineman, who seemed to have stepped out of the cornfields of *Oklahoma!* He made his way through the backyard tenements with yards of clothesline spiraled around his shoulder. He was a tall, lean, blond, middle-aged, handsome man, apparently of Anglo or Nordic stock. A light blue denim work shirt, freshly washed dungarees, and a navy blue knit hat complemented his rugged persona. The I Cash Clothes Man's territory was the street. The Lineman's domain was the backyard, where clotheslines spun on pulley wheels.

His signature call was, "Line! Line!" A tenant's frazzled clothesline and her shout of the apartment number brought him up the steps. He connected his new rope to the old one, then guided it through the far pulley attached to a tall wooden pole and the near pulley at the tenant's window jamb. After discarding the frayed line, he knotted the new one together using a series of concentric circles like a hangman's noose, all for $2, no haggling.

At the end of World War II, the launderette burst upon the scene. The Lineman couldn't compete with the dryer. Another voice from the East Bronx Chorus was eliminated. Where did he go? Maybe he returned to the cornfields of Oklahoma. The spiderweb of clotheslines in our backyards almost disappeared. One of the few remaining filaments was suspended from our apartment. Ma refused to surrender to technology. On her hands and knees, she fetched her rocking, corrugated metal washboard from under the bathtub, where it awaited its call to duty. She kneaded and rubbed our dirty clothes against its metal folds and then rinsed them. The launderette's dryer was no competitor to our line's production of fresh, air-dried clothes.

Quietly, another chorus member trudged along the streets, clutching the smoothly chiseled, projecting handles of his handmade, unpainted, gray, seven-foot wooden cart. What looked like a millstone was suspended on an axle spinning lazily at the center of the front. A few repaired but unclaimed umbrellas were tucked behind a strip of wood on each side of the cart. The housewives in the neighborhood knew that the sound of the gong from his pushcart meant it was time to gather their dull knives and damaged umbrellas. The Knife Sharpener had arrived. I ran to our apartment to announce his visit. If only Ma had a knife that needed sharpening. I knew she always sharpened her knives on the rough windowsill outside our kitchen window, but maybe this time she would give me one to carry to the sharpener.

"Ma, the Knife Sharpener is in the street."

"No, there are no knives to sharpen."

"But last night you said the knife was so dull you could ride a horse on the blade."

"Maybe next time."

The sharpener began his rhythmic pedaling, sitting on a bicycle seat at the end of his cart. The assembled knives waited their turn to meet the spinning wheel. We gathered in awe, ducking and dodging, as his wheel spun and sparks flew. Occasionally he repaired an umbrella, but that wasn't nearly as exciting as the darting sparks. Unfortunately, this poor man, too, couldn't compete with progress. Motorized sharpening wheels in a large green van drove him off the street. It was an example of a pro totally outclassing an amateur. The Knife Sharpener, his cart, and the sparks shambled into obscurity.

In the autumn, a simple black sheet metal wagon riding on small metal wheels creaked over the asphalt. It could easily have been constructed in Mr. Haller's sheet metal shop at Hermann Ridder Junior High School. Behind this wagon, straining and pushing, was an elderly gentleman wearing a black derby, a black jacket, and black pants, covered by a sparkling white bibbed apron. No matter that the street was level, his body leaned at a 45-degree angle, leaving the impression that he was guiding the cart uphill. A tubular three-foot metal chimney projected upward from the end of his cart, sending a gentle flow of black smoke into the air. He was the Sweet Potato Man. The scent of his baking potatoes crept through every unplugged nostril in the neighborhood. He kept opening and closing the three wide metal drawers in his cart to rearrange the potatoes. The bottom drawer held glowing charcoal. In the drawer above, were potatoes being baked, and in the top drawer were totally baked sweet potatoes kept warm while waiting to be sold. For 3 cents he would wrap a white paper napkin around the hottest and sweetest potato ever to excite a taste bud. A gentle pat on the rear sent you on your way. He eventually found the same lonely path as the Knife Sharpener, the path of no return.

Tony, the Jelly Apple Man, also made his debut in late spring. Tony had two polished copper vats set in the center of his cart, each holding heated red jelly. A crowded mound of small Macintosh apples in a wire basket separated the two vats.

If you didn't care for an apple, you could pick from a selection of other items filling glass partitions running along the sides of the cart: prunes, marshmallows, apricots, or "shoe leather" (pressed sheets of mashed and dried apricot). We pointed to our selection; then Tony impaled it on a round lollipop stick. With an arching loop, he removed the copper lid and ceremoniously twisted the fruit into the warm, red jelly. For 3 cents he placed your choice into your hand with a paper napkin wrapped around the stick. Then we gathered at his side to take inventory of our friends' selections. The item least requested was at the front left corner of Tony's cart—coconut slices floating in a translucent liquid against the walls of a square jar. I never saw Tony unscrew its lid. Did we know then that coconut contained saturated fat?

"So, what are you getting, Mutt?"

"I think I'll get the prunes."

"Ugh. The last time I had them, I couldn't get off the toilet seat."

"That's you. I'm me. I'm getting the prunes."

"I don't care what you get. But don't ask me for a bite of my apple."

"I don't like the apples."

"I didn't get it yet, did I?"

The bickering was aimed at getting in the last word.

As warm weather approached, Tony and the Sweet Potato Man deferred to an enameled white wooden cart with a red border and a green-striped canvas canopy. Inside this open cart rested a rectangular block of ice. To prevent its premature melting, the Ices Man placed a grungy sheet of water-saturated brown burlap over the block. The Board of Health was never consulted on the acceptability of his product.

It took 2 cents to have him create his masterpiece. With a cast-iron plane the size of a blackboard eraser he shaved and collected the ice. The shavings were slipped into a paper cone cup and then doused with your choice from a colored spectrum of flavors in containers resembling hair tonic bottles. With that soggy burlap cover indelibly imprinted on our minds, my friends and I were observers, never customers.

"Do you believe that kid is getting ices?"

"Look at that green flavor he picked."

"It looks like the chlorine water in Crotona Park Pool."

"He'll be at Dr. Kulock's office tomorrow."

"I hope he will be. I hate that kid."

When the street resounded with tympanic blasts, we knew that the One-Man Band had arrived. With an accordion in his hands, a harmonica braced at his mouth, and a parade drum strapped to his back, he tuned, harmonized, and energized the neighborhood. Each step activated drumsticks that pounded the skins of his drum while cymbals above it crashed together, accompanied by the harmonica and accordion. We slowly followed the booms and clangs enlivening the residents in their apartments. An aluminum cup, connected to the side of his drum collected coins from the music lovers. Out of step with the changing times, he, too, passed from this dwindling caravan of characters as the parade slowed to a crawl.

Another contributor to the sound of music was the Yardnik. In their old shtetls, the immigrants gave aliases to citizens, usually based on their occupations. The Yardnik got his moniker because he performed in the yards. Singing in Yiddish, Polish, or Russian, or playing his instrument, he worked the maze of backyards behind the tenements. My mother, in the midst of preparing dinner, would tear off a piece of newspaper and wrap 2 cents in it. When the song was over, I threw the package to the grateful singer awaiting a wave or a smile. Although the neighborhood ached from the sting of the Great Depression, and unemployment was the norm, the concept of charity was passed on from parents to children.

Our favorite Yardnik carried an old black case worn gray around the edges. Inside, in contrast to its shabby exterior, were his glossy, honey-colored violin and stringy bow. Sometimes he was a Yardnik, sometimes he played on a street corner. When he was a child, I'm sure, these were not the venues his parents envisioned as they saved their coins for his music lessons.

He wore an ironed white dress shirt whose frayed cuffs bounced off his wrists in tempo to the melodies escaping from the strings of his violin. Many of the tragic Yiddish songs he played lent themselves to the melancholy tone of the violin and of his appearance. The backyard airshaft provided an ideal conduit for the flow of these nostalgic tunes up to and through the open windows. Sometimes I would hear my mother sadly humming, occasionally muttering along with the notes. On the other hand, he could energize his violin, himself, and the tenants with a lively *Fraylach,* a tune usually played at weddings and bar mitzvahs. Newspaper-wrapped coins of appreciation fell at his feet at the end of the recital. With a "thank you," he gathered the packets and left to continue his gig on the tenement circuit. Whatever became of him and his violin?

Another neighborhood sight was a truck thundering music from a speaker at each side of the cab. On the rear platform of the truck sat a circular mesh fence about fifteen feet in diameter. It was covered by a multicolored dome like an umbrella. When the truck came to a halt, the proprietor opened a gate in the enclosure and flipped down three wooden steps that we could mount to arrive at five brightly colored miniature cars, each accommodating one driver. The cars were connected to a geared wheel at the center of the platform.

The volume of the music increased as mothers in housedresses brought their excited children to "drive" a car. Once the children were securely inside, the trucker shut the gate, stepped out, and manually turned the handle of a geared wheel at the side of the gate. The motorists were on a voyage to Oz. They pulled on ropes attached to bells. They squeezed black rubber honking balls at the sides of their cars. They spun the steering wheels to avoid road hazards. At the end of the journey, each motorist was given a lollipop. With the advent of World War II and gas rationing, this truck followed its little cars on a journey to Oz.

The Fruit Man's wagon was approximately twenty by twelve feet. Four large metal-surfaced wheels with wooden spokes slowly spun as a heavy-necked, wide-hipped draft horse pulled the produce-laden cart. Why was he the Fruit Man, not the Vegetable Man? Who knows? Frequently, his horse left a trail of compact brown spheres in the middle of the street, temporarily impeding, but not stopping, a stickball or punchball game. That was a given we lived with.

The fruits and vegetables, exploding with color, contrasted sharply with the gray- or brown-faced tenements peering down on the wagon. The Fruit Man's bounty was arrayed on angled boards so that it could be seen from a distance. Thin one-by-four wooden boards were nailed to a post behind each variety of produce. Brown paper bags displaying the name and price of the product were slipped over the boards. The prices could easily be changed as the merchandise aged or lost quality. To measure the weight of a purchase, a round-faced scale hung with three chains connected to a dangling steel pan. The customer placed her selection in a brown paper bag. The Fruit Man placed it in the pan. Both watched as the dial trembled and then came to a halt. He would invariably say, "I should charge you *X*, but for you, it's *Y*."

Of course, when supermarkets appeared in the area, the Fruit Man and his horse trudged off to oblivion.

It was early in the morning. I was preparing to go to school when there was a knock on the door.

"Ma, it's the Egg Man!"

With a dragging foot and a face misshapen from a stroke, he went door-to-door selling eggs.

"Order *mir* a dozen krex."

I turned to the Egg Man and ordered a dozen krex.

For years I had no idea what krex were. I thought they were a category like small, medium, or large eggs. In my teens, I finally asked, "Ma, do you remember the Egg Man? What were the krex you ordered from him?"

She told me that, in contrast to regular eggs, the krex had hairline cracks in them. Eggs sold for 25 cents a dozen at the grocery. Ma paid only 15 cents a dozen for krex. She bought them partly for economy, partly out of pity for the Egg Man. When she did go to the grocery to buy eggs, she bought the cheaper brown eggs because, as Dr. Carlton Fredericks had counseled, they were just as nutritious as white eggs. The Egg Man hobbled off to where?

Underneath pink, dirty, dank quilted blankets, in front of Adoff's drugstore rested three five-foot blocks of ice. Sal, the Iceman, was canvassing his customers. Seeing him at her door, the housewife lifted an oak lid at the top of her icebox to see what remained of her ice. After completing his calls to take orders, Sal returned to his horrible blankets, removed them, took his pick from its leather holster, and began to peck away at the block. A hunk of ice was separated. He fastened his tongs around the piece, placed it in a miniature wooden wine bucket, lifted it to his shoulder, and then carried it off to his first customer.

Every apartment had an oak icebox. A block of ice in the upper chamber chilled the contents in the chambers below. As the ice melted, the water was directed toward a small pipe leading to a drip pan below the icebox. If we forgot to empty the drip pan, it overflowed, sending a puddle creeping toward the curvy legs of our Quality gas stove.

In late fall, when there was a consistent chill in the air, my father placed a rusty sheet metal box with two sliding doors on our kitchen windowsill. He connected it with braided wire to two eye screws in the wooden jambs on either side of the window. Everything we had in the icebox was transferred to this window box. The chill of fall and winter refrigerated and sometimes froze our perishables. Our encounter with the Iceman came to a temporary halt until the following spring.

Milk, available only in glass bottles, was yet to be homogenized. Through the glass, you could easily see the separation between the cream and the rest of the milk. On very cold days, as the freezing water in the milk expanded, it would push up the cream, popping it up and out of the cardboard lid.

In the spring of 1939, a new blue-and-white enameled sign replaced the old, rusty one dangling from a twelve-inch metal pipe projecting from the facade of our building. It announced the availability of apartments including a perk—a Kelvinator gas refrigerator. Our oak was felled by technology. The Iceman slid into retirement. Iceboxes became storage containers in our small apartments. How were we to know that fifty years later these oak iceboxes would be expensive collectibles housing stereo sets or wine and liquor?

Who else marched in this passing parade? An occasional visitor was the Organ Grinder. At the end of his performance, his monkey darted from one person to another collecting coins in a small metal cup. In the summer, Simonize Joe, a smiling, jovial black man, would appear in khaki jodhpurs and a wrinkled white shirt, clutching a bottle of whiskey while singing a song familiar only to him. His voice sounded like Louis Armstrong's marinated in alcohol. As coins were thrown into a rumpled hat at his feet, he would declare, "Praise the Lord! Praise the Lord!"

In chorus, we would ask, "Who is the Lord?"

"Calvert is the Lord!" he replied, as he held up his inexpensive bottle of Lord Calvert rye whiskey.

The last time I saw Joe was in 1939 when the Detroit Tigers were at Yankee Stadium. He was a rabid Tiger fan. Walking along the aisles, he gesticulated at the ineptness of each Yankee batter who stepped up to the plate. Whenever Hank Greenberg came to bat, he would run toward the field boxes. With one hand he clutched tightly to the paper bag holding his pint of Lord Calvert, with the other he pointed to the bleachers. Joe tippled out of the Bronx never to be seen again.

The Great Depression brought the parade to an abrupt halt for some families in the neighborhood. In the 1930s, a common sight was a family dispossessed—removed from their apartment for nonpayment of rent. Their furniture, dumped on the sidewalk in front of the house, resembled Salvation Army rejects waiting for disposal. One day, my mother, holding my nine-year-old hand tightly, saw her friend Tillie, her two daughters, and her husband standing on the stoop of their apartment house. The family was dispossessed. Before moving to a shelter for defaulting on her rent, Tillie addressed a small crowd gathered between her and her possessions.

"How do we pay rent? How do we pay rent when there are no jobs?"

Turning to her husband, she went on, "Is this why he was gassed in France? Look at my husband. He hasn't worked in four months!"

My mother joined the sobbers around us. I looked at Tillie's husband's crumpled blue shirt with a worn, wilted collar, oversized pants, threadbare at the knees, supported by stretched, rippled suspenders. His dirt-impregnated calloused hands hadn't held a pickaxe, pushed a wheelbarrow, or loaded a truck in months. He was a poster child for the Great Depression. The sobbing was contagious, but I held back my tears. Big guys didn't cry.

Another day, the empty lot adjacent to my apartment house vibrated in tempo to the explosives used to excavate a foundation for a group of stores. We watched through holes in a wooden fence as heavy metal mats, covering the detonating area, heaved with each blast. Steam shovels loaded waiting trucks with the debris from the blasts. Finally, when the blasting was completed and the base of the excavation was flat, construction began on an A&P supermarket, the magnet of this small shopping complex. The mom-and-pop stores of the neighborhood were shoved aside by this giant. They joined the I Cash Clothes Man, the Lineman, the Sweet Potato Man, the Jelly Apple Man, the Knife Sharpener, the Fruit Man, the Iceman, and the Yardnik who once marched in the rich spectrum of the Passing Parade.

The parade's colorful cast of characters vanished, leaving only their memory, which will pass into oblivion when the surviving residents who "cheered" from the sidelines follow the same inevitable path.

Crossing the Border

Like a gentle wave rolling toward a beach, I heard Pa's low murmur surfing toward me from his bedroom. It broke with a reply, "Foist Hahmend-ehment."

A pause, then another flow of words elicited "George Vahshington."

A succession of waves, answered by "Prezident Ruhsehvelt," "Da Bill Uhv Rights," "Congress."

"Very good," said Pa.

I believe this was the first time I had ever heard my parents converse in English. They had immigrated to the United States from a shtetl in Lithuania where the Jewish inhabitants spoke only Yiddish.

My aunts and uncles, even my aged grandmother, from my mother's family in Montreal visited us occasionally, but I had never seen their children, my cousins. My brother and I were eager to meet them. But crossing the border for a visit to Canada required proof that you were either born in the United States or a naturalized citizen. Since Ma was neither, Pa was teaching and testing her for what she called "the *citizehner* papers test."

He coached Ma well. She passed the exam, raised her hand to pledge allegiance, and became a citizen. In a few weeks, her paper arrived with her photo affixed to the lower left side. She was proud; she was elated. This was a cherished document. She was a citizen of the United States, no longer a non-person, as she had been in her Lithuanian village.

I don't know whom Pa had consulted on his next maneuver, but I watched with interest as he smeared glue on the back of the citizen paper and quickly pressed a square of cheesecloth onto it. This was followed by trimming the fringes of cheesecloth extending beyond the edges of the paper.

"Pa, why did you glue that thing to the back of the paper?"

"Soon you will see."

My brother and I meet our Canadian cousins Helen and AnaLee in Montreal.

From a shiny, tan paper bag from Woolworth's, he removed a flat, black frame with a celluloid window and slipped Ma's citizen paper into it. He set the frame on the kitchen table and leaned it against the wall. Like an artist at his easel, he stepped back and admired his masterpiece.

"Pa, why did you glue that thing to the back of the paper?"

"So when you take it out and hold it, it wouldn't tear apart."

To my parents, the citizen paper was so valuable that Pa doubly protected it from damage—with the frame and with the cheesecloth backing.

After she finished reading the *Daily News,* Mrs. Suslow, from apartment 3, would give us her copy. Her husband was an employed furrier, so the 2-cent *Daily News* fit easily into his budget. Pa carefully read and reread the current events. Long after he should have been through with those he was still shouting at the newspaper's depressing news from Europe.

One day, when his rant had ended, he wet his thumb and forefinger and began flipping to parts of the newspaper he rarely looked at.

Left: The tuxedo kid, age 6, at Aunt Dorothy's wedding in Montreal, 1936.

Below: Formal portrait of my family at the wedding.

"What are you looking for, Pa?"

"I heard there are excursion prices to Montreal advertised in the newspaper. Would you like to go to Montreal?"

The only place outside New York City we had been to was Bayonne, New Jersey, and that had been an adventure on a real railroad car. Wow, Canada! We were going to leave our country!

It was the end of the school year. Pa read that the Delaware and Hudson railroad line had an excursion to Montreal. In a few days, our luggage was packed, and we were on our way.

The spaciousness and grandeur of Grand Central Station was an overwhelming sight for an eight-year-old. Pa and my brother, Harold, were carrying the bags as the four of us made our way toward the four-sided clock rising from the center of an information desk in the middle of this massive, tan marble hall.

"Where is the train to Montreal?" asked my brother.

"Track 14, lower level," replied the clerk.

My father kissed us good-bye and then returned home. He would have accompanied us, but he had found work for a few months. We entered the coach. Ma, as if she were a veteran of train travel, selected what she considered the choice seats—near the toilet. She grasped the back of one of the seats and pushed it forward so that the two long seats were facing each other.

The first order of business for my brother and me was to examine the toilet. But it was locked until we were underway, so our investigation turned to the water fountain adjacent to the toilet. We removed a flat paper drinking cup from its holder above the fountain, unfolded it, and filled it with cold, refreshing water. Then the tour continued to the other coach cars, to see who had joined us on the train. Like Business Class on an airplane, the sleeper was out of bounds. Returning to our seats, we anxiously waited to explore the bathroom. What is it about an unfamiliar bathroom that fascinates children?

Finally, the train was on its way. Strange names—Yonkers, Ardsley, Tarrytown, Croton, Harmon, Whitehall, Gloversville, Mechanicsville—were called out by the conductor. Since we had never left the city, the only vegetation we were familiar with was in the empty lot adjacent to our apartment building, Crotona Park, and the Bronx Zoo. We were traveling through a new world of greenery. The windows framed the Hudson River, green mountains, plains, villages, and a slowly darkening sky.

Lunch time! Egg salad or cream cheese on Litroff's delicious rolls. I opted for the cream cheese. Tan Postum as usual had its awful brown taste. Guided by Dr. Carlton Fredericks, Ma permitted neither my brother nor me to drink coffee.

She noted another family making a bed by slipping one of the seat backs into the space between their seats. We tried, we struggled, and then we had a bed. It was much harder than the new folding bed I slept on at home, however, and the seat cover's dense, stiff bristles mercilessly penetrated the skin exposed below my short pants.

After a sleepless night, I arose to a splash of dawn's colors. Backlit by the rising sun, the mountains were awash with blushes of orange and pink against a pale blue sky. Was this what Canada was going to look like? Finally, the mountains subsided into hills, and then we were riding on a plain as we approached the border.

A Canadian customs officer boarded the train and walked down the aisle conducting an inquest at each seat. This was to be Ma's first confrontation with a uniformed officer since she had left Europe. It was obvious she was extremely agitated. She fumbled with the lock to open the luggage. Once the valise was opened, there it was, right at the top, below the blue-printed paper lining of the valise. There it was, in its shiny new frame, on top of the folded clothing, with Ma's affixed photo staring up at us: her *citizehner* paper.

The customs inspector first addressed her in French. Holding the framed citizen paper and our birth certificates in a trembling hand, Ma looked up at him quizzically and then at us. He ignored the papers and asked in English what gifts we were bringing into Canada. Ma told my brother to tell him we were bringing three cornbreads from Litroff's Bakery for her family and a baked chicken for us. The inspector looked up to the ceiling in disbelief, and then suspended the inquisition.

Within an hour, our train arrived at Bonaventure Station in Montreal where my mother's youngest brother, Louis, my grandmother, and my cousin AnaLee were waiting for us.

Ma, her framed *citizehner* papers, and her two children had crossed the border!

The *Hindenburg*

Although 1937 was not a hopeful year, we seven-year-olds didn't—and weren't expected to—know it. Neighbors shared 2-cent papers, hot water visited our apartment only occasionally, and heat rose from the basement when a few sobering blows with a hammer on our radiator roused the janitor from his alcoholic stupor.

In the Bronx, unemployed fathers met in Crotona Park to extol the virtues of socialism. It appealed to workingmen in the garment industry, who considered themselves fortunate if they were employed five months a year.

Using rolled up newspapers, broomsticks, milk boxes, tin cans, rubber balls, the facades and stoops of our tenement buildings, we children occupied ourselves for hours with competitive games. To avoid the inevitable argument, before the game we gathered in a cluster around a sewer lid in the middle of the street.

"If we catch it off the car without a bounce, you're out. And don't try to punch the ball when you're halfway to first base. You have to punch it at home plate—the sewer—and then run to first base. That's how the big guys play it."

The ground rules were being settled for a punchball game between two neighborhood rivals, the Minford Place Tigers and the Seabury Place Pawnees.

"If the ball goes in Schmidt's cellar, you're out and you have to …"

"Wow! Look at that! Look up there!"

A zeppelin immediately became the focus of our attention, an unexpected intruder on an ongoing neighborhood rivalry. Our mouths were agape. We were stunned. The bright summer sky was eclipsed by the sinister appearance of this huge, oval object, which blanketed Seabury Place under a giant shadow. The airship hovered like a marionette suspended by strings. Why wasn't it moving like the airplanes that passed by every day? Jaws dropped, mouths were frozen.

"What? What *is* that thing?" cried Puggy, who moved closer to Milty.

"Get offa me, dummy. How should I know?"

"I don't like this. Let's get outta here," shouted Bernie.

We had seen the *Hindenburg* in newsreels, but who expected it to hang over Seabury Place? On its rudder, a black swastika in a white circular field encased in a red square assured us it was the *Hindenburg*.

Why was it flying at such a low altitude? Could it have come all the way from Germany? If there was a swastika on its rudder, were there Nazis inside? What would they do to us after they landed? Where was it going to land?

Our enthusiasm for the punchball game instantly chilled. Without a word, the Tigers gathered and quietly returned to the security of their turf, Minford Place. We retired to our dugout for ballgames: the running board of a parked car. For security, we squeezed closer to one another than usual, shoulders pressed against shoulders, knees coupled with knees. Puggy, still standing and shaking with fright, sputtered, "I'm going upstairs."

Bernie, who was just as anxious as Puggy, put on an air of bravado: "Oh, scaredy-cat is going upstairs to his mommy." With that, Bernie said he was going upstairs to ask his mother if she knew anything about the *Hindenburg*.

"How would she know?" asked Milty. "You don't buy a newspaper."

"I don't buy one either," I replied. "Mr. Suslow gives it to my father after he finishes it."

"Oh, yeah? I'll bet he doesn't know that the *Hindenburg* flew over Seabury Place today."

"When he comes home, I'll ask him."

The running board session was adjourned. Rapidly beating hearts and wobbly legs stumbled for home.

I opened the door to apartment 11. Ma was doing something with string beans. "Ma, did you see the scary zeppelin that flew over Seabury Place this afternoon?"

"How can I see anything when our windows show me Mrs. Koletsky's kitchen? Wait until Pa comes home."

An hour later, Pa dragged himself into our apartment. I ran to tell him about the *Hindenburg*. He became agitated.

"What? A swastika?" he said. "Nazis? How could it be? Harold, did you see it? The United States doesn't want those bastards here."

"I didn't see it," said my brother. "I was in the apartment doing my homework."

Pa followed news of the German threat throughout Europe. A large part of our family was living in a tiny village in Lithuania. Pa was about to turn on the radio when my uncle came home from work.

"Shrolleh, did you see the *Hindenburg* today?" asked Pa.

"What *Hindenburg*? Wasn't he a German general? What was he doing here in the Bronx?"

"Yes," Pa said sarcastically. "He came here to draft you."

The family gathered around our Gothic Emerson table radio. It was Thursday, May 6, 1937. An excited newscaster reported that the *Hindenburg* had drifted slowly over New York City heading for Lakehurst, New Jersey. At 7:45 pm, upon approaching its mooring at Lakehurst, it had exploded, killing thirty-five of the ninety-seven people aboard. A member of the ground crew was also killed. Rumors about the cause of this disaster persist to this day. Indisputable evidence is still lacking.

A Summer Haircut

What caused my hair to grow so fast? Perhaps it was a surplus of testosterone. Why would a nine-year-old have excess testosterone? Was it an endocrine disorder? Perhaps it was the fresh fruits and vegetables, or the chicken fat smeared on rye bread with garlic rubbed against its crust that caused my hair to grow faster than the hair sprouting from the heads of my friends.

In 1939, a child's haircut cost 10 cents at Colletti's. You couldn't wear it; you couldn't eat it; so at nine years old I was convinced it was a needless event that could be put off until next week.

Why did Ma decide I needed a haircut when I was in the middle of a punchball game? Why didn't she decide this when I was in the middle of my homework? She emerged from our apartment building, stepped between me and my friends, and said, "Your hair is growing over your ears. Come, you're going for a haircut."

"Get your mother off the field, Danny. She's blocking first base."

"Shut up, Marty. I didn't tell your mother to get off the field when she brought you a glass of milk and cookies last inning."

Then, turning to my mother, I argued "Ma, let's go next week. Can't I finish the game?"

"You said that last week. Come."

We left the boys and walked along Boston Road parallel to the trolley tracks. The only sound that passed between my mother and me was the squeak of my still-new corduroy knickers. The huge faded blue Consolidated Laundry sign wound around Wilkins Avenue and onto Boston Road pointing the way to the Loew's Boston Road movie theater. Scary Boris Karloff was featured in *The Bride of Frankenstein*. He gave me the creeps staring at me from the poster behind the display window. I picked up the pace when we passed the tiny store adjacent to the movie theater where that disgusting tailor with the nicotine-stained teeth had made my stiff knickers.

Mr. Colletti's barbershop was tucked between a corner bar and a hardware store on Boston Road just past Prospect Avenue. Upon entering, I could almost taste the sweet smell of aftershave lotion or some other exotic liquid poured on adult heads. I sat on one of the mismatched chairs, picked up a dog-eared *Police Gazette,* and waited for my turn. My mother looked over my shoulder and saw partially dressed girls posing on each page.

"Put that magazine down," she said. "It's not for young boys."

"What's wrong with it?" I asked.

"Naked ladies are not for you."

"Then who are they for?"

"They are for nobody. Pa doesn't read it."

Smiling, Mr. Colletti walked over and handed me a *Scholastic* paper.

The last customer left his chair and paid. As the man walked by me, I wondered why I didn't smell like that when I left the barbershop. And what were those hot towels doing inside that steel drum near the wall? Mr. Colletti never used a towel like that on me. And look at all those milk-colored bottles on the small counters in front of each barber chair. What was inside them? And what about the red and green watery liquids in those clear bottles? They never touched my head. Maybe it was because Ma paid only 10 cents for the haircut. That's why the towel, the sweet-smelling stuff, and the red and green watery stuff stayed where they were.

Mr. Colletti's "Next" woke me from my reverie. Ma rushed ahead.

"Mr. Colletti, you'll give him a summer haircut, please."

"It's nearly winter, Ma. I need some hair on my head."

"So, you want a fancy haircut? Give him a summer haircut or else we'll be here again next week."

Mr. Colletti shrugged his shoulders. I stepped up and slid into the big barber chair. The discomfiting warmth from the brown leather seat just vacated made me feel as if I was sharing the last customer's underwear. Mr. Colletti shook the remaining hairs from the previous patron's coversheet. He wrapped a narrow tissue paper around my neck, and enclosed me in the coversheet. I looked up. The embossed tin ceiling's gray cobwebs had disap-

My summer haircut, Harold, Ma, and Uncle Louis in his Dodge (1938).

peared under a new coat of white paint. Answering Mr. Colletti's gentle nudge, I lowered my chin until it dented my chest. I heard the buzz approaching. He never used his scissors to cut my hair. To my mother's satisfaction, his electric clipper mowed my head to the length of the bristles on my toothbrush. The razor trimming the ends of my sideburns indicated he was nearly through. Ma suggested that the clipper should cut the sideburns closer.

"Ma, if it's any closer, the clipper will be inside my head."

"Quiet, and let Mr. Colletti do his work."

With the haircut complete, Colletti removed a little wooden brush with long, yellowing bristles from a glass cabinet in front of me. He swept the cut hairs off the back of my neck and face. The final touch was talcum powder. In a very dramatic gesture, he shook the powder from its bottle into one hand, rubbed his hands together and then dabbed it on the back of my neck to loosen the stubborn bristles that wouldn't yield to his brush. The summer haircut complete, Mr. Colletti placed his oval mirror behind my head so that I might view his masterpiece. "OK, OK," I said. I wanted to leave quickly. Maybe the boys were still in the street. Reliable Ma brought a woolen knit hat to keep my head warm for the long walk home.

"Was that so bad that you had to complain in front of the whole neighborhood?"

"Why should I get a haircut when I don't need one?"

"Need? We need to eat, and we need to sleep, and, when hair grows over the ears, we need a haircut. Pull down the hat over your ears—a wind is blowing. You'll catch a cold."

I had a spring in my step as we walked home. Although my back itched from errant clipped hairs, I felt cleaner than when Ma and I had entered Colletti's.

Ma's Wisecracks

Many humorous episodes occurred in the dimly lit halls of 1540 Seabury Place. Ma's first encounter with our new landlord, an African-American, was on the stairway. We were descending when we heard from the landing, "Hello, this is Reverend Black, your landlord."

Ma turned to me and whispered, "*Zay zeinen ahlleh* reverends" (they're all reverends).

"Don't you say hello?" he asked.

"To tell you da troot, it's so dark in here, who could see you?" Ma answered.

This made me squirm, but Mr. Black had a good laugh.

Another time, when my friends and I were watching the *Ed Sullivan Show* on TV in my apartment, the famous Moiseyev Ballet dancers from Russia were scheduled to perform. When Ed Sullivan introduced the dancers, they came storming out on stage, jumping, stomping, spinning, and kicking. While they cavorted, a member of the troupe came from behind the ensemble, leaped high above the twirling dancers, and landed in front of the entire company. We gasped. There was silence. Then an aching voice from the rear of the room groaned, "*Oy! Oib ehr hutt gehatt meyneh fiss, vult ess zein dem letzten muhl vie ehr springt ahzay*" (Oh! If he had my feet, it would be the last time he would jump like that).

Ma had a cousin Anna who was married to a lawyer. They lived in the Bronx, owned a car, and were financially comfortable. Whenever Anna went to Montreal to visit her parents and family, she invited Ma to accompany her. They were returning from one of these trips when an American customs officer ignored Anna and her husband but asked Ma if she had bought anything and what was its value. As the car pulled away, Ma observed, "*Die reicheh tsheppenen zay nit, die ohremeh machen zay shvitzen*" (the rich they don't bother, but the poor, they make them sweat).

The Moiseyev dancer's great leap.

Late in life, Ma's heart gave her problems. After one episode that took her to the hospital, I made an appointment for her to see Dr. Bloom, a prominent heart specialist at Mt. Sinai Medical Center in Manhattan. His exam fee was $100; this was an extremely high fee in those days. Ma sat on Dr. Bloom's examining table as he moved his stethoscope to various parts of her chest.

"Good. Good. Good. Very good," he muttered as he listened to her heart.

"Good? Very good? Sure, for you it's very good. You tahp me mitt dat mirror and for dat you get a hundred dollars!"

Completely familiar with Ma's outrageous behavior, I should not have been stunned by the remark, but I was. Luckily, the doctor burst into laughter, and we joined him.

The Running Board

I didn't know anyone living on Seabury Place who owned a car, but usually there were two or three cars parked alongside the curb. A big, black shiny Buick told me that Dr. Kulock was making a house call. A black Dodge with New York license plate BB-142 told me that my mother's cousin Anna was paying a visit. The street was ours for a variety of games.

When the three o'clock elementary school bell rang, in spite of the pushing, shoving, and horsing around, we came home quickly, changed into Keds (sneakers), gulped down a glass of milk, and ran into the street with cookie in hand. Within minutes, all the boys were assembled to choose up sides for a punchball game.

Everyone was already focused on the game when suddenly a group of youngsters came running up the street following two young ladies in short, tight, green satin dresses. They each carried a small tray suspended from their shoulders. They were distributing samples of Kool cigarettes.

"Hey, guys, I'm going to get a pack," said Bernie.

"You can't stop our game," shouted Milty. "Anyway, you're a kid. They won't give you a pack."

"I'll tell them it's for my father."

"You father doesn't smoke."

"If it's for free, he'll smoke."

"Your father is cheap. If he wants to smoke why doesn't he buy a pack instead of mooching it from the girl?"

"Don't call my father cheap. He could beat up your father."

"Oh, yeah?"

Between the short, shimmering green satin skirts and Milty telling Bernie his father was cheap, the game was over. We retired to our headquarters, our meeting place, our dugout for ballgames, the running board. The running board was the supplement to our elementary school education. We discussed bubble gum cards called "War!" which depicted the horrible atrocities committed by the Japanese army in the Sino-Japanese War. A photo of a wailing infant in tattered clothing sitting alongside bombed-out railroad tracks left an indelible impression on me.

There were also pleasant cards, baseball cards. For 1 cent, you got a colorful wax-coated wrapper that held a card showing a baseball player plus a thin rectangle of pungent pink bubble gum divided into four strips.

We scrambled for seats on the running board of a parked car. Boys who didn't get a seat leaned against the front and back fenders. Once we were sitting on the running board, our laps formed the desk where our business transactions with the cards took place.

"I have a Red Rolfe in very good shape. How many cards will you give me for it?" asked Puggy.

"Very good shape my ass! I'll give you nothing. The edges are worn and there's a coffee stain on his uniform."

"Big deal. I spilled some coffee on it. So what?"

"My mother says you're not supposed to drink coffee. It'll stunt your growth and make you nervous."

"Oh, yeah? What does she know? I drink coffee and I'm taller than you and my hands don't shake."

Arthur, our current events authority, announced his latest bulletin. "Did you guys see the *Hindenburg* yesterday? It exploded in New Jersey and thirty-six people were killed and …"

"I saw it," interjected Milty. "It was so big and dark I couldn't see the sky. It scared the shit out of me."

"Ah, everything scares you. I saw you run away from Mrs. Stein's poodle last week."

"Did you see the teeth on that dog?"

"Yeah. They look like a half of a Chicklet."

"Hey, what about this Mel Ott? I used it in flipping cards, but it's valuable. How many cards do I get for it?"

"Valuable? Bullshit, the corners are bent. Keep it."

On the running board's rubberized shelf we formulated plans for stealing "mickies"—potatoes—from a stand in the Jennings Street Market. We

A recent photo of me sitting on the running board of an antique car.

speculated on what was going to replace the cobblestones that were being removed from Boston Road. We grumbled about the big guys who thought they owned the street when they kicked us off the field in the middle of a punchball game. We spoke of the wonderful free morning sessions at the new Crotona Park Pool.

Vital issues were debated, disputed, resolved, and sometimes interrupted by the car's angry owner with, "Get your asses off the car, and don't come back!"

The running board was a shelf about twelve inches wide below the car's doors and running the length of them. It was covered with a black, deeply grooved rubber mat serving as a threshold to the automobile. In summer, when everyone wore short pants, the grooves left a series of parallel bands, red in the indents, pink on the surface, pressed horizontally into the backs of our thighs, giving the impression that our legs were covered with pink corduroy.

If we inadvertently stepped into a mound of horse manure, we used the edge of the running board as a scalpel to scrape off the residue.

The running board was not our private domain. We shared it with the police of 1930s gangster movies. Glued to the running board and grasping the door of a commandeered vehicle, they emptied their pistols at criminals on mad circuitous chases over rural highways.

When technology created new designs for the automobile, the running board, like punchball and the *Hindenburg,* became a memory. At the end of World War II only a slight rubber projection extended below car doors. Like a vestigial organ, it was a relic of a functional structure from the distant past. As car models became sleeker, eliminating anything that might offer wind resistance, the feature that had played such a significant role in our lives completely disappeared.

Jennings Street Market

It was a multistage theater with performances in each venue as unique as the performers. Each act had a single booking, because it was impossible to replicate. Cecil B. DeMille's spectaculars could not compete with the dramas played out daily on the sidewalks of the Jennings Street Market in the Bronx.

The curtain opened on a red-cheeked gnome, tightly wrapped in a white starched apron. Jake the Pickle Man was the despot of this East European bazaar, the undisputed czar of the Jennings Street Market. He had no store; he merely rented a patch on the sidewalk, approximately six by eight feet, from which he, his wife, and five barrels captivated audiences.

Each of three barrels had a different degree of fermentation—from bright green half-sour to olive drab completely sour garlic pickles. A fourth barrel held green tomatoes, and the fifth, shredded cabbage undergoing the same process. He coordinated the fermenting flora like a maestro to produce the most delicious sour pickles, sour tomatoes, and sauerkraut in the Bronx.

The year was 1939; I was nine years old. Going to Jake's on Friday was as routine as tenants hiding from the landlady on rent day. One day when my mother was next in line waiting to be served she became distracted by a friend across the street. Ma's slight delay before making her request was unsatisfactory to Jake. His beady eyes glared, and his thin voice shrilled, "*Nu*, did you come to your big decision?"

Ma was sensitive. She was not willing to be addressed in that aggressive manner. After that exchange, the pickle jar was passed into my hands. Since every mother in the neighborhood bore at least one scar from Jake's blistering tongue, a queue of their offspring would form alongside his barrels waiting for him to fill their jars and send them off to their Sabbath meal. Inexplicably, Jake loved children. As far as I know he had none of his own.

The bustle of Jennings Street Market in 1939.

The respect he should have shown to the ladies, he showered on the young ones. He squeezed every pickle he could into their jars.

"Only pickles for *Shabbos* [the Sabbath] can fit into this jar. Your mother doesn't have another one?" He told me to bring a bigger jar next time and sent me on my way.

Ma wasn't the only patron to nurse the bruises of Jake's slings and arrows. A woman in front of me announced, "Ah full jar *mitt* pickles right up to da top. End you should give me a good price."

"You came *mitt* an empty jar; you go home *mitt* an empty jar. No pickles for a *chazer* [a pig]!"

In another incident, a woman a few places in front of me declared:

"I vahnt sour pickles but dey should be hard vuns. Da lest time you gave me pickles, dey fell apart on mine fork!"

"You vahnt a hard vun? Go esk your husband. Maybe for *Shabbos*, *mitt* some *mazel* [luck], he'll give you a hard vun."

At that time I didn't understand what he was saying but I could tell by the *oys, veys,* and *tsk tsks* from the women around me that this was a gem worthy of storage.

It was a very busy day before the Jewish New Year. Jake was besieged by the usual horde at this time of the year. As I was about to leave with my pickles, the woman behind me presented him with a jar that had a very narrow neck.

*The site of Jennings Street Market in 2004. Jake the Pickle Man's stand
was located behind the bushes to the right of the car.*

"Dis is a jar for pickles? Your *hahldz* [neck] should be as narrow as this
jar and you should have a *geshvirr* [an abscess] in it."

Most of the women tolerated his insults as the toll paid for his wonderful pickles. Jake's generous portions were determined by an eyebrow—his
wife's. As soon as it gained altitude and described an arc, he stopped stuffing the jar. Aside from her eyebrow, I could not determine her role in the
operation. She never held a jar. Her hands were constantly marinating in
sauerkraut juice or among the pickles, turning them down and around like
a convection current. When her hands emerged, a sparkling emerald-cut
diamond on her ring finger glistened in sharp contrast to the drab brine
and pickles surrounding it. This, of course, led to all sorts of rumors about
Jake's wealth. Some women claimed he owned all the real estate on
Jennings Street. Others said he earned the money for the diamond from his
other enterprises, which were much more profitable. This was ridiculous.
The man spent his entire day and a good part of the night tending to the
inventory in his oaken barrels.

Late in the evening, behind a wrought iron gate, he could be seen in his
laboratory, his backyard. His pink, cherubic Rubenesque face was bathed in
the yellow glow of a single low-wattage bulb as he checked his barrels of
newly fermenting pickles, tomatoes, and cabbage. He sampled the brine in

each barrel, dropped in some bay leaves, or perhaps added dill, salt, or garlic. When he was satisfied, he pulled the string on his lightbulb and went up to his apartment to rehearse his tirade for the following day.

World War II veterans, who benefited from the GI Bill of Rights, abandoned the neighborhood. The suburbs were blossoming as our neighborhood withered. On weekends, the vets made a pilgrimage with their children to the czar—Jake of Jennings Street. They parked their shiny cars along the curb opposite the familiar oaken barrels. Their once leaky jars were replaced by rubber-gasketed Mason jars sealing in the smells and nostalgia of the old neighborhood. I'm sure these vets shared their Jake the Pickle Man stories with their wives and children.

While Jake was spicing the atmosphere with his pickles and verbal lashings, a *shochet* (ritual slaughterer) in a flapping white but bloody apron shlepped through the streets with a freshly killed chicken, displaying its rear end while directing prospective customers to his stand in one of the many indoor markets. Freshly killed still-warm chickens were waiting to be plucked, eviscerated, and then roasted in the oven.

One indoor market was directly across the street from Jake's pickle stand. As soon as you entered, your salivary glands began working overtime as the intoxicating aroma from the heartburn-inducing fare at Feuer's Appetizing overwhelmed your nostrils. Squeezing past his barrels of salted herring, trays of pickled herring, slabs of smoked salmon begging to be sliced, platoons of smoked whitefish, and tubular salamis aligned like artillery shells, you came upon the chicken stand. It consisted of a long white-tiled counter with a cash register at the left end. Prone and limp lay the warm, recently slaughtered, feathered carcasses. A woman at the far right of the counter sat on a wooden milk box. Unaware of carpal tunnel syndrome, she placed her wrists in overdrive as she plucked the feathers from a chicken for 10 cents.

"Good morning. How are you, Mrs. Wolfe? How did you like last week's farmer cheese? Did you use it in your blintzes? It was a new brand." Unlike most of the market's entrepreneurs, whose single corrosive insult could dissolve all the rust on the George Washington Bridge, Mr. Beer, at the dairy counter, was a gentleman with a refined vocabulary. His veined gray marble counter was on the right as you entered the building. Behind his counter were three refrigerated sections enclosed by vertical sliding glass doors. Through the glass, Mr. Beer's entire inventory was exposed to his customers. Two large wooden tubs filled with bright, golden yellow butter beamed out.

"A half-pound of butter, please."

It always amazed me how he was able to plunge his trowel into the butter and remove a portion of precisely the requested weight.

In front of the wooden tubs were two twelve-inch rectangular wooden boxes holding Breakstone's cream cheese. Cream cheese then was not available in neatly folded aluminum foil eight-ounce packages. With his trusty trowel, Mr. Beer sliced off the amount requested and then placed it on shiny translucent paper he ripped from a bulky roll at the end of the counter. I thought his deft folding of the paper was a trade secret. As soon as I came home, I tried to duplicate the folds. Somehow, the package never closed.

The third refrigerated section burst with color. A bright gold-toned five-gallon tin can, tipped at an angle like a cornucopia, contained gleaming white pot cheese whose curds seemed to flow out of the can. At either side, a round cheese wrapped tightly in red cellophane prevented the can from rolling sideways. I think Mr. Beer positioned them solely for support and color effect. I never saw anyone buy a wedge of that cheese.

I was familiar only with Mr. Beer's cream cheese and farmer cheese. The cream cheese was like mortar between two slices of a bagel. For twenty-three consecutive years, my father's daily bialy roll for work held a square of farmer cheese between its two halves. All the other cheeses in Mr. Beer's medley were either too expensive or too foreign to test.

Stepping out from Beer's dairy and to the left, at the corner of Jennings and Wilkins Avenue, resided the market's trophy fruit and vegetable stand, Miller's. Possibly Matisse's brush could have done justice to the yellows, oranges, purples, reds, and greens exploding from various angles. The beautiful fruits were lined up in the morning as if they were awaiting inspection by a general on the company street. Then the customers came, squeezing, examining, fingerprinting, and replacing the fruit in mounds of disarray.

An elderly employee rearranged them as he cursed out the women digging for prime fruits. By the end of the day, a few lonely pieces were left in front of the brown paper bags displaying the prices.

To show off the brilliance of the fruit's colors, Mrs. Miller removed the thin, soft, translucent papers in which some fruit was wrapped. She saved the wrappings in a brown paper bag for my mother, who collected them on Sunday—the day she bought her produce, because the prices were lower. We used these papers as toilet tissue.

At the intersection of Jennings and Charlotte Streets was Ruby's junk store, a poor man's Woolworth's. It was cluttered with merchandise, much of which neither he nor his patrons could identify. Regardless of the season, the odor of camphor permeated the store. If OSHA had existed, it would have condemned his store as unsuitable for human respiration. Ruby's entire inventory could be found on the floor in open cardboard boxes or scattered on a long wooden table at the center of the store. Nearly every piece of merchandise was buried in a box of sawdust. So, it was potluck when a customer's hand dove into the shavings prospecting for a bargain. The specialty of the house was mismatched dishes made in Japan. Today, with a genuine pre-war "Made in Japan" stamp on the bottom, these dishes would be collectibles.

Running a close second to the dishes in quantity were sheets of long brown oily camphorated paper. In summer, we lined the clothes closets with this paper to prevent damage to our pathetic woolen garments. A moth with all her faculties would think twice before she deposited her eggs in our clothing. Her larvae, feeding on the fibers, would either expire or suffer from terminal malnutrition.

Shoe polish must have been held in awe by Ruby. This was one of the rare items that perpetually occupied the same area at the left side of his front window for years. After purchasing liquid Shinola and finding its dauber frozen in dehydrated solution, I discovered that Griffin wax shoe polish was the wiser choice. Legislation requiring expiration dates was forty years in the future.

A remnant of the Jennings Street Market in 2004. The butcher whose sign decorates the fence had his store in a piece of this building.

Ruby was a congenial man with a ready smile. Usually, he could be seen walking around the tables with a mysterious object in his hand trying to determine how it could serve his customers.

In later years, Ruby's merchandise was still in demand—but in demand at the point of a knife or a finger on a trigger. After a few such incidents, Ruby shut the door on his landmark.

Another entrepreneur was my mother's tomato man, Benson. A thin sheet of plywood, about three by five feet, supported by two sawhorses was the showroom for his merchandise. One section held overripe tomatoes, another ripening green tomatoes, and, at stage center, the crown jewels of his inventory, the firm ripe red tomatoes. Since he was a *landsman* (someone from my parents' shtetl), he saved the not-quite-overripe tomatoes for my mother and charged her overripe prices. The difference was only a matter of pennies, but these were years when a penny bought a blank stamped postal card.

A voice that had a Parkinsonian effect on every shopper in range came roaring down the hills and over the moguls of a display of oranges, grapefruits, lemons, and tangerines. It emanated from the resonant vocal cords of Milton, the Pavarotti of Jennings Street Market, performing his aria on a wooden skid, surrounded by nature's bounty. Its magnetic field drew shoppers like the Piper's fife drew mice. Further confirmation of his operatic talent came from the fact that hardly anyone knew what he was shouting. Many years later, while he and I were reminiscing about the old neighborhood, my friend Al Lakind, whose dilapidated house was opposite Milton's stand, decoded his refrain. It was in Yiddish: "*Zetz uhp di mimeh!*" This can have two entirely different meanings: "Beat up your aunt!" or "Have intercourse with your aunt!" The shoppers had their choice.

Behind Milton and a few stores to his right was a small store that eventually evolved into a supermarket chain. A large green sign with white lettering let the East Bronx know it was Daitch Dairy. Its logo, "The Symbol of Quality," was painted below a sparkling diamond. Inside, compressed twelve-inch, parchment-wrapped farmer cheeses were stacked like bricks near a scale, waiting to be mortared into a building.

"Get a half-pound farmer cheese, and ask them to cut it from the thick side."

Inevitably, the piece was three-quarters of a pound.

"It weighs a little more than a half a pound," the counterman informed me.

"Why doesn't it ever weigh less than a half a pound?" I asked.

"Could I control the knife? Sometimes it goes this way, sometimes it goes that way."

I left with the cheese in a white paper bag knowing that Pa would be carrying that white bag to work with his bialy and cheese the next morning.

Across Jennings Street from Miller's fruit stand and about fifty feet up the street was the neighborhood culinary institute, Meager's Bakery on Wilkins Avenue. No insults, just the best-tasting rolls, rye bread, cornbread, and onion rolls that ever slid off a wooden paddle from the oven. My relatives would return to Montreal with a canvas sack full of cornbreads, telling each other "Don't drop them. They might split a tile or break your toe."

The neatest and most immaculate store in the market was the pork store. A large, ceramic head of a smiling pig dominated the center of the window display. Not a welcome smile to most of the passersby, who kept kosher homes. A heart bypass could have been performed here without the risk of infection. It looked as if Mr. Salerno threw fresh sawdust on the floor every fifteen minutes. All his merchandise was refrigerated in a sparkling glass case. Commercially packed and store-sliced meats were neatly aligned behind one another like rows of dominos. Silence from within came roaring at you when you passed the store. Quite a contrast to Brodsky's, my mother's butcher shop. Its proprietor held a seminar with each incision he made on the torso he hauled from the refrigerator. When my mother asked him to remove more fat and gristle from the chuck roast, Brodsky replied, "Mrs. Wolfe, I'm only a butcher; I'm not a surgeon."

His store was the official source of neighborhood gossip. With his steel sharpening rod, he divined a *shidach* (marriage match) for a worried mother. Phone numbers were exchanged, and Mr. Brodsky announced news of its progress.

We knew Miller's fruit and vegetable stand was on the corner of Wilkins Avenue and Jennings Street. We knew Jake was cursing out the women in the middle of Jennings Street. We knew Milton was straining his vocal cords opposite the intersection of Charlotte and Jennings Streets, but where was the Newspaperman? He could be somewhere between two fruit stands or in front of a closed stand in the evening. His newspaper stand consisted of a plywood board suspended over two empty milk boxes. Nervous—or, as my friend the Creep called him, Noiviss—related this Jennings Street story:

> On a chilly wintry evening, the fruit and vegetable vendors were blanketing down their inventory with heavy canvas tarpaulins. Jennings Street Market was being put to sleep. There wasn't a soul in the market but the Newspaperman. Under a rock and flapping in the breeze were the few remainders of the *Daily News, Daily Mirror,* and *Forward.*

A spacious gravestone for Jennings Street Market. Note the inspirational inscription by a local graphic artist.

I left Steinberg's Bakery with my hands in my pockets and a rye bread under my arm when I noticed the Newspaperman hunched over his stand, his hands in his armpits and a wool hat pulled over his ears.

"It's an empty street. It's freezing. The stands are closed. Why don't you go home?" I said. [This was highly unusual for Nervous, who rarely spoke to anyone he didn't know.]

"Listen, shitass, don't give me a weather report," said the newspaper vendor, while bouncing from one foot to the other. "I've been at this long before you were born. Who are you to tell me how to run my business?"

So the Newspaperman was another voice contributing to the congeniality of the Jennings Street Market. Even a casual vendor was sure to sustain the belligerent reputation of the street.

As a precursor to the demise of Jennings Street Market, Jake's wife passed away. After a period of mourning, Jake returned to his barrels. A few months later, barbarians broke into his apartment. They forced a hand towel down his throat. The czar was dead.

Today pickles can be purchased in sterile glass jars at the supermarket, but will your change be spiced with an insult to make shopping for these poor imitations an event? String beans can be purchased at Balducci's, where they are called *haricots verts*, but will Milton's vocal cords mesmerize the air? A plucked and cleaned free-range chicken can be purchased at Lobel's Meat Market, but will its feathered rear end be launched into your face for evaluation?

The immigrant families of the Jennings Street neighborhood inculcated their children with a love for learning. As the members of this first generation succeeded, with the help of the GI Bill, they moved to the suburbs. The vacuum created by their departure brought radical change to the neighborhood. It was silenced by crime. The Jennings Street theater played to an empty house. The curtains closed, the pageant was over.

Rent paid for the surrounding apartments did not cover the cost of vandalism. Landlords abandoned the buildings. The somber shells of the structures stood like ashen gravestones inscribed with illiterate graffiti in an abandoned cemetery.

In 2004, my friend Alvin and I returned to Jennings Street, looking for the market. A wall two blocks long confronted us—a gray, cinder-block, graffitied wall that resembled the cold, gray Berlin Wall. I saw a man sweeping the sidewalk in front of his butcher shop, the only store that had survived. The chipped facade cornice above his store was a pathetic vestige from the past. I asked him if he had owned the store when this was a bustling market. He had no idea what I was referring to.

Today, the shards of Jennings Street Market lie only in the fading memories of residents who once made it a community.

A View from the Stoop

We were not schooled in the aesthetic nuances of architecture, but as long-term residents, my friends and I agreed that the men who had designed our tenement buildings were neither valedictorians nor salutatorians of their graduating classes. Their attempt to create an appealing and welcome entrance fell flat on its facade.

Rarely was the entrance door to a tenement on street level. Ours sat above three one-by-four-foot slate gray steps. At the top, two chipped brown-painted doors inset with filigreed wrought iron swirls opened to a white and brown mosaic floor in the hallway.

The three gray steps constituted the stoop. If Mr. Tekula, the janitor, was sober, the stoop was verboten. If he was sleeping off last night's bender, we would scramble for choice seats. A choice seat was one where it was unnecessary to rise and step aside for a tenant or visitor entering or leaving the building. If there were only three of us, we would make a dash for a seat on a car running board where we wouldn't be hassled by the janitor or tenants and visitors.

On the running board we were able to use four-letter words and raise our voices without the neighbors' complaints. The same weighty issues were debated in this forum as on the stoop. How many baseball cards can I get for a Jimmy Foxx card in good condition? Ebbets Field has installed lights for night games; will the Yankees do it? Have you ever seen Mrs. Koletsky walk in front of her kitchen window in her bloomers? Why don't they make Chicago Racer wheels fit onto Union Hardware roller skates?

The stoop also was useful for one of our games—Off-the-Stoop—a game that had the residents screaming "Go to the park, bums!" and had the janitor chasing us with "Koom on! Get the hell outta here!" The player ran up to the stoop, threw the ball at it, and raced to bases drawn with chalk on the street, as fielders tried to catch the ball. This game was initiated with the full expectation that a ground floor tenant would sooner or later appear on the stoop to call a halt to it.

I suspect that our building stood proud and tan on an open field when it was built in the late nineteenth century. But its porous bricks absorbed every pollutant the Bronx had to offer. The pristine tan evolved into charcoal gray on its way toward becoming jet black. But that didn't interfere with the color scheme. It blended in well with the black cast-iron fire escapes forming a zigzagging scar down the belly of the building's facade.

From the stoop, a panorama unfolded before us. Jerry's five-story apartment house was to the left, and the six-story New House with an elevator was at the far right. Filling the void between these buildings were small, one-story shops, giving an overall appearance of two giant lower molars with immature teeth growing between them. The first of these "teeth" on the left was Pinsky's pathetic vegetable store, where a shaky gray wooden table in front displayed his wilted greens, soft onions, wrinkled, aging turnips, and shriveled parsnips for Friday's chicken soup.

"Hey, Krebs. Does your mother buy at Pinsky's?"

"No. She says Mrs. Miller in Jennings Street throws out better vegetables than the crap he sells."

"My mother goes there," said Bernie. "She feels sorry for him."

"Feels sorry for him?" Peanzy remarked. "He oughta close that dump. That place stinks like our toilet after our boarder took a crap in it."

Adjoining Pinsky's was Henry Lee's Chinese laundry. Lee had the misfortune of opening this laundry in a neighborhood whose residents had one change of clothes and did their laundry in a bathtub.

Following Lee was Luboff, the kosher butcher. Since he lacked the charisma of Brodsky, the butcher around the corner, his business was always hanging by a thin tendon.

"Luboff's place stinks, too. My mother doesn't go there," Peanzy continued.

"Where does she go?"

"She goes to the A&P that just opened."

"They don't sell kosher meat," Puggy pointed out.

Peanzy was getting annoyed, "We're not kosher," he said.

"My father said if you're not kosher, you're a communist," said Puggy.

Ma coming home with bargains from Jennings Street Market, 1941.
You can see the awning of Litroff's Bakery in the far rear. A little closer
is the hydrant where we left our jackets, and Nick the Shoemaker's store is to
the right of the hydrant. Pinsky, in a white apron,
is standing with a customer in front of his vegetable store.

Peanzy, lunging at Puggy, replied, "Your father is full of shit. We're not communists."

The stoop became a tangled mass of wrestling ten-year-olds. After we brushed ourselves off and took our seats again, we continued our review of the capitalist commerce going on across the street.

Adjacent to Luboff was Kosloff, the grocer, who sold sour cream and milk by the measure. The measure was a long-handled, one-pint metal scoop that hung from a hook near his cash register. It was a playground for pathogens, but no one knew it. Off to the refrigerator he went with his measure to fill an empty quart bottle. He lifted the circular metal lid from a tall milk can, scooped out two measures, and poured them into the patron's quart bottle. Only the fancy people could afford to buy milk bottled at the plant. Because of his limited inventory, Kosloff was one of the few grocers in the Bronx who did not own an extender to grasp boxes shelved high up out of reach. His entire inventory was within arm's length.

From glory to dump. Charlotte Street in a 1977 article.

To the right of Kosloff, occupying a two-store space, was the Harley-Davidson Motorcycle Club. We didn't know these folks. Their only contact with the neighborhood was producing resounding booms and black smoke from their exhaust pipes as they took off in black leather jackets and goggles to places where people with black leather jackets and goggles go on motorcycles on Sundays.

"Peanzy, did you ever speak to any of those guys on his motorcycle?"

"They look dangerous. I'm afraid he'd kick me in the ass. Did you?"

"No," said Julie. "I wouldn't know what to say to them."

The door nudged me in the back. Mrs. Lader was trying to leave the building.

"Danny, your mother should know you sit on the steps. Go to the park."

In the distance I saw my father walking toward our building. This was a good time to recess our summit meeting. It was close to dinnertime.

Thirty years after I moved from the Bronx, I decided to take a detour on my way home from work to visit the sweet memories of my childhood. In the distance, I saw the New House (the apartment building across the street). Venetian blinds and shades were suspended behind its windows. It had survived the blight! Yes, my stoop was still there but no rear ends would ever rest on it. Like gravestones, the shells of the tenement buildings

*Seabury Place in 2004. The New House is on the left, and
Hermann Ridder Junior High at the rear. But 1540 is gone.*

stood in somber silence where once a vibrant community had exploded
with the energy of daily lives; where mom-and-pop entrepreneurs slavishly
eked out a living in competition with itinerant pushcart peddlers; where
children of all ages overpopulated the sidewalks, stoops, and streets. Now
the gloom escaping from empty tenement windows draped a gray curtain
between the past and the present. I snapped a photo and quickly drove
away, with a lingering distaste for the desecration.

One year later, President Jimmy Carter visited my neighborhood to ini-
tiate Charlotte Gardens, a rehabilitation program. The area was to be razed.
The New House remained, and construction was to begin there, in the
place where I once knew every brick, every crack in the sidewalk, every
neighbor. The *Six O'Clock News* showed the president standing among the
skeletons of the tenements. A few months later I drove to a sad pile of
bricks and twisted metal where my home, my building once stood. Maybe
I could photograph the stoop? There was no trace of it, just the rubble of
iron and bricks. I picked up two bricks and drove home.

Then, in 2004, my friend Alvin and I returned to the cradle of our youth.
From Boston Road I turned left onto Seabury Place. The surrounding area

appeared to be a middle-class suburb. The Carter and Reagan administrations had successfully eliminated the skeletons and the rubble and had built modest single-family dwellings. Neatly clipped lawns surrounded the small homes that now replaced our shattered tenements.

A new broom had swept clean. It had swept away a sweet, pleasant, fun-filled era and left in its wake first fear, terror, vandalism, and murder, and then this green patch blooming in the South Bronx. I hope it will impart pleasant memories to the children who are now living there.

The New House

Ours was a humble building, like its string of sister tenements leaning against one another on Seabury Place. A row of dominos, all with the identical number of windows pressed into them, these four-story buildings formed a depressing brick wall on the east side of the street. Atop the walls, projecting copper cornices overhung the black zigzagging fire escapes. Slashes of oxidized green, streaking through the paint of these cornices, begged for but never received a fresh coat.

Directly across the street, rising majestically above its poor cousins was a tall tan brick art deco apartment building, the New House. It was the only building on the street with an elevator. From its inner courtyard, four wide gray granite steps boldly proclaimed their presence by aggressively projecting onto the sidewalk, daring us to sit on them. In the evening, two coach lights flanking the steps illuminated the path to the entrance.

Nobody, but nobody, ever sat on the steps of this building. This was the only stoop on the block untested by rear ends. Mr. Schmidt, the janitor, and his frothing German shepherd scoured their domain with the intensity of guards patrolling the electrified fences at a concentration camp.

Milty lived on the fifth floor of the New House. Although the Depression affected most of the families in the neighborhood, money was not a problem in his household. His parents generously supported his hobbies.

"Come up to my apartment. I have a new crystal set with headphones," he said.

This was a fascinating and entertaining gadget for an eleven-year-old. When a vertical copper needle at the end of a pivoting shaft was placed onto a sensitive area of a crystal, the sound of a radio broadcast could be heard in earphones connected to the device.

The New House as it appeared in 2004. My apartment house stood where the parking lot is.

It wasn't the first time Milty had invited me, but there was no way I would step into that building as long as Schmidt and his hound guarded the area.

"Schmidt and his wife leave the building every Sunday," said Milty. "Come up next Sunday. We'll have fun."

I was eager to hear his crystal set and see his other gadgets. He convinced me that Adolph Hitler and Eva Braun would be gone for the day.

Sunday arrived. The door to Schmidt's street-level apartment, usually ajar, was closed. I looked toward the adjacent cellar gate: neither the Nazi nor his beast was in sight. Cautiously, I walked up the granite steps and passed through the entrance doors. With apprehension, I stepped into the elevator, slid the inner scissors gate closed, and squeezed button number five. I was on edge. The elevator's three metal walls and the gate in front of me reinforced my fright. The cab was on its way. Can't it move faster? I worried. Will it ever reach the fifth floor? Suddenly it stopped between the third and fourth floors. I froze. Then the elevator reversed direction. Herr Schmidt's vulgar German grunts and his snarling dog's growls came thundering up the shaft from the basement. The elevator was being pulled downward, downward toward the cellar. Frozen with terror I passed the third floor. What was I to do? I was imprisoned in this metal cage. When the elevator was directly opposite the second floor, I slid open the scissor gate. The elevator stopped. I pushed the door open, rushed down the steps and out the front door, streaked through the sunshine, and ran up to my apartment.

Ma was rinsing spinach when I came panting by her. "Look at that pale face! How many times do I have to tell you not to run up the steps? Young people get heart attacks, too."

If she knew how many near heart attacks I had had in the past ten minutes, she would have carried me up the steps to our apartment on her back.

Secure in Pa's chair but still trembling, I swore I would never, ever go near the Reich Chancellery again.

"Are you breathing like a normal person again?" Ma called from the kitchen. "Maybe Mrs. Miller grew this spinach at Orchard Beach. Come help me rinse out the sand."

The sand resembled little blackheads as they settled on the sink's crackled white porcelain. One flush from the faucet had them scrambling down the drain.

I returned to Pa's chair wondering what I ever did to Schmidt to make him so evil. What had my family in their tiny village in Lithuania done to his heroes that we could no longer send packages to our relatives? I'd ask Pa when he came home.

Germany had overrun Poland, conquered the Baltic States, and was marching through Russia. It wasn't long before Schmidt, his wife, his daughter, and his frothing monster disappeared from the neighborhood. My friends and I were convinced that somehow he had returned to the Fatherland to become an adjutant to Heinrich Himmler, and his wife had become an aide to Ilse Koch, the Bitch of Buchenwald.

Today, in 2006, the New House is still standing and the elevator is still carrying passengers to their apartments. I would like to join them and tell the story of my elevator ride, but I am still afraid that the ghost of Schmidt and his vicious hound might be lurking at the bottom of the elevator shaft.

Ma's Hammer

The radiator stood in the corner of our living room like a brat being punished for a misdeed. In a vacant apartment, it was the centerpiece of a bare bedroom or living room. Spruced up with a new coat of silver paint, it shone to greet a new tenant. The landlord spared no expense in hiring a Michelangelo to douse the radiator and anything that happened to be on it with a veneer of silver. Consequently, tangles of cobwebs, a roach taking its constitutional, or paint chips that had abandoned the ceiling were laminated under the new silver exterior. Like layers of sedimentary rock, each coat of paint contained a history.

Who had designed this device? It should have been placed near a cinder block wall of a warehouse, complementing a tangle of exposed wires, rusty pipes, and meters. Its credentials for dispensing some heat allowed it to barge in and ensconce itself in the far corner of our living room.

My Bronx tenement building had been built in 1894. I guess this tubular, cast iron device was a state-of-the-art fixture at the time. It did not corrode; it did not erode. As Shakespeare said of Cleopatra's beauty, "Age cannot wither her, nor custom stale her infinite variety." So, here we were, forty-five years later, with this silver apparatus unaffected by age, indifferent to fashion, defiantly standing tall and proud.

Some unhappy tenants hid the intrusive radiator with creative camouflage. The common disguise was a punctured sheet metal veil, allowing heat to escape but concealing the eyesore behind it. In winter, the radiator's top doubled as a shelf that Ma used for reheating her cuisine. Tenacious food stains became a permanent part of this appendage. In summer, when the radiator was at rest, Ma adorned it with her annual failure: an avocado plant grown from a brown, golf-ball-sized seed. The plant struggled to survive and then dropped its leaves as if it knew it could not compete with an occasionally whistling radiator in autumn.

If Ma saw this radiator, she would have sung, "If I Had a Hammer."

"Maybe next year, it will be better," Ma would say. It never was.

With the arrival of cold weather, steam heat was meted out sparingly. After all, coal came from trees, it did not grow on them. A hiss from a shiny, chrome-plated valve connected to the side of the radiator announced that Mr. Tekula, our janitor, was sufficiently sober to locate the aperture of the furnace with a shovelful of coal. In his usual comatose state, he was awakened by a cacophony of clangs from the tenants' hammers striking their radiators. This Tenant Symphony informed him that we were shivering in the tundra.

Ma played first hammer in the percussion section. She stepped up to the instrument in her uniform: a cotton housedress, an apron, and felt slippers. As tender as she was with her children, as devoted as she was to her husband, she defiantly held her hammer, dug in her heels, snapped her wrists, swung her hips, and followed through like Joe DiMaggio to pound the radiator for a home run. Shards of silver paint darted in every direction, leaving Rorschachlike depressions on the radiator in their wake.

Pa, in his bathrobe, shivering on his shaky club chair, made sure he played a part in the recital. "Rose, go easy on the radiator. Tekula may be sleeping."

"If he's freezing like I am, he shouldn't wake up."

Pa's major role was as the grip for the concert. With his tiny brush and little jar of silver paint, he healed the scars on the machine after Ma's solo.

When three years had elapsed, the landlord was mandated to paint the apartment, radiator included. The scarred martyr was smeared again by an artist's supersaturated brush, leaving puddles of silver droplets in its wake. The radiator then stood within a rectangular silver outline of itself on our linoleum floor covering, prepared to take a beating for three more years.

If I had foreseen the Tenement Museum in Manhattan, I would have bronzed and framed Ma's hammer, engraved its history on a brass plate, and submitted the package to be spotlighted above a similar radiator in that collection.

Today, buyers of a two- or three-story brownstone sometimes inherit these radiators. With a substantial investment they usually replace the antiques with baseboard heaters or grates for forced-air heat or heated foils, improvements in thermal device evolution. They melt into the landscape of the living room.

Our radiators are history; Ma's hammer is history. We are left without an inebriated janitor, without a clanging cast-iron radiator, without a hissing valve, without a hammer. What tales can vents or heated foils tell?

An Additional Perk

Who would have guessed that our tenement building would have a dumb-waiter? From a rusty twelve-inch pipe sticking out from the outside wall of the house in the East Bronx dangled a new blue and white enamel sign in the shape of a shield. Creaking and rocking in the wind, it announced the availability of one- and two-bedroom apartments. Below, bold letters proclaimed that a Kelvinator gas refrigerator graced the empty, roach-infested apartments. But how would you know that another perk was the luxury of a dumbwaiter? A dumbwaiter to ease the burden of carrying our brown paper garbage bags to the pails in the cellar.

Mrs. Dolnik, the landlady, paid her monthly visit to collect $25 for our one-bedroom apartment. Most of the tenants paid on time. Mr. Packman, our neighbor in apartment 2, called himself a seasonal worker. Which season he worked was a mystery everyone tried to solve, especially Mrs. Dolnik. When rent was not available, neither was Mr. Packman. When he was able to scrape up the cash, he reappeared as mysteriously as he had disappeared.

Mr. Freidman, in apartment 7, was a painter—an apartment painter. He was another seasonal worker waiting for the right season to call him to duty. I believe the painter's hat, which was bonded to his head, was the precursor to today's fashionable baseball hat. In the hallway, adjacent to his apartment and apparently frozen to the wall, leaned his unopened ladder. It never budged. The Great Depression had willing workers awaiting the call. Very few were summoned.

Some of the tenants' garbage bags were as anemic as their incomes, but, with five mouths to feed, Ma was able to generate a full oil-stained bag daily.

We could depend on the dumbwaiter bell to intrude while we were eating. This was no accident. Mr. Tekula, the janitor, detested the tenants; the tenants despised him.

Our family was seated at the table dining on Friday night's chicken. Shrolleh as usual pointed to a large brown-stained pipe curving downward from the apartment above us and disappearing into a bulging wall leading to the basement. "The Toilet," he called it and claimed that all the toilets in the building led into this pipe. His narrative, of course, whetted our appetite for the next course.

He was chewing up a chicken leg bone, rolling the macerated pieces over his tongue, and expelling them onto his plate. The table was so short and narrow that, although I tried, I couldn't look away. When he spit out the shards, I nearly gagged on my derma. The grating of the dumbwaiter bell interrupted this repulsive sight. Everyone and everything in the kitchen vibrated to its tremors. Mr. Tekula was collecting the garbage.

Ma, who was serving the stewed prunes for dessert, said, "Sit. I'll get it."

She rushed to grab the bag under the kitchen sink, and sped to open the dumbwaiter door. We braced ourselves for the pungent whiff of rot that diffused from the shaft into the kitchen. The dumbwaiter was a six-by-three-foot open wooden rectangle divided into two square compartments, one on top of the other. Each compartment was generously laminated with a history of the tenants' spillage. Upon opening the dumbwaiter door, we beheld bulging brown paper bags ripe with garbage, desperately clinging to each other in an attempt to prevent a spillover. This was the visual complement to the stench.

Leaning forward, with a tight grip on a thick, braided sisal rope, Mr. Tekula pulled the dumbwaiter up to each apartment. Frequently, his abrupt tug on the rope caused some bags to topple. The contents could travel in only one direction—down onto the head of Mr. Tekula. Baptized by garbage, he emitted a flow of Polish invectives that, unaffected by gravity, scaled the shaft and passed into each apartment through the dumbwaiter doors, whether open or closed.

Tenants could have walked their garbage to the empty drums in the cellar free of bells and taunts. But why should they? That would be a ceasefire, a white flag of surrender. Tekula would win without an insult being fired.

One evening, we had a visitor. Standing at our door was Mr. Tekula himself. He certainly hadn't dressed for the occasion. His grimy, gray chino pants and ragged plaid flannel shirt were not the attire of a gentleman caller. His oversized pores pocked the purple-red skin of his face. Somewhere in the center of this landscape a mottled nose, sprouting hair, supported silver-rimmed eyeglasses. Slicked-back gray hair was streaked with yellow patches from when he had been blond in the past.

Without a word, he walked past us, strode toward the dumbwaiter, opened the door, and painted a foul-smelling Iron Glue onto the door-jambs.

We sat in silence. What was he up to? What emergency had brought him to us this evening? Wasn't this the first time he had entered our apartment?

He closed the dumbwaiter door making a seal with the Iron Glue and, with a sneer of triumph, warned, "No open door no more."

As soon as he left, Ma closely inspected his work and then solemnly said, "Our cockroaches are not going to like this."

The dumbwaiter was decommissioned. After that evening, it lay suspended in its shaft for forty-two years.

A Shower for Apartment 11

Technology was moving forward at a rapid pace. The World's Fair of 1939 at Flushing Meadow Park in Queens, promised a life of leisure, but apartment 11 on Seabury Place, trying to climb out of the Great Depression, marched in place.

For breakfast, Ma assigned me a seat near the stove to make sure the toast didn't burn on our collapsible tin toaster. The flames from our gas stove poked through the toaster's perforations, but I was there to signal that the toast was turning brown.

"Ma, can I turn over the toast? It's brown."

"The last time you tried you burned your fingers. Let Harold do it. You get the milk."

"Let Harold do it." "Let Harold do it." He was twelve, three years older. Would I ever be able to do anything around here? I went to the icebox, pulled up on the door handle, took out the milk, and gave the bottle a good shake. The cream mixed well with the milk. Harold removed the toast and then fried two eggs for the two of us in our Wearever aluminum frying pan.

With a cookie in hand, Harold left for Hermann Ridder Junior High School across the street, and I went off to P.S. 61. After the two-block walk, my corduroy knickers had pushed my knee-high stockings down to my ankles. Before entering the classroom, I pulled them up again, adjusted my white shirt, and straightened my red knitted tie. I entered the room as neat as any girl in the class.

Ma still scrubbed our clothes on her wobbly, corrugated metal washboard, bleached and blued the whites, then rinsed the wash, and hung it on a clothesline to dry. Our incontinent oak icebox left a telltale puddle of water meandering on the kitchen floor. Why couldn't we have a refrigerator like the tenants across the street in the New House? Our collapsible toaster soon was replaced by a chrome pop-up Toastmaster, but the icebox continued to flood the kitchen floor.

A knock brought Ma to the door. "Who is it?" she asked.

"It's Mrs. Dolnik, the landlady."

"I paid the rent last week."

"No, Mrs. Wolf. I am sending a plumber to you tomorrow. He will …"

Ma opened the door and interjected, "Yes, yes. The water in the tank above the toilet seat drips on us when, you should excuse me, we move our bowels."

"No, no. The plumber will install a shower. Would you like that?"

"For a raise in rent, I don't like that. We can clean ourselves in the bathtub."

"It will only be a dollar a month. Isn't it worth it?"

"For a dollar, I could get a plucked chicken for Friday … but we'll take it."

Last month Dolnik gave us a new valve for the radiator. Now we're getting a shower? At the Crotona Park Pool, we had a shower. At my aunts' building in Brighton Beach, they had a shower. But a shower in our own apartment? With such a luxury, would we ever leave the house?

In the evening, my father dragged himself into the apartment after a day of hand-finishing ladies' overcoats. "Oy! That boss of mine is ripping the skin off my bones. Where's my chair?"

Like a magnet, gravity pulled him into the crater of his upholstered armchair.

"Morris, do we need a shower?" Ma asked.

"A shower? Why do we need a shower? We have a bathtub."

"So I'll tell the plumber tomorrow not to put up a shower."

"Maybe he could make the water go down faster in the bathtub? I sit there soaking like a tea bag in a tub of *shmutz* [dirt]."

"But a shower, you don't want?" asked Ma.

"All right. Let him come in and put up a shower."

Two days later, the plumber knocked on our door. His heavy leather plumber's bag, slung over his shoulder, had him leaning at a 30-degree angle to the right. When he put the bag down, he was still leaning 30 degrees to the right. He aligned an assortment of narrow cast-iron pipes on the floor outside our apartment. Ma showed him to a bathroom almost entirely occupied by a sink, a bathtub, and a toilet bowl. The rusty stains in the sink below the hot and cold water faucets were the first to greet him. A water tank, high above the toilet seat, was performing its drip concerto while the water in the toilet bowl below gurgled with delight. The claw feet of our tub held their tenacious grip on the undulating mosaic tiles beneath them.

The plumber dropped his bag into the tub and then told us to do what we had to do with water, because he was shutting it off for a few hours. I turned on the tub faucets full blast to mute any embarrassing sounds I might emit with the odor seeping under the door.

Banging and clattering began with the installation of water pipes running from the shut-off valves to the faucets. The plumber then connected a single arching pipe capped with a perforated six-inch disc showerhead. An oval curtain rod, following the outer edge of the tub, was secured to the wall and ceiling. A white cotton shower curtain was suspended from this rod, hiding the chronically peeling paint on the wall behind the tub.

In the evening, I was ready for my first spritz. Would marinating in a tub full of dirty soap bubbles come to an end? I eagerly anticipated that orange-red cake of Lifebuoy soap skimming over every plane, curve, and crevice of my body. This would be followed by a surge of water from the showerhead, energizing my lathered body and leaving it squeaky clean. Then I would step out, wafting that he-man Lifebuoy scent. I turned on first the hot and then the cold faucets. A tentative trickle came out of the showerhead. I could count the drops as they squeezed through its perforations. Soon a cascade of water will burst through the showerhead, I thought. No, the trickle was it.

The spray from the showers at Crotona Park pool nearly knocked me over. But the city had built those showers. My aunt's shower tickled my back. But this? Was this our new shower?

In spite of this minor defect, it was our shower, and Pa paid for it. Now we had a shower, a phantom of a shower, in our apartment.

The shower was used daily by my family without complaint. Nineteen years later, my fiancée spent the night at our apartment. The following morning, she stepped into the bathtub for her shower. After a minute or two she ran, wrapped in a towel, into the kitchen where I was having breakfast.

"How do you clean yourself in this thing you call a shower?"

"Why? We've been using it for years."

She led me to the bathroom and turned on the faucets.

"Is this what you call a shower? When does the spray come out?" she asked.

"That is the spray," I replied.

Through no fault of her own, at that moment, she made me realize that I had been cheated out of a real shower throughout my sprinkling years.

Street Games

Three o'clock—school's out! I ran upstairs for a glass of milk and a piece of honey cake; then I rushed into the street. Why run two blocks to Crotona Park when we had the street in front of our apartment house as a playground?

Street games were determined by our physical development and the architecture of the neighborhood. At ages five and six, Hide and Seek, Tag, and Running Bases, with the "big guys" throwing the ball, were as much as our bodies could manage in competitive sports. As our muscles developed and reflexes sharpened, the rubber ball played a major role in our street games. The ball at this time was white, sweet smelling, and stamped with scripted "Leader" inside an oval disc.

Sidewalks were constructed of four-foot concrete squares separated by half-inch expansion joints. A penny, a key, or a soda bottle cap was placed on the joint as a target. Each player stood at the far end of one of the two adjacent squares and threw the ball at the target. A ball that hit it, earned a point. The first one to score ten points won the game.

"That's a point for me."

"Why? You didn't hit the penny."

"I did so. It was heads, and now it's tails."

"It was tails before, and it's tails now."

"I quit. You're cheating."

"Go quit, baby. I won't play with you again."

Scoring ten points could take forever, so an argument was a good way to stop the game.

On the same concrete squares, we played Box Ball. Each player stood in an adjacent square and hit the ball without a previous bounce into his opponent's square. A bounce or a hit outside the square scored a point for the opponent. Stupid? No. It kept us occupied.

Some of the older boys on Seabury Placein 1940. Mrs. Baretz's candy store is to the left, and Hermann Ridder Junior High at the right rear.

With sharpened reflexes, we moved ahead to Off the Point as our game of choice. There were two different methods of playing, depending on the number of players. The exotic architecture of the tenement building had rows of horizontal bricks, one row indented, the next row projected. The projected row created the "point." With a minimum of two players, we stood at the foot of the curb and then threw the ball at the point. If the ball hit the point, it would rise in the air and return to the thrower. If the thrower caught the ball without a bounce, he earned a point. The first player to get ten points won the game.

Punchball, our favorite, used the white rubber Leader or a solid sponge ball (the pink Spalding was yet to arrive on the scene). This game was played in the street. Since very few people in the neighborhood owned a car, traffic was no problem.

First, second, and third bases were drawn with chalk. Usually a sewer lid was home plate. The number of boys in the street determined the number of players. The two best players were the captains. One captain selected "odds," the other "evens." On a signal, each captain extended one or two fingers. If the total was three, the captain who selected "odds" had the first pick; if the total was two or four, the "evens" had first pick. This assured equally balanced teams.

Standing near the sewer lid, the "batter" punched the ball onto the field. The puncher was out if the ball was caught without a bounce. As in baseball, a ground ball had to be caught and sent successfully to the first baseman before the puncher arrived, to make an out.

"Your foot was off the base!"

"It was not!"

"You didn't see it. You were trying to catch the ball."

If one of the "big fellas" was nearby, he would make the decision. If there wasn't anyone to issue a verdict, it was a "do over." If neither side bent, the game came to an abrupt halt with each side accusing the other of cheating.

Seven innings completed a game. The score was written in chalk on the asphalt of the street. The diagram of the score resembled a fish's skeleton with its vertebral column and ribs. The spine separated the names of the teams and the score they earned. The ribs separated the innings.

Triangle was a similar game, played when only a few players were in the street. There were two bases. The field, chalked out from home plate on the street's asphalt, was shaped like an isosceles triangle. The pitcher tossed the ball underhand, pinching it so that it would curve or back up after it bounced. The hitter used the palm of his hand to send the ball into play. From then on, the game resembled Punchball.

In autumn, one of the boys took a newspaper, folded it, rolled it up, tied it with a piece of twine, and—voila!—an eight-inch football shaped like a large frankfurter roll. The game, Two-Hand Touch, was played on the street, like the others. Opposite sewer lids were the goal lines for the teams. No tackling, of course; two hands placed on the runner ended a play.

"You never touched me!"

"Yes I did, but you didn't feel it. Next time I'll blast you."

"Oh, yeah? Just try it, liar, and you'll go running home with a bloody nose."

After a heated scholarly debate on whether it was sacrilege to use a rolled-up Jewish newspaper, the *Forward,* as a football, the sages made a decision, with Talmudic logic as their guide. "A rolled-up Jewish newspaper tied with a shaggy twine is perfectly compatible with the ethics of our fathers provided that you don't kick it. So, when the play calls for a kick, throw the *Forward* with the opposite hand as far as you can."

Many a rolled up paper provided hours of fun during the chill of autumn. This game gave our less agile friends an opportunity to play and distinguish themselves. For example, Hopalong (Abe), crippled in his right leg by polio but strong and beefy, was one of the first players picked because of his excellent line play. Bull (Stanley) could not catch a ball if it was placed in his hands but gave a very good account of himself as a blocker and defense man. Puggy was picked only when we needed an extra man. Peanzy's agility was amazing. How he was able to outmaneuver an opponent on those narrow streets mystified all of us.

There was no bias among my friends but there definitely was a hierarchy based upon our performance in the street games. Peanzy was the fastest. Moish was the best hitter. I was best at Off the Curb and best pitcher in Pitching In. And we knew that no street game would be possible if the rest of our crowd were not there to play and enjoy the sport with us.

The curbs of a four-way intersection formed the Off the Curb field and bases. No one owned a car, and our neighborhood wasn't a tourist attraction. Consequently, the street was clear to play this game. On rare occasions, a car *was* parked on the field of play. If its doors were unlocked, one of the "big fellas" would shift the car into neutral, and we would push it off the field. If we couldn't move the car, we had specific rules, modified over the years, to decide what was a base hit when the ball hit or went under the car.

In Off the Curb, the "batter" threw the ball at a wide chip in the curb. It flew up and out toward the infielders and outfielders. The rules of baseball then applied.

Julie, who was three years younger than we were, was one of the few neighborhood boys physically handicapped by "the awkward age." He never traveled at a smooth pace. His sneakers managed to bump into any rise in the sidewalk, light pole, or hydrant that should not have been there.

One day, as we chose up sides for Off the Curb, we needed another man. As a last choice Peanzy picked Julie. Before it was Julie's turn to throw the ball at the curb, Peanzy warned, "If you fall down, Julie, I'll kill you!"

Julie threw the ball at the curb. A base hit! He rounded first base and headed toward second. As he approached that base, he tripped and sprawled out in front of Adoff's drugstore. Peanzy ran over to Julie, gently kicking and stomping him as he screamed, "Didn't I tell you not to fall down?"

We were rolling with laughter.

At about age ten or eleven, we started to play the game that was the crown jewel of all street games, Stickball. The Leader rubber balls we used lost their bounce after a few games and ended up in the hands of the younger neighborhood athletes. The stick came from an old broom or, when we were desperate, a mop.

Another notable event was the day the neighborhood bookie, Leo, came strolling by with his newborn in a carriage while we were playing Pitching In. The ball was hit in the air and floated down into the carriage. Was the ball a hit or an out? Whether the infant was hit was of no concern to us. Since the ball had landed behind the pitcher's mound in fair territory, it might have been scored a double. Since the fielder couldn't catch it, it might have been a do-over. The debate continued into the candy store. We referred our problem to the "big fellas." No solution. To this day, when the boys discuss the dilemma, they still disagree.

I shudder when I think about one Pitching In game we played on a weekend afternoon. I hit a ground-rule double that landed on top of a series of one-story stores running from 172nd Street around and down Seabury Place. We were democratic. If you hit the ball onto the roof and were agile enough to climb the clothesline pole adjacent to the stores to reach the roof, you retrieved the ball. If not, a volunteer went after it.

I started climbing up the projecting spikes on the pole. It was about a thirty-foot ascent. Just as I left the last spike and jumped from the pole to the roof, the rotting pole snapped at its base and fell against a fire escape on the building behind it. I stood on the roof shaking in my sneakers and looking at the rotted pole collapsed against the fire escape. Would I have to remain on the roof until the Fire Department rescued me? Fortunately, at the far right there was another pole that I climbed down, slowly and with great caution.

Julie and Trench Feet (Jerry) decades later point to the location of
the old curb where Peanzy warned Julie not to fall down.

Another game played in the street was the Fine Game. Two cans the size
of baked bean cans were placed facing each other on opposite curbs with
their open ends toward the players. To score a goal, a player had to kick a
ball into the can. After a few days of battle-scarred ankles and black-and-
blue shins without a goal to show for it, Moish called a halt to the game.
He then attempted to place the ball into the aperture of the can by hand. It
did not fit—the ball was wider than the can!

"This is a fine game!" he exclaimed.

Did we stop playing the game? Of course not! We played for weeks thereafter, calling it the Fine Game.

What could we do with a ball at night? Leave it home? Keep it in a pocket for the next day? Oh, no! We put it into action. We played Over the Light. Any number can play. Each player represented himself. A player threw the ball over the streetlight and into the evening darkness. As it descended from the blackness into the halo of the streetlight, the opponent stood poised to catch it. If he caught the ball, it was his turn to throw it. If the catcher dropped the ball, the thrower scored a point. The first player to get ten points was the winner.

During World War II rubber was at a premium. The familiar white Leader rubber ball used in our street games was no longer available. Just as Lucky Strike Green had "Gone to War!" the rubber in the ball was drafted. Quickly slipping in to fill the vacuum was a black ersatz-rubber ball. It bounced much higher than the Leader but was extremely vulnerable. If it was hit on the seam, the ball would split. From this emerged the game of Half-Ball. The split half of the ball was pitched to a batter, with neither pitcher nor batter having any idea of its path. Like a knuckle ball, sometimes it would sail upward, sometimes it would curve, and sometimes it would dip as it approached the plate. Most of the time it never reached the batter. When it was hit, it didn't travel very far. The ball was an interim trinket for the war's duration, later replaced by the classic pink Spalding.

Hockey on Shoes was another favorite. No skates? No sticks? No problem. All we needed was anything the size of a puck. A piece of ice became a puck in winter. Shoes replaced skates; shoes also replaced sticks. We passed the puck to our teammates with kicks. The pebbles embedded in the cement sidewalks were like sandpaper on the soles of our shoes. No matter. Nick the Shoemaker was ready to replace them with Cat's Paw soles.

Immediately after World War II the gem, the pearl, of street game equipment, the pink Spalding, made its debut. It was perfect for Stickball. It was a high bouncer, it did not split when hit on the seam, and it held a true path when it was thrown. Building architecture, parked cars, and women sitting on fruit boxes in front of their buildings determined rules for the game that were carefully worked out and passed on to each next generation.

Among the many street games I have not yet mentioned were Street Hockey, Skelly, Ringaleevio, Johnny on the Pony, Three Feet to Germany, Flipping Cards, Pitching Pennies, Kick the Can, and our friend Mutt's personal creation: guessing the number from one to ten that he had written on a yellow slip of paper. If we guessed it, he paid twice the number he had written.

Following World War II, signs of prosperity began to appear. The once empty streets became congested with cars, mostly pre-war relics. The Beck brothers bought a pre-war DeSoto yellow cab that had more miles than a subway train. They dismantled the motor, leaving its parts lying on the street as they worked on it for a few weeks. Finally, when it was reassembled, veiled in a cloud of black smoke, it puffed once around the block and then expired in front of their building.

Veterans returned from overseas. They went to school or to work, but the appeal of Stickball persisted. On Sunday morning, teams were chosen and the pink Spalding went flying off cars, tenement buildings, and sometimes residents. The women were still sitting on the sidewalks, still yelling their old refrain, "Bums, go to the park!"

The bums went on to become accountants, chemists, teachers, mathematicians, postal employees, and builders of luxury homes. All of us long for those carefree days when our pockets were empty but our days were full of laughter.

P.S. 61

Directly across the street from the abandoned powerhouse on Boston Road, perched atop the huge cement foundation that formed the schoolyard, loomed this gloomy three-story red brick structure. Its architecture would have meshed very nicely with that of the somber, late-nineteenth-century New England textile mills. On the top floor, curved sand-colored arches capping the tall classroom windows tempered the depressing red bricks. This was our elementary school, P.S. 61.

My earliest recollection is of the kindergarten class. We carried small, mission-style oak chairs to form a semicircle in front of our teacher, Miss Kogan. From her perch on a high oak chair, she read, told stories, and instructed us. Her animated rendition of the now verboten *Little Black Sambo* could have earned her a starring role on Broadway. When weather permitted, she would lead us to the schoolyard. The first test of our physical agility and rhythm was to form a circle. Then the boys reluctantly selected a female partner, bowed, and sang:

> How do you do my partner?
> How do you do today?
> We will dance in a circle.
> I will show you the way.
> Tra-la-la-la-la-la.

After we recovered from this choreography, number two on the Hit Parade was, *Did You Ever See a Lassie?* the precursor to aerobics at Gold's Gym. Again we formed a circle and sang while gyrating and twisting:

> Did you ever see a lassie, a lassie, a lassie,
> Did you ever see a lassie go this way and that? (gyrations)

P.S. 61 in 2004. The dark buildings in front of the brick school are portable classrooms.

Go this way and that way (gyrations)
Go this way and that way (calisthenics continue)
Did you ever see a lassie go this way and that? (twisted in a knot)

At the beginning of the year I had difficulty communicating with my classmates. My Yiddish interspersed with fractured English kept my conversation to a minimum. Consequently, I sat quietly in class and rarely spoke unless spoken to. Frequently I did not reply because my responses in the past had been met with laughter.

"Bring two wooden hangers to class tomorrow. We will make them pretty for Mother's Day," said Miss Kogan.

We covered the hangers with her Kelly green enamel paint. When they dried, I thought I had created a work of art. Apparently Ma thought so, too. They were to hang, undressed, in my parents' closet displaying their young artist's masterpiece for fifty years. Whatever became of them?

Was it my language handicap, shyness, or a combination of the two that kept me from speaking to the girls in the class? They spoke English without a trace of an accent, while I was struggling with the language. But one thing brought them down a notch in my esteem: the heavy, institutional, long taupe jersey stockings they wore in the winter. These stockings appeared to be very itchy. I was certain my fingernails would have been in perpetual motion collecting the skin off my thighs and legs had I worn them.

How did they stay up? They seemed to be stapled to something under their skirts or connected to their skin with mending tissue (the precursor to Scotch tape). The stocking ran smoothly along the leg until it reached the knee. At that point, when the knee was straight, the jersey bulged into a slight protrusion, a lump, as if an abscess were festering behind it. This hollow lump filled with the kneecap as soon as the girl sat down.

Mrs. Hyman was my first and second grade teacher. By then, my language skills had greatly improved. I learned to read quickly, while Ernie Gitlitz continued to place a yellow slip of paper under the line of words he was struggling to decode. For showing the most improvement, I was rewarded by Mrs. Hyman with a book called *The Little Swiss Wood Carver*, which I have to this day. Although I was still shy, the award gave me the confidence to mingle with my classmates.

Our third grade reader was *Peter and Peggy*, whose lives bore no resemblance to ours. They lived in a house, they ate in a dining room, and they had a dog. The family owned a car, and on weekends they would go for a drive to the country. In spite of their unheard of lifestyle, we learned to read.

After our adventure with *Peter and Peggy* we moved on to arithmetic. By this time we had mastered the basics. Now that we had the ability to read, practical problems challenged us. Miss Adelman, our teacher, watched carefully to see if we were looking for the correct answers at the back of the book. I had a great feeling of satisfaction when I was able to sneak a peek there to confirm a correct answer.

My hand went up when the teacher called for a volunteer to be the cracker monitor. Little eight-ounce containers of milk were delivered daily to students who ordered them each week. Upon their arrival, I went to the second floor gym, whose cork tiles had absorbed dust and odors since the late nineteenth century. A volunteer mother placed a variety of crackers in a square red tin with a press-down lid, which I took to my classroom. For a penny, students could choose from Oreo-type vanilla cookies, brown cookies with peanuts popping out of the surface, fig newtons, or thin white crackers embedded with pressed raisins. At the end of milk break, I returned the pennies and unsold cookies to the woman in charge. She rewarded me with the shards of broken cookies.

We graduated from a pencil to a pen: a metal pen point pushed into a tapered wooden dowel, which we dipped into ink periodically. The pencil, our writing instrument for first and second grade, was now to be used exclusively for arithmetic problems, where many erasures were anticipated. To prepare us for writing script, Miss Scraley, the school's writing specialist, entered the classroom for her cameo role.

Because I was a left-handed scribe, my pinkie and the side of my palm would smear the wet ink as I wrote. By the time I left school, my left hand resembled an Arab woman's henna-decorated palm.

With the completion of the Palmer cursive exercises, Miss Scraley left the class to Miss Adelman. She rolled down a six-by-twenty-inch white chart with the phonics, AY, EE, AI, AW, OH, OO emblazoned in bold black letters. With her black-rubber-tipped wooden pointer, she indicated the phonic we were to vocalize. It was a futile attempt to exorcise New Yorkese from our larynges.

When the weather cooperated, we went outdoors. I think I can attribute my present wrist problems to the schoolyard game in which we used miniature bats to strike rubberized softballs the diameter and weight of the moon.

I dreaded the arrival of a monitor carrying a buff-colored chart. She was Satan's messenger assigned to lead a victim to the torture chamber, a den worthy of the Inquisition, the dental office.

The dentist's drilling apparatus appeared to be constructed from an Erector set. Movable metal sections resembling a construction crane pivoted overhead. This enabled the dentist to penetrate the ailing tooth. A thin cable moving through the sections activated his slow, primitive drill.

Hairy knuckles and forearms moving toward my mouth told me the drill was airborne and zeroing in on a tooth that had caused neither him nor me harm. My damp shirt stuck to my back and to the back of the leather seat. I gripped the two ceramic arms of the chair preparing for the hurt. My knuckles turned as white as the chair arms, my rear end became intimate with the seat, I opened my mouth, and the drill began twist into my tooth's enamel. Every pain receptor in my body was excited. By the time I left elementary school, I had twelve fillings in my baby teeth and utter contempt for the dentist.

Friday was assembly day. This meant white shirts and knitted red ties for the boys; middy blouses, red scarves, and navy skirts for the girls. Our class lined up in the hallway outside the auditorium and then marched to our seats in cadence to a martial tune played on a piano by Miss Mahler. The entire auditorium sat down to a shout of "Seats!" Typewritten words to a song were beamed onto a screen from a slide projector. A sea chantey called *Blow the Man Down* was one of our favorites.

A memorable assembly program was the one in which we were taught Gilbert and Sullivan's song *Tit Willow*. The words are as follows:

> On a tree by a river, a little tom-tit,
> Sang "Willow, titwillow, titwillow."
> And I said to him, "Dicky-bird, why do you sit ..."

Upon hearing this, Irving Kizner, sitting directly behind me, stage-whispered, "What is this, with 'tit' and 'dick' "?

The students nearby, as well as the teachers in the area, went into a panic. We were dismissed—end of assembly.

The rich kid in our class was George Kaifig from the upscale Crotona Gardens apartment building overlooking Crotona Park. In winter, he would arrive in a tan camel's hair overcoat, a brown plaid scarf, and brown leather gloves, while most of us sported our older brother's outgrown and stretched jacket with knit woolen gloves.

During the summer, George and his parents went to Europe on the ocean liner *Queen Mary*. We were treated to an unexpected luxury when they brought an 8 mm movie projector to class with color movies of their trip. In 1938, most movies were black and white. Accompanying the film was Mrs. Kaifig's narration.

Why doesn't she have an accent? I wondered. My parents and my friends' parents slaughtered the English language.

My fourth grade teacher, Miss Mahler, was a stately, beautiful honey blond. One day she accompanied us on a trip to the Sheffield Farms milk bottling plant on Webster Avenue in the Bronx. We saw a film about milk, *From the Cow to the Bottle*. When I saw the sanitary conditions under which the milk was processed and bottled, I thought of Mr. Kosloff, our Seabury Place grocer, who used an unsanitized metal scoop to transfer milk from his battered cans into his customers' unsanitized quart bottles. Before we left, we were treated to squares of ice cream in small, folded cardboard boxes. I tried to save some of it for dessert after dinner but it melted on the bus back to school.

It was in this class that I met Donald. He towered over me and was undisciplined, outrageous, and fun to be with. We spent a lot of time together in and out of school. At the end of the term, Miss Mahler told me she would place me in the same class as Donald the following term if I promised to behave myself. I told her that I could make no promises. She laughed and pulled my head to her breast. At this point I realized there was an opposite sex but I had neither the mental nor the physical wherewithal to do anything about it. This was my first encounter with a mature female's anatomy. I continued to seek this Holy Grail—with not much luck.

At the end of the term we were happy to learn we'd been promoted, but we were assigned to Mrs. Buckner's fifth grade class. She was the school librarian. Her pale, rouged face contrasted with her intense jet-black dyed hair and black-penciled eyebrows. She frightened me. Once a week she read a proverb and then asked the class to write a story showing that we grasped its meaning. Invariably, Jeanette Yokel was called upon to read her story. I deliberately wrote something awful because I knew I'd be too shy to read if called upon.

The United States entered World War II when Donald and I moved on to sixth grade. The war was not going well for the Allies. Bowlegged, cigar-smoking Mr. Klein was our homeroom teacher. He stressed the importance of helping on the home front by collecting newspapers and tin cans. I never knew and still don't know what their role was in the war effort. Don concocted a clever scheme. He asked for, and got, permission to return late from lunch if we came back with a substantial pile of newspapers. We canvassed the high-rent buildings facing Crotona Park, where the residents bought magazines and newspapers. We returned about an hour after the noon class had begun, lugging a load of newspapers in two cardboard boxes, much to the delight of Mr. Klein. By then, classes were preparing for dismissal. This patriotic effort ended the following term, when we graduated to junior high school.

My seven pleasant years at P.S. 61 were nudged gently to the rear as the excitement of entering the modern art deco building of Hermann Ridder Junior High School 98 consumed my thoughts during the summer.

Sixty years later, in 2001, I stood on the lawn of the defunct powerhouse opposite P.S. 61. Portable classrooms in the schoolyard obscured the view of my elementary school. The once pristine cement wall of the foundation upon which the school stood was smeared with incoherent and unsightly graffiti. Perhaps the school was going through the same stages as my expired apartment building. That had been first graffitied and then vandalized by its new denizens. After a few years it was abandoned and became a hollow shell. Then it was razed to make way for small, private homes.

Will P.S. 61 be razed and replaced? When I attended it, the building was old, but the rooms were immaculate. Above the blackboard, rectangular black cardboard sheets beautifully illustrated proper upper- and lowercase script. Obviously, the graffiti writers had learned neither grammar nor their ABCs.

The Pens in My Life

There it is, lying on its side behind my thesaurus to the right of my key-board, a product of modern technology, my ballpoint pen. Its history began when crushed, pigmented minerals slipped off the fingers of Cro-Magnon Man as he painted images on the walls of his cave.

My introduction to producing the written word in P.S. 61 was by way of a sharp, yellow Eberhard Faber No. 2 pencil with a quickly eroding brown eraser on the end. The pencil was for novices. The serious work of writing began with a metal pen nib pushed into a circular slit at the end of a dowel called a penholder. The ink supply came from a glass inkwell, fitted into a hole located at the upper right-hand corner of my oak desk and covered by a brass lid. We sat anxiously in our seats as a monitor walked to each desk with a large bottle of blue-black ink to fill our inkwells. The pen, the ink, a piece of green blotting paper, and an ink-stained chamois pen wiper pre-pared us for Palmer penmanship exercises.

Miss Adelman, our third grade teacher, stepped out of the classroom, allowing Miss Scraley, the writing specialist, to perform her weekly featured role. A navy blue crepe dress hung from her shoulders below a tan cro-cheted collar in the style of the teacher in a Little Rascals comedy. Black nurses' shoes completed the ensemble.

Anticipating her arrival, I pulled my sagging argyle socks up to the knit-ted cuffs of my knickers and tucked in my shirt. Although her own stale outfits were fading from fashion, Miss Scraley wouldn't hesitate to tell us that our socks drooped, our fingernails were dirty, our stretched red knit ties resembled shoestrings, or our shoes needed a shine.

Karl Small was brightest and fattest student in our class. His penmanship paper was always spotless. Under his shirt, a disgusting gray woolen sweater was glued to his skin by the brine of his perspiration. It generated a halo of fumes that diffused in every direction. As Miss Scraley quickly tiptoed past him she gasped, "When you get home, Karl, if it's possible to peel off that sweater, please give it to your mother; have her wash it and hide it. Then, see if you can find it next winter."

Who would dare to laugh?

The exercise was about to begin. Her illustrations on the board could have been lifted and set into a textbook on the Palmer Method. She snapped her commands. "Up and down, up and down. Don't stop until I tell you. Up and down, up and down."

No one dared to stop. This was serious business. We were stumbling over a threshold from the childish pencil into the domain of the adult's ink pen.

Miss Scraley paused, rested her chalk on the sill of the blackboard, and began the inspection. We fixed our eyes upon our papers, hoping she would pass us by without an embarrassing comment.

"Blots! Blots! You don't have to drown your pen point in the inkwell. Let it swim gently on the surface, George."

"Squiggly lines, Shirley. Rest your arm on the desk when you write."

Shirley began to cry, saying that she would never be able to write with an ink pen. Miss Scraley gently offered a handkerchief and then told Shirley that she wrote well but just needed a little improvement.

I was so relieved when she went by. It was one of the rare times I had no blots or finger streaks on my paper, but her passing comment was, "Make sure when you get home that you wash those hands, and don't forget to clean under your fingernails."

Miss Scraley returned to the blackboard. With pursed lips, she surveyed the classroom. In terror, I sat with my heels dug into the floor while my spine was pressed against the back of my seat.

"Now a circle," she commanded. "Up and around, up and around, again and again. Don't lift your pen from the paper, up and around. Stop!"

Barely stopping to catch her breath, she went on. "Now let's try an upper arc, back and forth, back and forth, back and forth. Stop!"

"Pass the ends of a lower arc through the ends of the upper arc, back and forth. Don't press too hard, back and forth. Stop! Let's repeat the exercise."

What fate awaited anyone who dared disobey her? We never knew. Her every command was heeded by a classroom of terrified eight-year-olds.

How often did I look up and scan the upper walls of the room illustrating the beautiful white alphabet script on a black background, wondering if or when I would duplicate it?

This was the torment I endured before I would be permitted to write words with the pen. I wonder if scientists have found a penmanship torture chamber somewhere in the Lascaux Caves where Cro-Magnon Man practiced his warmup exercises before he sketched on the walls. Were there spots on his loincloth or stains on his fingers like my spots and stains when the exercise was completed?

A genetic handicap guaranteed that blue streaks would marble my paper: I am left-handed. As I wrote, my soft outer palm and pinky trailed over my script, smearing the wet ink over the words I had formed. Consequently, I had the cleanest blotter, the sloppiest paper, and the bluest left hand in the class.

At the end of the lesson, we used the chamois pen wiper to remove the remaining ink from the pen point. We flipped the brass cover down over the inkwell, placed the pen in the groove at the front end of the desk, and then anxiously awaited Miss Scraley's departure.

In fourth grade, we finally graduated from a dip pen to a fountain pen. I had a shiny black, white-capped Morrison fountain pen. It wrote smoothly, but the curse of the left-handed persisted. Smudged letters and words continued to plague my writing and my left palm.

One evening, while I was doing my homework, the bladder in my pen ran dry. I ran across the street to buy a 5-cent bottle of blue-black indelible Waterman's ink at Mrs. Baretz's candy store. Harry, who was a numbers runner for his mother, was playing the pinball machine. When I asked for the ink he sarcastically interjected, "What are you gonna do with that ink, Danny? Bring home a test with an A?"

"I don't know. I brought home A's when I wrote in pencil."

The ink bottle had an interesting angular shape. When the ink reached a low point, I could set it on a tilt, gathering the few remaining drops for the rubber bladder to suck into the pen.

I reloaded my fountain pen to prepare for the next day's skirmish. There was a problem with my pen. When the bladder was full, beads of ink would escape from its nib and leave mini-pools on my paper. At a distance, my smeared, blue-blotted paper resembled a Jackson Pollock monochrome. If I absentmindedly placed my pen in my pants pocket, the gray pocket lining was dyed blue—along with my thigh, which absorbed the surplus.

In 1947, when I was a high school senior, Milton Reynolds found a solution to the random blots on my paper. He flew around the world in his small jet, leaving samples of his revolutionary ballpoint pen at each stop. It sold for $19.95, wrote under water, and performed equally well 30,000 feet above sea level. What was I going to write under water, and why would I write it under water? How often, if ever, would I be 30,000 feet above sea level? At that elevation, my trembling fingers inside heated gloves would never have been able to grasp the pen anyway.

When the outrageous price of ballpoints was substantially reduced, all the students bought them. Although this pen did not produce blots, it did skip frequently, leaving an inkless, shiny outline of a letter in a word I was trying to write. I would return to the invisible letter and press harder. The letter was then replaced by a gash in the paper.

Not long after, the ballpoint was no longer in the hands of the elite alone, and it no longer skipped. Now it can be purchased for a few cents in any third world country.

We have come full circle. Ads for fountain pens are found in the *New York Times.* Department stores have locked counters displaying an array of expensive fountain pens ranging from $50 to $500. Antique dealers sell old pens for excessively high prices. Now I should collect ballpoints. If fountain pens have returned, with their leaks, blots, smears, and smudges, can a clean palm, a clean pocket, and a ballpoint be far behind?

My Leather Mackinaw

From the front door of the first subway car, it seemed as if the speeding train generated its energy from the disappearing tracks it consumed. There was a busy exchange of entraining and disembarking passengers at Grand Central Station. My heartbeat accelerated. Next stop, 14th Street, Union Square. On the way to the 14th Street station, the partially empty cars had very few passengers to absorb the rumbling clatter. It was the sixth time this week that Pa had ground out a tedious subway ride. Five days a week he boarded the train with his bialy-and-farmer-cheese sandwich for the chaos called the Garment District. Today, Saturday, he was on another mission. He was accompanying me, as my father and my maven, to select my first new winter jacket. Ma came, too—always welcome for her pithy comments and clever observations.

Finally, Union Square. The subway doors opened. I could hardly restrain myself from leaping up the stairway leading to the store. But Pa was not in good physical shape. Sitting and sewing his entire working life was not an exercise in weight training or a challenge to his cardiovascular system. I restrained myself by keeping pace with him and Ma, who were slowly climbing the stairway, one step at a time.

Upon opening the doors to S. Klein, we were confronted with bargain-laden racks of clothes suspended over creaky wooden floors that sagged under the weight of garment-littered counters. This was S. Klein, "On the Square," the Saks Fifth Avenue of the immigrant shopper.

Pa was our point man, maneuvering us through the cluttered aisles. We arrived at the boys' clothing section, where Ma announced the strategy.

"Who buys anything that fits? The way he's growing, by the time we get home the jacket will be too small."

This maxim was to become my fashion template from elementary school through high school and would have continued had I not been drafted into the army. I inherited my shirts, pants, and anything underneath them from my older brother. Since the purchase of clothing was infrequent, my body was normally draped in costumes of overwhelming proportions. A one- or two-inch seam sewn into a sleeve shortened dangling cuffs to my wrists. Hanging from my hips, my brother's pants formed a multitude of pleats around a waistline that was yet to expand. As I grew, the seams in my sleeves and the pleats in my pants gradually disappeared. Consequently, the population in my closet remained static, with complete disregard of style and season. We conceded fashion and quantity to poverty. There were no complaints. All of my friends went through the same cycle.

The woolen mackinaw with a heavy corduroy collar at the end of the rack was a perfect fit. Red, green, and yellow plaid was a bit loud, but I could adjust to that.

"A woolen mackinaw?" asked Ma. "Your Uncle Louis, when he was a boy in Montreal, had one like that. The cuffs, they wore out the first winter! The collar? This is a collar? This collar couldn't keep you warm in the summer! Try on the leather over there."

She threw it over my shoulders. My knees buckled. I was certain I wouldn't be able to bear the weight of this millstone for an entire day. That woolen, plaid mackinaw on the far rack shone and beckoned to me. Its vibrant colors completely eclipsed the gloom of the black pelt Ma had draped over me.

My father, the expert and neutral observer, was calculating the pros and cons of leather versus plaid. He stood silently by as Ma approached the bench.

"Well, Morris, what do you think?"

"The woolen wouldn't live to grow with him. The leather he'll have a long time."

Our judge had issued his ruling. We agreed that, in spite of its higher cost, the horsehide was the prudent purchase. With some difficulty, the cashier folded the leather mackinaw, placed it into a gray cardboard box, and tied the bulging cardboard with a red-and-white candy-striped string. She connected the string to metal loops at each end of a round wooden handle to ease my grip on the box and then pushed it across the counter toward me. Had it fallen off the counter I would have had at least four broken toes to contend with.

The box rested on my knees until we reached the East 174th Street station. I kept pace with Ma and Pa on the two long blocks home. When we arrived at the entrance of 1540 Seabury Place, I couldn't contain myself. I had a new jacket! With box in hand I raced up the stairs, two at a time, to apartment 11, second floor. Before I heard the door slam behind me, I had loosened the knot and untied the string. Soon the string became part of a large cotton ball in our kitchen junk drawer.

The open box was no surprise. It revealed a somber shiny maroon lining complementing the funereal black leather to which it was joined. Longingly, I focused back on the bright plaid mackinaw we had left hanging on the rack.

When Pa was settled in his chair, he said, "Put on the jacket. Let's take a look."

Ma chimed in, "Let him sit down. He just ran up the steps. It's no good for his heart to be so busy."

Pa looked at me, made a face, then looked at Ma, and said, "Put on the jacket."

The sleeves extended well beyond my fingers. Pa folded the ends inward toward my wrists and then painfully tacked them down with his fur needle. The horse that had furnished this pelt had certainly outlived its life expectancy. The hide could best be equated with a sheet of stainless steel. I knew that the same animal had not contributed the belt. It had some flexibility and was to become a tourniquet around my diaphragm. A double row of flat, shiny black buttons were probably sewn in with a jackhammer. What else could have penetrated this armor? Two pockets rakishly tipped at a forty-five degree angle and adorned with tubular piping scarred the chest. Two flapped horizontal pockets below the belt completed the jacket's style details. This garment was to become the elder statesman of my sartorial inventory for many winters. The soft plaid mackinaws insulating my friends sent me to the bleachers in the fashion game. Each one of their multicolored jackets seemed to shine like a beacon alongside mine.

With the arrival of autumn, inmates gazing out of their tenement windows saw our gang competing for forward and defensive street hockey positions.

My mackinaw installed me as the uncontested goalie of Seabury Place. Although my shins were bare, the horse's hide provided superb protection against the sharp edges of the puck, which was made from the two jagged wooden ends of a Breakstone's cream cheese box. Pucks bounced off my mackinaw the way a pink Spalding rubber ball bounced off the wall of a handball court.

Winter followed autumn. A long-sleeved, thick woolen sweater separated me from the hard, near-freezing black hide that was supposed to insulate me from the cold. The sweater was the insulator; the mackinaw played only a minor role. When I removed the jacket and bent it to fit over a coat hanger, I thought and hoped it would crack.

Although the jacket did not shed water, it was reliably waterproof. It absorbed and retained every moist molecule that hit it. Water softened its rigid, black surface to the consistency of heavy rubber, and it became as flexible as the belt. But there was a price to pay after it dried. It then looked and felt like it had been baked in a kiln, unglazed but stiffer than it had ever been. With each drizzle or downpour, the jacket also lost some of its dye. By the time I reached seventh grade, all points of wear were gray. The flaps over the horizontal pockets fluttered like loose shingles in the wind. The piping of the breast pockets resembled dangling pieces of licorice. At that point, Pa made his final repair on this fading beast.

Springtime with its sunshine was a welcome arrival after a long, cold winter. At the far right of my hallway closet, next to my corduroy knickers, an empty wooden hanger awaited the eyesore, but the loyal, worn guest never appeared. My mackinaw had finally become a candidate for a ride on Mr. Tekula's dumbwaiter to the garbage pails. A sleeveless sweater replaced the black albatross. My new Davega handball sneakers relegated my Coward shoes to the rear right of the closet floor. I felt like an Olympic contender as I ran off, bouncing a pink Spalding, to meet the boys at the candy store.

Let the games begin!

The Little Engine That Stood

Living in the New House placed the Wieners a few rungs higher on the economic ladder than the rest of the residents of Seabury Place. Their building, six stories tall, stood over its poor cousins. Some of the Weiners' neighbors were Milty, whose father worked all year as a furrier; Mr. and Mrs. Bord, bookies and numbers runners; Miss Winter, who gave us a nickel tip for calling her to the candy store telephone; and Rosalyn Fuchs, who was always starchily dressed when she came to school or stepped into the street. To my nine-year-old eyes, the Wieners seemed out of step with the rest of the residents in their building. They had a shy, docile son my age, who never laced up a pair of sneakers to play ball in the street, never wrinkled his pants on the hard rubber running board of a parked car, never joined our weighty discussions on the stoop. Perhaps he was too timid to ask if he could join us? One day, when he made one of his rare appearances in front of his building, he nearly dissolved into its tan bricks as I approached him.

"Hey, Itzy, we need another man for punchball. Do you want to play?"

"No," he said, "I don't want to."

"We can't have a game without you."

"No," he mumbled, "I don't want to."

I returned to the boys. If he didn't want to, what else could we do? The extra man played for both sides. What a peculiar kid, I thought.

After the game, we made a dash for the stoop of my building to speculate on our next visit to New York City's 1939 World's Fair. With that topic exhausted, I asked the boys if they knew anything about Itzy. Milty replied that, whenever he saw him, Itzy was with his mother, and she was holding a small jar of milk for him.

"Who drinks milk from a jar?" asked Bernie.

"Don't be stupid," said Milty. "Do you want her to hold the milk in her hands?"

The sun went down, and it was getting chilly. I saw my father coming home from work, so I left the boys to join him in the climb to our apartment.

Ma was there to greet us. "Morris, yesterday he didn't wash his hands. Do you think maybe he could wash them now before he eats?"

"Go wash your hands," said Pa. "Who knows what's doing under those nails."

After dinner, the image of Itzy's "I don't want to" still bothered me.

"Ma, what does Mr. Wiener in the New House do that he can afford to live there?"

"The big *macher* [money maker] shares the apartment with his sister-in-law and her family. That's how they are able to pay the rent."

"Do you know their son, Itzy?"

"How would I know him? Sometimes I see him by his mother. You should know him. He's your age. Why do you ask?"

"He lives on our street but he doesn't play with us."

"So, you don't have to marry him. Ask him to play ball with you and your friends."

"I did today, and he said he didn't want to."

My father joined in, "Danny, not everyone likes to play ball."

I left to watch my brother do his homework in his loose-leaf notebook. When he was finished, he turned on the radio to the *Fred Allen Show.* One of the residents in Allen's Alley was a comedienne, Mrs. Nussbaum. If my mother had improved her English but kept her accent, she, too, without a script, could have been a resident in that alley.

The weekend arrived. I was an early riser. My friends were fast asleep, so I brought a *Daily News* with me to the stoop. While I was reading the comic strip "Smokey Stover," I was distracted by a voice imitating the clanging of a fire engine and then its siren. It was Itzy, barreling down the block, slapping his rear end while his wailing siren and gongs warned any pedestrians that a fire truck was racing to douse a fire.

What was this all about? He could be a fire engine but he couldn't play ball with us?

With Seabury Place's population density, the odds weighed heavily in favor of having a peculiar resident. Although this was the first time I'd seen Itzy tearing down the block to put out a fire, I expected some reruns in the future. I wasn't disappointed. He was usually driving his engine early on weekend mornings.

Two years later, when I was in sixth grade, math evolved from adding, subtracting, and memorizing the multiplication table to more difficult word problems. One Tuesday after school, I passed Itzy standing beside his mother as I was on my way to Mrs. Baretz's candy store to buy a bottle of ink. Mrs. Wiener called to me, "Maybe you could come upstairs and help my Itzy with his mathematics?"

I could see Itzy squirming with embarrassment. It was so sad to see him edge behind and almost into his mother.

"Oh, no," I said. "The last time I was in your elevator, Mr. Schmidt tried to pull me down to his cellar. I was so scared, I'll never go into your building."

"So, maybe he could come up to your apartment tomorrow?"

"Not tomorrow. Eddie Cantor and the Mad Russian are on every Wednesday night."

So Itzy came up to my apartment on Thursday, and he tried. He tried very hard to make sense of a math problem: if the first building on a street was 841, what would the next five building numbers be? When I discovered he couldn't read and couldn't possibly do math, we folded our books and played a simple card game of War. Then he went home.

He continued to be a shadow in front of his building most of the time, but on weekends he certainly was a presence as a fire engine clanging down the street. I went on to junior high school. That was the last I saw of him.

Almost. Twenty-six years later, my wife, children, and I were visiting my parents in the Pelham Parkway section of the Bronx when I came upon Itzy. He was still slight but bent over and shrouded with the same blank expression he had had on Seabury Place.

"Hello, Itzy," I said. "It's been a long time since we were on Seabury Place."

"Yes," he replied."

"Are you working?"

"Yes," replied.

"What do you do?"

"I'm a presser. I press women's dresses on 38th Street."

He was a fire engine in his youth. I was happy to hear that he'd evolved into a presser in the garment district.

A Ride on the Subway

The East 174th Street elevated subway platform was an easy sneak-on. The 5 cents we saved would be invested in a crock of baked beans or coffee at the Automat. We squatted below the window, adjacent to the cashier, in the corridor that led to the platform.

"Hey, Krebs, get your ass down. The change clerk could see you."

"I am down. I can't get any lower."

"If we don't get to Broadway, blame it on your fat ass," whispered Peanzy.

The Seventh Avenue Express arrived. The gate at the end of the corridor slowly opened, allowing the exiting passengers to bypass the turnstiles. We dashed past them, through the open gate, onto the platform, and through the open train doors. Another free ride!

The seats gave every appearance of being uncomfortable. This was confirmed as soon we sat on them. A basket weave of glistening thin yellow bamboo strips covered springs that felt as if they had been forged from igneous rock. As the bamboo strips aged, stiff threadlike barbs rose from the surface. They pierced delicate skirts or dresses and shredded expensive silk stockings. They embossed the art of the basket weave onto the seat of a man's rayon pants until sitting on a smooth surface ironed out the pattern.

Speeding toward the turn at Simpson Street station, the train seemed as if it was charging headlong into the squalid Bronx Hotel.

"How does anyone get any sleep in that hotel?"

"Krebs, you dummy, no one goes there to sleep."

"Why not? They have beds in the rooms, don't they?"

"It's a whorehouse. You don't sleep in a whorehouse."

"If you don't sleep, then why are there beds?"

Jerry was exasperated. Alvin and Peanzy were doubled over in laughter.

"Krebs," said Jerry, "this is too much. Go find a seat in another car."

As the train moved on, a painting by Moses Soyer, who was influenced by the Ashcan School of art, came to life. Wash hanging from lines, tenants gazing out of windows, open garbage pails, windblown litter, and kids playing in the streets animated a neighborhood bruised by the Great Depression.

The train raced into the darkness toward the Third Avenue station. Once it was inside the tunnel, the clatter of the wheels ricocheting off the walls reached such a pitch that it was impossible to carry on a conversation without sharing it with strangers.

There was very little activity at the Third Avenue station. Moving on, we approached the long, winding curves leading to the East 149th Street and Grand Concourse station. As the subway negotiated the bends, centripetal and centrifugal forces sent passengers sliding on their seats toward, then away from, the windows behind them. The thickness of our knickers shielded us from the seats, but the unfortunate youngster opposite us, wearing short pants, had his thighs stamped by the bamboo strips as the train rode these infamous curves. To ease his discomfort, the little boy stood up and extricated the pants from the crack in his rear end. Then, holding onto a white enameled pole, he vigorously rubbed at the temporary pink and red surrealistic mural imprinted on the back of each thigh.

Newsboys ran through the aisles shouting the headlines of the 2-cent *Daily News* or *Daily Mirror.* The evening edition of the *Daily Mirror* featured a light green or pink outer page. Despite this attention grabber, the *News* outsold it substantially. Horseplayers pored over the last two pages of the *Mirror,* which were devoted to the track program and the results from the previous day. The 3-cent, stodgy *New York Times* was like a physics textbook for most riders. It was for the men wearing suits and hats.

If the newsboys were here, could the amputee seated on a wooden dolly be far behind? Pushing himself along with what appeared to be a small, cast-iron household iron in each hand, he adroitly maneuvered from car to car. He would stop, offer pencils to the passengers, and then extend a tin cup for coins. The amputation appeared to be very high on his torso.

Peanzy turned to me and whispered, "I wonder how this guy goes to the bathroom."

Uninvited, Krebs, chimed in, "He goes to the bathroom the same way you do."

Peanzy was stunned. "I don't believe this idiot. I don't piss from a board. How does he take a leak, I asked, and the shmuck tells me he pisses like I do."

"Then maybe he has a tube that carries it to the bowl," replied Krebs.

That was the first sensible sentence to escape from Krebs's mouth since we'd boarded the train.

Sometimes a blind singer accompanying himself on the accordion would pass through as his young daughter solicited coins from the passengers. She approached with such pathos that it was difficult to deny her a few cents.

"Should I give her the 3 cents I brought for the bittersweet chocolates in a vending machine?"

I replied by parting with a penny.

Next stop, Times Square. We paused at our oasis, the 1-cent vending machines connected to the subway's vertical steel girders. One offered two Chiclets in a little yellow cardboard box. Another provided a single strip of Wrigley's Spearmint gum wrapped in silver foil and green paper or Juicy Fruit in yellow paper. A third machine had small, silver-foil-wrapped squares of Suchard chocolates, sweet or bittersweet.

With two bittersweet squares slowly dissolving in my mouth, I joined the boys in climbing out of the darkness and into the bustle of Times Square, "Crossroad of the World." Wherever we turned, lights, odors, and people excited us. We spent some time watching men on stools rolling balls toward holes in a penny arcade. Our heads were spinning from looking at giant neon signs. A large screen projected jerkily moving figures created by flashing lightbulbs. Perfect smoke rings escaped from the mouth of a soldier pictured on a block-long Camels sign.

We peered through the windows at the fancy people dining in expensive restaurants such as Child's or Lindy's. The centerpiece in the front window of Jack Dempsey's restaurant, lit by a spotlight, was the pair of bloodied boxing gloves worn by Abe Attel in his fight for the featherweight championship in 1911. The tempting odors of broiling hot dogs and hamburgers, frying French fries, and popping popcorn suggested it was time to visit

Horn and Hardart's Automat. I stopped to watch how the cashiers threw an accurate handful of nickels at the customers who handed in a dollar. How did they do it?

At home, the closest drink to coffee I could get was tasteless tan Postum. "Coffee is not good for children," my mother would say. Now I was on my own, no restrictions. I placed a coffee cup under a beautifully sculptured silver faucet, deposited into the slot the nickel I had saved by sneaking onto the subway, and turned the handle. The most delicious coffee in the world came steaming out of the mouth of a polished silver lion's head.

How did it know when to stop pouring? I wondered.

At our table, although we were only twelve-year-olds, Alvin, Jerry, Peanzy, Krebs, and I felt on a par with the adults around us. We didn't embarrass ourselves with bad table manners or immature conversation until Krebs shouted, "Hey, the Heinz beans at home don't taste like these beans. I'm going to tell my mother to buy them in the A&P."

"First of all, dummy, they don't sell these beans in the A&P, and second of all, they have bacon in them," said Alvin.

"How do you know?" asked Krebs.

"My grandfather told me they flavor almost everything with bacon at the Automat."

"Aah, your grandfather never leaves your apartment. What does he know?"

"Krebs, I'm warning you. Not another word."

We walked to the Museum of Science and Industry in Rockefeller Center to see if there were any new exhibits. They never changed. With that mission completed, it was time to return home.

We could not devise a scheme to avoid paying for the return trip. The area was well policed, and U-shaped bars prevented anyone from sneaking under the turnstiles. Reluctantly, we paid our fare along with the other passengers.

The long ride home gave us a chance to review an adventure in the big city.

It Came with the Shoes

"What do you mean, it came with the shoes? When I buy shoes, they put them in a box, and I go home."

"They gave me a baseball glove when my mother paid for the shoes," said Jerry.

"Can I see it?"

The person who designed the shoes obviously was the one who designed this glove. It had laces with eyelets, it had a heel, but it also had a thumb as long as the tongue of an L. L. Bean woodsman boot. The remaining four fingers, resembling discarded banana peels, huddled together in fear of joining the mammoth thumb. I christened his glove The Thumb, but I wouldn't tell him. He was a lefty; I was a lefty. He had a glove; I didn't. Whenever we played Stickball, I prayed he would be on the opposing team so I could borrow his glove to catch those nasty ground balls without bobbling them as they came rocketing toward me at third base. Jerry always offered The Thumb, and I gratefully accepted.

As the four fingers continued to soften, the thumb began to calcify and became an impediment to catching a rubber ball. Before a ball had reached the glove pocket, it was speared by the thumb. This would never do. I had small hands. I needed a glove to catch a spinning rubber ball. Jerry was the only lefty. All the other boys were right-handed. They had their own gloves, except for The Creep, whose hands dangling from his wrists were the size of a baseball glove, so a glove for him was moot.

My father didn't have a lefty glove. What would he have done with it if he'd had one? Probably squeezed it into the kitchen junk drawer. He wouldn't have hesitated to buy me a glove had I asked. But I believed that I had to present a logical argument to satisfy the investment. I told Ma I was short and my hands were small, so I had difficulty catching the ball. She

Alvin and I suited up for the Bronx Y baseball team in 1948.

sagely counseled, "So, when you grow, your hands will grow and you'll catch the ball."

At thirteen, the boys hit the pink Spalding hard and fast.

"Ma, I can't catch the ball now without a glove, a lefty glove. Are you left-handed or right-handed?"

"Ich kenn shaierenn tepp mitt beideh hent" (I can scour pots with either hand), was her reply. "Oh, so it's a glove you want. Why didn't you say so? Morris, he wants a baseball glove. Let's go with him."

Across the street and around the corner from my apartment building, Crotona Felt Sporting Goods occupied three contiguous stores on Boston Road. They had two pathetic lefty gloves. The oil on one did not mask its use. It probably was a return. The other glove was for a major leaguer.

"Let's go to Southern Boulevard. They have sports stores there," suggested my father.

It was about a mile walk under the Southern Boulevard el to the Vim and Davega stores. With a spring in my step, my parents at my side, I set out.

Visions of sugargloves danced in my head when suddenly my happiness was crushed by remembering my panic the previous night. It might have been an asthma attack. Whatever it was, I awoke and couldn't breathe. I thought it was the end. A few frantic deep inhales put a stop to it.

What if this happens again and I die? I thought. Why should Ma and Pa be left with a baseball glove? Pa doesn't play Stickball. Should I tell them what happened last night?

Oh no, that would frighten them. I'll let it pass this time, but if it happens again and I live, I'll tell them for sure.

The tall, art deco, multi-tubed red neon lights of the competing Davega and Vim stores outshone all the other signs on Southern Boulevard, even the Loew's Spooner movie theater. Davega was large and brightly lit. I was wearing their black high-top handball sneakers with big black rubber bumpers in the front. Maybe they had a glove that would hold up as well as those sneakers. We were directed downstairs to the baseball equipment. We looked around. Where was a salesman? I guess we were disturbing his break—he darted out from behind a door with a strong scent of tuna fish on his breath. He handed me a lefty glove and assured me that this was the best one in our price range. I looked at the inside liner—it had a rough nap—and then looked at my father.

"Pa, it looks like it needs a shave." It resembled the gray leather gloves Mr. Tekula wore when he rolled his garbage cans to the edge of the sidewalk.

On to Vim, a few doors to the right. A friendly salesman showed me two dark brown gloves that were perfect. The larger one was a $5.99 Red Rolfe; the smaller one a $3.99 Ken Keltner. I placed my right hand in one and punched its pocket a few times. Then I punched the other.

"Which one do you like?" Pa asked.

"I like both of them."

"So, take the better one."

I looked at the two gloves. What if I get the $5.99 glove and that frightening breathing problem returns? I thought. Pa will be left with the expensive glove. What will he do with it? Should I tell him to give it to Jerry?

"The $3.99 Kenny Keltner glove is smaller, but it will be fine. Yes, I like the $3.99 glove."

The following day, I burned my name onto the back of the glove with the help of the sun and a magnifying glass.

Jerry was left with the glove that came with the shoes, but he could borrow my glove whenever he needed it. My Kenny Keltner joined The Thumb and all the righty gloves on the Stickball field. Now, I felt, I really belonged.

A World Out of This World

We were at the threshold of a technological leap, from the manual kitchen to the mechanical kitchen, from the ice-box to the refrigerator, from Tar Beach (the tenement roof) to the "Cool as a Pool" air-conditioned Dover theater. Rectangular airplanes and automobiles matured and developed sensual curves.

I laced up my black high-top canvas Davega sneakers, took the cream cheese sandwiches from the refrigerator, and pocketed 10 cents for the round-trip subway fare from the kitchen table. I was about to leave for the 1939 World's Fair when Ma, who was hanging wash on the line from her bedroom window, called out, "Take off your sneakers. Put on your shoes. You'll be walking all day. You'll need support. You'll be a cripple!"

To bolster Ma's argument, Pa chimed in, "When I was your age, I never wore sneakers."

"Pa, when you were my age you didn't own shoes."

Ma knew that, if there was a choice, I always opted for sneakers. These were the days when men wore suits, fedoras, and leather shoes to watch a ballgame at Yankee Stadium. Sneakers were exclusively for playing ball. Some said they were bad for the eyes.

I ran downstairs to join the big guys, my brother, Harold, and his friends. They were twelve, I was only nine. They attended Hermann Ridder Junior High School, I was in elementary school.

"Stay close, but don't bother us," was my brother's warning, to dampen the beginning of what I expected to be an exciting day.

It was a long two-block walk to the East 174th Street subway station. Everyone placed a nickel in the turnstile slot. If anyone were caught sneaking on without paying, that would end his day.

Sitting very nicely was not in my repertoire. How many nine-year-olds could plant themselves on a stiff bamboo subway seat and sit for an hour?

"Harold, I'm going to the front of the first car. I want to see where we're going."

"If you leave this car, you'll get off at the next stop and go home."

This curt warning from my brother forced me to remain in my seat.

At the first underground stop, the cast of subway characters made their entrance. The newspaper boys were carrying Saturday papers as thin as a leaflet. There were few buyers. The notes of *Lady of Spain* escaping from a pearlescent accordion startled the man sleeping next to me. Next came a Negro with a beautiful deep bass voice singing in Yiddish. I wished I had a few extra pennies to show my approval, but these were the days when our pockets had lint resting in their seams where coins should have been.

In half an hour we arrived at Grand Central subway station. My brother and Ernest led us down the steps to the lower level. A train came, and we were on our way again. Soon we were out of the tunnel, out of the darkness.

Why does the ride seem quicker in the daylight? I wondered.

In fifteen minutes, we had reached the Willets Point station. The doors flew open to a wide, wood-plank boardwalk. Like a pop-up in a children's book, the 1939 World's Fair rose above us consuming the entire horizon. Multicolored flags snapped in the breeze. Curved buildings, rectangular buildings, wide boulevards, green meadows, caravans of cars changed the area from an ash dump into a fantasy world. "From Dump to Glory" was how the pamphlets described it.

Standing tall, above the pavilions and amusement rides, as if they were aware of their importance, were the bright white symbols of the Fair—the tapering *Trylon,* piercing the sky alongside its mammoth white globular partner, the *Perisphere.* I raced down the boardwalk to the ticket booth, then past the turnstile, and into the future.

Which way to go? I hesitated. I'll wait for the big guys to decide. How could a nine-year-old lead men of twelve and thirteen?"

The open metal steps spiraling around the circumference of the *Perisphere* were dense with people waiting to see *Democracity,* "A Perfect Model of a Perfect World." At an exorbitant 25-cent admission, the perfect model remained perfect without us.

Although we took the same path and saw the same exhibitions as we had on our previous visits, each trip was wrapped in a new experience. This time, we were told, the King and Queen of England would be there.

"It's the King and Queen of England, let's go!" said Alex.

"I don't give a shit about them," said Nadey. "Who are they? Let's go to the General Motors *Futurama* exhibit."

"I heard it's great. What do you think, Harold?"

"The heck with the King and Queen. Let's go to *Futurama*."

That did it. *Futurama* was in our future. I wasn't consulted. That's the price you pay for wearing short pants and being nine years old.

The notes of *East Side, West Side, All Around the Town* accompanied a chain of long blue-and-orange open cars snaking visitors through the crowd. Where were they going? Where did they come from? Why bother with an answer. We were on our way to *Futurama* in the General Motors building!

The General Motors Highway and Horizons exhibit.

Visitors were lined up at the pavilion to see what General Motors had planned for our future. Suspension systems, cross sections of motors, batteries, and a variety of tires were on display, but the civilian autos, which would soon be replaced by military vehicles, drew the greatest interest.

Enough, let's move on. We stepped into a darkened vestibule and sat down in soft, lush, velvety seats mounted on a track waiting to carry us to the future. The buzzer went off. As we moved through the darkness, a massive, colorful diorama of the United States was spread out before us. Miniature automobiles were traveling on litter-free roads, crossing the country from the East Coast to the West. They motored through forests, agricultural areas, and cities. Overhead walkways separated pedestrians from the roads. The motors, the suspensions, the new cars, and the diorama were too much to absorb. OK, next time I'll just concentrate on one area. I waited for all the boys to assemble. A little kid could easily get lost in the crowd.

"I'm getting that convertible when I get a job," said Ernest.

"What are you talking about? Your father has a job. Does he have a convertible? Does he own a car? No one on our block owns a car," said Harold.

Thus a dream escaped through the exhaust pipe of a convertible.

The next stop was the water fountain.

"Hey, Nadey, doesn't that thing that the water is coming out of look like a pecker?" I called out.

"It doesn't look like mine. Does it look like yours, Danny?"

I was so embarrassed, I was sorry I'd said it.

In the General Electric exhibit there were two lifelike robots: a husband in the living room, his wife in the kitchen. Life was easy in a kitchen surrounded by modern GE appliances. A refrigerator, a pressure cooker, a steam iron, and a pop-up toaster promised to bring the kitchen out of the Dark Ages. Did I know that these unimaginable luxuries would eventually be part of our kitchen? An oaken icebox was our refrigerator. My father placed a damp rag over the woolen pants he ironed—that was his steam iron. Our toaster was a collapsible wire device placed over the gas burner on top of our oven, with slices of bread set on it. A chipped white enamel pot with a lid was our pressure cooker.

Onward to the Bell Telephone exhibit. At home, our phone was in a booth behind folding glass doors at the candy store. The modern black phone, with a handle resting on a cradle, was on exhibit. The handle had an earpiece at one end and a mouthpiece at the other. The visitor could pick up the phone, talk into the mouthpiece, and hear his voice in the earpiece. I didn't recognize my voice. I sounded like a boy soprano.

The older guys had had enough. We left for fresh air. On top of a tall column stood the statue of a young man stepping resolutely forward, raising a red star in his right hand. Inside the building behind him were large black-and-white photo murals of farmers on tractors, close-ups of women in babushkas doing something agricultural, and a panoramic view of fields of grain. One or two actual tractors were lost on the huge floor of this barren, gray hall. We were in the Soviet pavilion. We decided to get out.

"Let's go to the Heinz exhibit. They pass out free samples," said Nadey.

"I don't like the crap they dish out," said Alex, "but they give you a little green plastic pickle. It will be the ninth or tenth pickle in my collection."

We picked up our pickles; then we left.

Time to eat. It was getting late. Our sandwiches were getting warm. My favorite rolls, Litroff's, were smeared with cream cheese. We made no dent in the food vendors' inventory. Ma would say, "Who knows what kind of junk they put in their sandwiches. From home, you know it's good."

We rinsed the sandwiches down with a drink from the nearby water fountain. Now it was time to explore.

Nadey suggested we go to Billy Rose's Aquacade. It played a prominent role in the promotion of the Fair. In all our trips to the Fair, we'd never visited the amusement area. We simply had no money for entertainment or to watch Billy Rose's wife, Eleanor Holm, swim around in a pool.

"How about going to the Aquacade?" Nadey persisted. "I heard naked girls are in the show."

"I don't have any money for that," replied Alex. My brother and Nadey nodded. The only place I could go was the subway train. I had a nickel for the return fare.

Toward the evening, we made our last stop at Consolidated Edison's *City of Light.* Massive generators dwarfed visitors as they opened the doors to the exhibit. The caption said that these monstrous round things with miles of copper wire inside produced electricity.

"How does electricity come out of those things?" I asked the boys.

Silence. I could see from their annoyed expressions that I had better keep my mouth shut. However, the large mock-up of the Manhattan skyline above a cross section of the streets below it was self-explanatory. Power lines, pipes, and subways in motion filled the caverns under the ground. A voice from speakers told us how much power it took to energize the city. The room darkened. It was nighttime. Tiny bulbs, like miniature diamonds sparkled within the buildings. The insides of the subway trains glowed as they completed their circuit underground. We were overwhelmed with statistics about the contributions of Consolidated Edison. The lights went on. We left the building. It was dark outside; time to go home.

He was always there. How many times had we passed him ignoring his presence? But in the evening, when most objects were obscured by darkness, he served as a beacon, silhouetted against the illuminated *Perisphere,* about forty feet high, in his long, draping coat. This imposing statue of George Washington was the assembly point, should anyone get lost.

All of us were present and accounted for. Weary legs trudged past George to the Willets Point station for the long trip home.

In August 1939 the Soviet Union and Germany signed a non-aggression pact. One month later, September 1, 1939, Germany invaded Poland. Because Poland was totally unprepared for modern warfare, Germany slashed through this country toward the U.S.S.R. in three weeks. This was the beginning of World War II. The following year, ten countries, including the Soviet Union, Poland, and Germany, withdrew from the Fair.

The Fair went on in spite of this. Perhaps it was the war, perhaps it was overfamiliarity, but the glory of the 1939 World's Fair had faded. There were fewer visitors. The temporary buildings looked jaded, like candidates for the dump on which they were built. The Fair had opened on April 3, 1939; it closed on October 27, 1940.

We returned to spending our time on our dependable streets, using the running board and the candy store for our education, stimulating conversation, and entertainment. World War II took center stage for the next five years.

Silver Skates

The Indian Rock stood sentinel on a hill overlooking Crotona Park Lake. In the summer, it was a sanctuary for workers escaping from their sweltering apartments. The lake had an expanse of ten acres. In summer, a bearded elderly man in a derby shuffled along the gray stone boundary around it selling sunflower seeds—two shot glasses of seeds for a penny. The pretzel man, wearing a filthy apron and emitting a vocabulary to match, followed the sunflower seed man, hawking his stock from a braided wood basket. On weekends, sweltering laborers living in the area sought some relief by renting a rowboat.

Winter's freeze changed the lake into a sheet of black ice. I ran there daily to see if the white flag with the red ball in the center was hoisted, the signal that the ice was safe for skating. I couldn't wait to get on the ice and challenge the winds attacking from every direction. I skated like a National Hockey League veteran carrying the puck on a penalty shot. I became an instant celebrity. "Hellos" came from people I did not know—the more well-to-do crowd who skated there. Eyes were focused on me as I sped around the lake. But I let no one ever see me put on my skates.

They were oversized and dated back to the Hans Brinker era. My parents had bought them for me in the winter of 1937 at a secondhand store under the Third Avenue El in the Bronx. Although their blades were entangled and their laces knotted, I managed to fish them out of a large cardboard box. They were so worn that their black boots appeared to be made of rough suede. Aged brown streaks highlighted the folds in the leather. Their blades, a half-inch wide, were excellent for a goalie but an impediment for speed. In addition, they were two, maybe three, sizes too big.

"Don't worry about it. He'll grow into them," the sage of the second-hand shop had declared. "Meanwhile, he can wear three pairs of socks, and stuff the remaining space with cotton. That way, for a quarter, you'll have them for a long time."

I glanced at my parents beside me. My father, tired from a day's work, my mother, who wouldn't treat herself to a new apron, and here I was sitting on a chair, indulging myself in a pair of ice skates I would use only two, perhaps three, months out of the year.

Pa didn't hesitate. He took a quarter from his pocket, and off we went to Crotona Park Lake. It was nightfall. The tranquil soft yellow glow from the lamps surrounding the lake reflected off the ice; the sharp sound of blades cutting into the surface was my seductive initiation to the sport. I couldn't wait to lace my oversized boots. Never mind the absence of cotton stuffing in the toes, never mind the wide blades, never mind the roomy boots. I was going to skate!

I raced in and out of the skating crowds. No one was able to keep up with me regardless of age. My parents, standing at the edge of the lake reaped the dividends of their 25-cent investment.

Woolen socks at that time were not reinforced with a synthetic fiber at their toes and heels. Those areas, suffering most of the abrasion, quickly developed holes. My mother remedied this. She stretched the sock over the open end of a *yahrtzeit* (memorial candle) glass to expose the hole. Guiding a thick needle threaded with whatever color wool was available, she wove a patch. This left a spectrum of patches illuminating my toes and heels. Joseph had his Technicolor Dreamcoat; I had my Technicolor socks. Fully aware that they were not de rigueur with the bourgeois skating crowd, I would lace my skates secretly in a stall of the men's boathouse bathroom. With my socks safely hidden in my skates, I confidently stepped onto the lake and sped to admiring glances.

A few weeks later, Mr. Solomon, the "Parkee" (park attendant) chased me around the lake after his whistle had signaled to end the skating session. When he caught up, he told me to apply for the Silver Skates, a race sponsored by the *Daily News*. The finals were to be held at Madison Square Garden. The winners of each age group would be awarded engraved silver skates.

I filled out the coupon in the *Daily News* and ran down to the mailbox. A reply by mail instructed me to be at the Brooklyn Ice Palace in two weeks. At age ten I was placed in the Midget Group.

"Ma, I entered a speed skating contest."

"Where? In Crotona Park?"

"No, it's at the Brooklyn Ice Palace in Brooklyn."

"In Brooklyn? That's in *Yenneh Velt* [another world]," she said. "Who knows who lives there!"

I knew I was in trouble. Like our immigrant neighbors, she felt insecure outside our ghetto.

"The letter says that the subway station is only two blocks from the Ice Palace. Can't I go?"

My language, especially my body language, showed my disappointment.

She made her concession. "You go with me or you don't go. And after, we go right home."

Two weeks later Ma and I boarded the subway train for a one-hour ride to the Brooklyn Ice Palace. My nervous anticipation stretched the minutes until I thought the train would never arrive on time. I wandered to the front of the first car and watched the tunnel's lights coming at me like tracer bullets. When this grew tedious, I decided to sit down and rest my legs—on the chance that we *would* arrive.

Finally, the stop for the Brooklyn Ice Palace! Ma and I climbed up the station steps and into the inviting sunlight only to encounter a sinister display in the two front windows at a corner bookstore. The featured book had an ominous red and black cover with a swastika emblazoned at the center. Adolph Hitler's *Mein Kampf,* his instruction manual for World War II and the Holocaust, assaulted us from both windows. My mother grabbed my hand.

"*Ay, ah finsternesh* [a darkness]!" she said. "Let's get out of here. It's a bunch Nazis!"

"But Ma, we're only two blocks from the rink. I waited a month ..."

Reluctantly, she conceded, although I could see in her demeanor the trauma she had suffered from the sight of the book.

Nearly every contestant at the rink had a colorful, form-fitting knit jersey uniform. The name of a skating club was emblazoned on the back of the uniform; the contestant's name was embroidered on the upper left side of the chest. The skaters had long, narrow, sharpened racing blades protected by gray leather scabbards. My Third Avenue junk store figure skate blades were three or four times as wide and half the length of theirs. I had no idea that blades could be sharpened or be protected by scabbards.

My competitors were standing in little groups plotting strategy with their coaches. What advice could my mother give me? She was an immigrant from a tiny village in Lithuania. Ice-skating there consisted of sliding on layers of cotton rags wrapped around a person's feet in place of shoes during winter. What did she know about racing tactics?

A buzzer sounded for the warm-ups. Some of my opposition, skating leisurely, had tan camel's hair coats draped over their shoulders. Perhaps I should have draped my leather mackinaw over the cotton flannel shirt on my shoulders.

My blades had never slid over ice such as this. It was like skating on glass. My dull blades skidded sideways when I pushed, while I could hear my competitors' blades biting into the ice with every stride.

A second buzzer announced the end of the warm-up session. Stepping off the ice, I passed the favorite of my age group, Johnny Wiegal. I recognized him because the *Daily News* had given him quite a bit of coverage in the weeks leading up to the contest. His maroon-and-gold uniform fit as if it were painted on him. The narrow, saberlike blades on his boots made mine resemble trolley tracks. Many parents, immigrants like mine, were speaking in boisterous German. This sent my mother darting to the other side of the rink.

We were brought to the starting line in groups of six. Our group, the Midgets were to complete the course by racing twice around the oval. I was relieved to see that Johnny Wiegal wasn't in my heat.

The gun went off! To my surprise, I had a substantial lead after finishing the first lap but I didn't know how to pace myself. I had expended most of my energy in the warm-up and the first lap, but I was still in the lead going around the second time. The group moved substantially closer to me. I could hear the names of my competitors being urged on from the sidelines. My mother, an *auslander* (foreigner) wouldn't dare call my name. I felt like an intruder on alien turf. Trying to outdistance them, I pushed harder. My wide, dull, stupid blades couldn't bite into the ice. They skidded sideways when I pushed. My skates slid, and then I fell, bringing my two closest competitors down with me. The three skaters at the rear of the pack coasted in to first, second, and third place, making them eligible for the quarterfinals.

I returned home with a bruised ego, water-soaked woolen pants, and a damp cotton flannel shirt, from my venture outside the cocoon, my ghetto.

Did I disappoint my mother? If I did, she never mentioned it. I think she was simply happy to leave an area that would tolerate such a blatant display of *Mein Kampf.*

My skating resumed in the comfortable confines of Crotona Park Lake, whose rough surface enabled my blades to dig in and push me through the refreshing breezes wafting among friends, not rivals.

Climb Every Mountain

What was this? The hockey season was poised at the top step of the cellar, waiting to make its entrance onto the Seabury Place asphalt, and I was supposed to go learn to read and write Yiddish after a full day at P.S. 61? There was no compromise. I had to learn to read and write the mother tongue.

I followed Ma through the tumult and trash of Jennings Street Market, hopped over the trolley tracks of Southern Boulevard to a narrow building adjacent to Carlucci's Pizza. She opened the door. Each step had its unique groan and squeak as Ma and I tried to conquer the final flight. Why are Yiddish schools located in an oxygen-deprived garret at the top of a steep staircase?

Seated at his desk was Chaver (Comrade) Shtrugahtz.

Ma spoke. "I want my Danny to learn to read and write Yiddish. To speak, he knows already."

"Yes. It's $5 a month, no bargaining. You're getting something for nothing." Then, pointing to me, he said, "You, sit down over there."

Ma left me with Chaver Shtrugahtz and a classroom of strangers. After a few minutes, I could see that I had an advantage over most of them. The class was conducted in Yiddish. Yiddish was my language when I entered kindergarten. Yiddish was the language at home.

Chaver Shtrugahtz reviewed the colors by pointing to a shirt, a tie, or something tacked to the bulletin board. Then he cupped his hands as if he had something inside and asked in Yiddish, "What does a bird do?"

I pictured those revolting pigeons below my apartment liberating their waste onto their toilet, the A&P roof.

"It shits," I said to myself.

He walked up to me, uncupped his hands, and watched "the bird" fly away. *"A feigeleh fliht!* [a bird flies]," he shouted, and he pinched my arm.

We were then asked to write in Yiddish "A bird flies" fifteen times in our notebooks. I had neither a notebook nor a pen.

"I don't have a notebook and I don't have a pen, Chaver Shtrugahtz."

"He comes to my classroom without a pen, without a notebook? I never heard of such a thing!"

The Seventh Avenue Express came screeching by, rattling our windows in cadence to the chaver's simmer.

"Do you go to English school without a notebook or a pen? Don't I deserve the same respect as your teacher in that school? You will not answer any questions today. Go home."

He wasn't finished frothing when I turned and rushed for the door before he could change his mind. I ran all the way home.

"Ma, Shtrugahtz kicked me out of his class, and I'm not going back."

"Why?"

"I didn't bring a notebook. I didn't bring a pen. The subway drives by as if the tracks are in the classroom, and he pinched me."

"Why did he pinch you?"

"To show that a bird flies."

"This calls for a pinch? Don't go back. He's a *meshugener* [crazy person]."

I was a one-day dropout from Yiddish school. The boys were waiting at the candy store to choose me for a hockey game.

Three days of bliss came to an end when Pa discovered Workmen's Circle School 4 on Wilkins Avenue. Two flights of dark brown wooden stairs, their treads yellowed and worn to the bare wood at the center, challenged us to make the ascent up a narrow hallway.

Mrs. Silverman, an attractive, well-dressed, and well-perfumed woman tested my Yiddish. She taught the beginners. After our brief tryst, I was disappointed to be assigned to Mr. Dorin's advanced class.

Mr. Dorin, a middle-aged, congenial man, smiled and shook my hand. He told me to return tomorrow with a pen, a notebook, and a thin Yiddish text called *Stories and Legends*.

"I can't read Yiddish," I told him.

"In two weeks, you'll be reading better than Mr. Dorin," he assured me.

This was quite a contrast to Chaver Shtrugahtz with his pinch and his bird. By the end of the third week, I was well acquainted with the five boys and two girls in my class and was on my way to reading and writing Yiddish.

My class began at 4:30, immediately after the beginner's class. Most of my classmates arrived early. Our favorite pastime was playing King of the Hill on top of a massive six-foot safe in a corridor outside the classroom. In order to mount the safe, we placed a foot on the handle and hoisted ourselves up by gripping the top of the safe. The one who was on top by the time class began won the game.

We tried to be as quiet as eleven-year-olds bursting with excitement could be. Mrs. Silverman visited twice to tell us to quiet down because there was a class going on. As our class time approached, I was on top of the safe, and my shouting classmates were trying to dethrone me. Mr. Dorin passed the chaos on his way to his classroom. In his attempt to get me off the safe, he accidentally grabbed my shirt pocket. As I came sliding down, he was left with my pocket dangling from his hand. My pencil tumbled from the pocket, but I caught it before it hit the ground.

"Oy, what a ballplayer!" he said, as he crumpled the square that had once been a pocket.

The end of the term approached. The class was reading and writing at an acceptable level.

"In two weeks, we will put on a play for our friends and family," announced Mr. Dorin. "This time we will be on the Hermann Ridder stage. It has a fancy auditorium, which costs a lot of money to rent. It holds a lot of people, so we have to sell a lot of tickets. They're 25 cents apiece."

He gave ten tickets to each student. Jokingly he said, "If you don't sell all of them, don't come back!"

"What is this play about?" asked Shirley.

He passed out mimeographed Yiddish scripts. We read the script once.

"Any questions? Velvl, you will be the *melamed* [teacher]. Beatrice, you will be the *melamed's* wife. Dovid [that's what he called me], you will be Yussel. The rest of you will be students in the class."

Shirley barged in, "I can't be in the *melamed's* class, ha, ha, because I am a girl, and girls don't go to Yeshiva."

"It's not a Yeshiva, it's a *cheder* [elementary school], ha, ha. You will put up your hair under a *yarmulke* [skullcap], and you'll be a boy without a *bris* [circumcision], ha, ha," replied Mr. Dorin.

"Read the play again. Velvl, you read your part to the class, and Beatrice you read yours. Dovid, you don't have much to say but a lot to do. The rest of you will be students in the class. Just raise your hand when Velvl asks a question."

The next two weeks were devoted to rehearsal. We had no props, no makeup, and no costumes. These accoutrements would be there on the evening of the play, we were told.

Early in the evening on the day of the play, we entered Hermann Ridder Junior High. I was impressed with the marble floors and shiny brass railings at the entrance. This is where I would be going to school next term, directly across the street from my apartment house. Maybe I'd be a better student, if Donny wasn't in my class.

Down the aisle I went and backstage to review my role. I didn't notice the scenery. Velvl and Beatrice were in a room getting their costumes. Mrs. Silverman stepped out in front of the drawn curtains to promote the cultural activities of the Workmen's Circle. To illustrate this, she introduced our play.

The setting was a classroom in a tiny shtetl in Poland where a *melamed* barely eked out a living teaching and tormenting his students. The *melamed's* wife generously took in a starving Yeshiva student but then nagged the *melamed* about their poverty. She suggested that they raise tuition in order to have meat to feed another mouth on the Sabbath.

"They don't pay now, and if we raise the price they still won't pay," said the *melamed*.

"We need some wood for the stove. By tomorrow all of us will be freezing!"

"Maybe I should go out tonight to ask a *poyer* [farmer] to chop down a tree? Oy, what do you want from me?"

"I would like to live in a nice house in a city and have food on the table."

"In a city? In a city? God doesn't live in a city."

"So, he must be here in this shtetl freezing and starving like we are."

The students came running, pushing and shouting, into the *melamed's* classroom. They settled into their seats. I had not yet made my entrance. I was the brat who was always late and disrupted the class.

The *melamed* was shouting at the class for their stupidity. That was my cue to enter. I came running in with a trip and then a fall. I was stretched out on the floor when I could hear from backstage, "Oy! Get a doctor!"

It was Zelda, the woman who cleaned our classroom. She had never watched a rehearsal and probably wouldn't have known what was going on if she had.

I stood up, pulled Shirley's braid, and knocked off her yarmulke. The *melamed* waited with crossed arms. I sat down. He called on me to read. Naturally, I mispronounced every word. The m*elamed* charged toward me. He grabbed and twisted my ear. I looked up at him and couldn't believe what I saw. Pasted to his face were a rust-colored beard, a mustache, and eyebrows in one dense, continuous piece, just like the features of a villain in a Charlie Chaplain movie. I couldn't contain myself. Burying my face in my chest, I burst into uncontrollable laughter. The audience, thinking I was crying, decided I deserved an Oscar. To a burst of applause, the play ended with the *melamed* thanking God for giving him his wife, his Yeshiva student, and his *cheder* students.

At the end of the term, secure in my ability to read and write Yiddish, I left Workmen's Circle School 4 to return to the nurturing pavement of Seabury Place.

My after-school education did not end with the Workmen's Circle. Bar mitzvah time was approaching the following year. Although Ma kept a strictly kosher home, we did not observe the Sabbath, and we attended synagogue only on the High Holy Days; however, orthodox or not, every thirteen-year-old boy in the neighborhood observed this rite of passage into manhood.

One block from my building, on Minford Place, was Congregation Ein Jacob, a large synagogue that offered religious instruction and preparation

I report for duty in my brown Keds sneakers, 1943.

for the bar mitzvah. In five months I was to celebrate my bar mitzvah. So I began my third round of supplementary education.

The classroom, of course, was on the top floor of the synagogue. The caretaker showed Ma and me the steps leading to it. After a successful perpendicular ascent, we were met by a low ceiling. Hunched over, we made our way into Mr. Kohler's classroom, where the ceiling allowed us to stand upright again. Could it be that our three challenging treks to the peaks contributed to Ma's health and longevity?

Mr. Kohler's students were taught to read the daily and Sabbath prayers. In winter, the musty room was heated by a hissing space heater, and the air was stifling. But with friends like Harold Zap, Marty Aranoff, and George Liker in the class, the stale air was irrelevant to me—until the day someone farted. The combination of heater fumes and human ones made me feel as if I were sitting in an outhouse instead of a classroom. I looked over my shoulder. Aranoff was holding his nose. Harold Zap, sitting next to him, had a smile on his lips (I think he did it). Mr. Kohler, without saying a word, moved closer to one of the cold, drafty stained-glass windows. Now, that was adolescence at its zenith.

A week before my bar mitzvah, my three uncles, two aunts, and grandmother arrived from Montreal in one car. As soon as they entered the apartment, my aunts, mother, and grandmother started cooking for the occasion. But where were they to sleep in our two-bedroom apartment? Uncle Shrolleh was not going to share his bed with a relative. My father crawled into bed with me. My grandmother and Aunt Esther slept with my mother. My youngest aunt, Dorothy, and her three brothers, Morris, Hymie, and Louis, slept on the floor.

My mother, grandmother, and two aunts cooked and baked all the food for this "catered affair," unlike the usual bar mitzvah today. The meal was rich in nutrients and cholesterol, but, more important, it was rich in love.

A year and a half later, I went on to James Monroe High School, where my only after-school activity was the football team. No more mountains to climb.

Fannie's

Too old for a three-wheeler, too young for a dream (a real automobile), we had only two options for transportation: our legs or a two-wheeler.

None of the boys in the neighborhood owned a two-wheeler. Mickey Rooney rode one in an *Andy Hardy* movie, but his father was a judge and owned a house—not like our fathers.

When would I learn to ride a bicycle? Would I ever own one? How does a person remain upright on two thin wheels, one directly behind the other? It must be possible. I'd seen many of my schoolmates do it. I'd even seen girls ride two-wheelers.

Hidden within the shadows of the elevated subway, opposite the Radio movie theater on Southern Boulevard, stood the cheapest bike rental shop in the neighborhood, Fannie's.

When we entered her store, the evil smell of some solution penetrated our nostrils, coating our tongues and stinging our eyes. Surplus bicycle chains hanging on their sprocket wheels were soaking in this foul-smelling elixir at the bottom of a galvanized steel tub. The oily darkness of the shop mixed well with the clutter and stench. A few bicycles leaned on one another against a wall, waiting to be fixed. Wheels, chains, splayed leather bicycle seats, and tools lay scattered on the floor nearby.

The front wheels of narrow-tire truck bicycles and, the centerpiece of Fannie's collection, balloon-tire bicycles poked through the pickets of a short wooden railing. For 15 cents an hour we could rent the trucks; for 25 cents, the state-of-the-art balloon-tire bicycles.

Out of the reek and gloom and into a shaft of light stepped Fannie. Jet black dyed hair framed a pasty, jowled face studded with islands of brown mottled growths of varying shapes and sizes sprouting hairs. In spite of her gruesome appearance, she was a gentle soul. We tested her patience while

Peanzy, Herman, Mutt, and I deliberated over whether to rent a truck or splurge on the balloon.

"Will she rent us a balloon tire for a half an hour?"

"Is a half an hour enough time for all of us to practice? We'll have to walk the bicycle to Crotona Park, since we don't know how to ride it yet, and maybe have to walk it back to Fannie's. That'll take too long."

"No, the most each one could ride, then, is five minutes. We need more time."

"OK, we'll rent the balloon for an hour."

"That's 7 cents each. There are four of us, what will we do with the 3 cents?"

We decided we would share brown licorice sticks from Leff's candy store on our return to Fannie's. Fannie waited quietly while these critical issues were being settled. I'm sure this was not the first time she was party to such a caucus.

We paid in advance, wrote our names and addresses in her book, and were on our way. The problem of walking the bicycle to Crotona Park, a distance of five long blocks, took the edge off our excitement. It was embarrassing to be seen walking instead of riding. The neighborhood boys were brazenly outspoken when anyone stimulated their creative expression. One day, Mr. Beck was seen being dragged by his brown-and-white terrier, his leash arm straight as a yardstick, his body leaning backward at a thirty-degree angle, as the dog zeroed in on a hydrant. The shout was, "Is Beck walking the dog, or is the dog walking Beck?"

A similar barb would certainly be aimed at us, as we guided the bike toward the park. We reached a compromise. Each one would walk the bicycle for one block; the last one would walk it the final two blocks.

Peanzy, Mutt, and I walked the bicycle without incident. As Herman guided the two-wheeler along his block, his neighbor's daughter asked if she could ride it. Without breaking stride, he curtly replied, "It's not mine. I rented it," and moved on.

Finally, Crotona Park. The practice area was a large round asphalt rink encircled by a tall cyclone fence. Perfect! No cars to threaten us; no people to laugh at us.

Herman went first. Leaning to the right side, where he anticipated his fall, was not productive. He pedaled twice and fell to the right just as he had planned. Three coaches began shouting instructions.

"Look straight ahead!"

"Don't lean to the right!"

"Keep pedaling. Don't stop!"

"You're out of control. You're going too fast!"

"Shut up! You never rode a bicycle."

He went off by himself. In five minutes he returned smiling confidently while circling his trainers. That smile did not score well with me. He was able to ride a two-wheeler; I was waiting and determined to learn.

A few stumbles told me that I had to keep pedaling and look straight ahead to avoid a fall. Once that idea was passed on to my legs, the bicycle moved along smoothly. Occasionally, I was able to glide along without pedaling. I felt on a par with any two-wheel rider. It was more satisfying than solving an algebra problem in Miss Clarke's class.

Soon Peanzy and Mutt were racing around the rink, too.

On our return to Fannie's, a rider took the bicycle for each of the five blocks. The brown piece of licorice swimming in my mouth had never tasted better. I could ride a two-wheeler! What a great feeling! The mystery of remaining upright on two thin wheels, one behind the other, had vanished. This was one of the sweeter steps in my struggle toward maturity.

As the weeks passed, I went on to solve the mystery of riding in traffic, as well—all thanks to Fannie and her greasy bicycles in that dark, smelly store.

Early Adolescence

Junior High School

The blue ink stains on my left hand announced to the lower grades in elementary school that I had graduated from a pencil to pen points. Blots created by those sharp pen points came to an end when I advanced to a fountain pen. Blots on my psyche were made by the masochistic school dentist, who had honed his skills from a torture manual written in blood by Torquemada. All of these were now history. I graduated from P.S. 61 and moved on to Hermann Ridder Junior High School on Boston Road, across the street from my apartment house. It was a massive art deco building occupying an entire block. Its distinctive silhouette could be seen from any rooftop in the East Bronx.

Junior high school was a bridge connecting the short pants and knickers I wore in elementary school to the long pants the big guys wore in the upper grades. Junior high school engaged in the hopeless task of shaping a rowdy early adolescent into a well-behaved older teenager.

Having Donny in my class did not speed my conversion. He had taught me how to hang onto the back of a trolley car to avoid the 5-cent fare. He was frequently mentioned as my mentor when a teacher called my mother in to discuss an offense I had committed. We had identical programs.

On the first day of our general science class, our teacher, Mr. Rosenthal, lined us up around the room to assign seats in alphabetical order. He looked up and saw Donald and me talking to one another.

"Before anyone sits down, I'm going to separate you two."

Donny stage-whispered, "What's that, Baldy?"

That was it. He was immediately transferred to Miss Spagnol's general science class.

Donny was tall, handsome, nervy, and totally undisciplined. Mr. Kavenoff, our homeroom teacher, was always reprimanding him for lateness.

Ma and me in 1944. Check out those six-pack abs.

One day, when Donny was about to step into class late, Mr. Kavenoff rushed to the door and locked him out.

"You can't come in," he shouted. "This is the third time you were late this week. Go to Mr. Hawkins [the assistant principal], and get a late pass."

When Donny returned with the late pass, he was allowed to enter, but, like a lion hidden in the tall grass, he patiently waited for his prey to falter. The occasion came on a rainy day when Mr. Kavenoff arrived late to homeroom. Don ran to the door, leaned his body against it, and said, "You can't come in. You're late. Go to Mr. Hawkins, and get a late pass."

Of course, he quickly relented and let the door open, but he drew admiration and laughter from our class for his gall.

Much to my parents' regret, he was the friend I most admired. He was tall; I was short. He had no respect for our teachers; I did. His mother couldn't control him, and his father was totally blind, so he couldn't control Don either.

Donny rang our doorbell one afternoon. My mother, knowing I looked up to him, sarcastically called out from the doorway, "Danny, your father is here!" This was one of the rare times I did not enjoy her humor.

The gym locker room was an endless scene of adolescent buffoonery. The hissing radiators in the winter sounded the call for slobs to urinate on their sizzling cast-iron pipes. The bouquet sent dawdlers rushing up to the gym floor partially dressed. One warm spring day, George, peering out of the locker room window, saw an insurance agent walking alongside the school building. He was neatly dressed in a tan cotton chino suit, a yellow shirt, and a maroon tie. George directed us to strafe the agent with the wet wads of toilet paper he had soaked in a sink. We locked, we loaded, we fired for effect. The saturated paper sailed through the air and exploded at his feet splattering his suit with water shrapnel from his waist to his ankles. Then we zoomed upstairs to join free play on the gym floor. Within minutes, the gym doors at the far side flew open. The insurance man, with pants resembling General MacArthur's chinos after he waded ashore at Luzon beach, burst through the doors brandishing his maroon insurance book. He exploded, "Where are those rats?"

Terrified, we melted into the mob of students at the center of the gym. Mr. Janoff, our gym teacher, blew his whistle. Play stopped. He asked the salesman what he was doing in the gymnasium. Stepping forward, leaving wet footprints, his pants clinging to his legs, the man shouted that some students had thrown wet toilet paper at him. Fortunately, Mr. Janoff said he was sorry and then explained that he was supervising about seventy-five students so it wasn't possible for him to determine who had been missing at the time of the incident. The insurance man left to seek satisfaction from the principal. That was the last we saw or heard of him.

Reading and writing were most memorable with Miss Medler. At a time when obesity was considered neither a health hazard nor a humiliation, the dial was embarrassed by its lack of movement when she stepped on a scale. At the fitness center she would have been rated number one in body mass ratio. She was Superman's counterpart, a Woman of Steel. As a teacher, she had no peer. By the end of the term she had honed our scalpels to dissect a sentence as if we were fine surgeons.

As a teacher, Miss Clarke was Miss Medler's clone in the math department. With her patience, kindness, and dedication she kneaded lumps of clay into above-average math students.

Miss Rothstein, my senior-year English teacher, was another swatch of the precious fabric from which Miss Medler and Miss Clarke were fashioned. She was totally committed to her profession. Her preparation for the day's lesson was a contagion passed on to her students. We wouldn't dare step over her threshold unprepared. The work ethic she elicited from our group of undisciplined adolescents resulted in an appreciation of and enthusiasm for William Shakespeare's *Julius Caesar,* Sir Walter Scott's *Rebecca,* and Samuel Taylor Coleridge's *Rime of the Ancient Mariner.*

In contrast, there was Mr. Kavenoff. Donny called him Mr. Cabbagehead. He was our math teacher in eighth grade. For the first ten minutes of the class, a passerby would have thought it was a gym class. Dangling arms could be seen swinging in unison. What was going on? At the beginning of the period, he would challenge us to determine the time lapse between two taps of his ruler. Our swinging arms were pendulums measuring the seconds between the taps. Obviously, he spent little or no time reworking his lesson plans.

I was moving along very smoothly through junior high school when algebra became the new kid on my program card. Miss Clarke distributed thick algebra textbooks along with mending tissue (the precursor to Scotch tape) to repair torn pages. After mending the fragile yellowed pages of my aging text, I thumbed through it. In the past, the language of my mathematics classes had been perfectly clear. English was spoken there. However, in the algebra classroom, English was a second language. Miss Clarke was very patient with her students, who spoke English in class and whatever language their parents spoke at home. After two weeks, Donny and I were wrestling hard with the vernacular of x's, y's, and equations. We were good students, but with algebra we hit a wall.

"Come over to my house, and we'll make sense of this math," said Don.

In the evening we met at his apartment to decipher our homework assignment. Stepping into the kitchen, Don pulled the string for the ceiling light. Roaches darted over the walls like people fleeing a fire. I rolled a newspaper to swat them before they could return to their nest.

Don held my arm. "Leave them alone. They have a right to live. Let's get to the homework."

I opened my algebra book with one eyeball on the wall. I had the uneasy feeling that hordes of roaches were lurking in its crevices to witness our struggle.

> There are 24 green and red apples in a bag. If there are three times as many red apples as green apples, how many
> a. red apples are in the bag?
> b. green apples are in the bag?
> Show your answer as an algebraic equation.

"I don't like apples," said Donny, tearing the page out of my textbook.

Well, he wasn't going to get away with that. The next question about a locomotive did not please me. I tore the page from Don's book. As the evening wore on, our thick algebra texts came to resemble the thin spellers from our English class.

Don's father, who was blind, was sitting on a club chair in the darkened living room. "What's going on in there? You're not tearing up your textbooks, are you?"

"No," Don answered. "Danny wanted to kill some roaches with a newspaper. I pulled it from his hand."

Don's mother did not let her husband's blindness ruin her social life. A heavy scent of perfume drifted into the kitchen followed by her appearance. She looked as if she had spent the evening preening for a date. With hands on her hips she spun around and asked, "Well, Don, how do I look?"

"I still can't tell the difference between you and my ass," he replied.

"Did you hear him? Did you hear that rotten kid? Is that the way you talk to your mother?"

I was not about to get into the middle of this.

"Don, I'll see you tomorrow in class."

I quickly gathered my books and left before I was drawn into the battle.

Within another week or two we could easily translate the new language. Algebra was fun. We looked forward to the challenges offered in each week's word problems.

Mr. Rosenthal was one of our general science teachers. Donny called him Mr. Roseyballs. By the end of the period, general science could have been called general confusion. Uncontrollable shouts from Murray Drasner, an unfortunate victim of Tourette's syndrome, agitated Mr. Rosenthal to a point where he was constantly anticipating outbursts even when Murray was silent. When the shouts did come, Mr. Rosenthal lost his concentration, lost his place in the lesson, and struggled to control a disruptive group of crazies. His attempt to inspire the class after these incidents fell flat on his lesson plan.

We were not a class of delinquents. We were merely expressing the growing pains of adolescence. On one foot we had a sneaker racing around in puberty while on the other foot a shoe was plodding calmly toward maturity.

For a week Jerry had been planing a piece of pinewood in Mr. Muller's woodworking shop in a vain attempt to produce a straight edge. Finally, after shaving the piece down to two inches, he brought it in triumph to Mr. Muller. The teacher glared at the piece and growled, "Get this dog bone out of my sight! We'll have to empty a lumberyard before you make a straight edge!"

Before he had entered the woodworking shop Jerry had never seen a plane. Like the rest of us, he had no tools at home except a screwdriver and a hammer, and he lacked the skill to use either one. Now, with a plane in his hands, he had to produce a straight edge or he would fail. What to do? The answer lay in the golden hands of Lunchee Blum, whose talent shone in the wood shop but was hidden in his academic classes. Lunchee could always be found wandering the halls of Hermann Ridder. Jerry stepped out of the classroom with a bathroom pass. He looked down the hall, and there was Lunchee! With one sweep of Jerry's plane, Lunchee turned the dog bone into a straight-edged plank.

In June every year, our school was invited to a baseball game at Yankee Stadium. Tan school buses were lined up along Boston Road waiting to transport us. But we were not released until Mr. Maguire, the principal, had stood at the dais in the auditorium performing his annual rendition of *Casey at the Bat*. He delivered it in a low, hoarse, soaked-in-alcohol monotone. Squirming in our seats, we waited for Casey to do his thing. As Mr. Maguire came to the end of the recital, his bulbous red nose lit up and glowed when "mighty Casey had struck out." This was our signal, the green light to stand up and leave for the buses.

The year was 1944. Philip Brody organized a 10-cent pool to guess the date of the D-Day invasion. Upon learning of the pool, Miss Sanderson accused us of gambling and brought Dr. Litwin (who had now replaced Mr. Maguire) to threaten dire consequences: we wouldn't graduate if the gambling continued. As if he had been in the war room planning the invasion, Philip selected the correct date, June 6, 1944.

Good news about the war on both the European and the Pacific fronts made our summer vacation more fun than in previous years. After spending our days at Orchard Beach and Crotona Park Pool, our class 9A2 returned in September as 9B2. We were seniors!

Miss Sanderson was our teacher for official class and economics. She resembled a Salvation Army officer, wearing a black crepe dress with a white collar. In contrast, we resembled a class in a Lower East Side settlement house, with every stereotypical immigrant face and outfit imaginable. We were above-average students but were not placed in the elite rapid-advance class. While most students in our school carried notebooks, many in our class also carried conduct cards assigned by the school court. We were directed to have each subject teacher sign them and enter a comment about our conduct. In two weeks, if our conduct was good, we returned the cards to the court and were warned not to be seen in court again. The court was composed of our peers—students who campaigned for and were elected to the student council at the beginning of each term. One was chosen as mayor, and members of the council were judges in the court. A teacher was their adviser.

We were proud of 9B2's disobedient reputation. So, how could we identify ourselves to the rest of the school? A select group of teacher-tormentors called an executive session at Donny's apartment: Donny, the grand mufti, whose blotter of crimes against the peace and tranquillity of the school could have papered the floor from our classroom door to Hermann Ridder's entrance two floors below; Leon Teager, who, when assigned to write a business letter to a city service in his English class, chose to write to the fire department requesting that they come as soon as they could since his apartment was on fire; Gilbert Barr, who had left a condom on Miss Medler's desk at the end of the period and caused the thin skin on her pale face to finally blossom into a bit of color; George Liker, who, in a fit of rage, threw his loose-leaf notebook at our music teacher, Mrs. Bornstein; Red Hecht, who carried a bottle of Something in the Air, which actually polluted the atmosphere with its aroma; and myself, a minor offender compared to these big-time felons.

The meeting was called to order.

"This is our last term at Ridder," said Don. "We have to leave an impression on the teachers and the rest of the students without getting into trouble."

Red volunteered "I'll bring my Something in an empty fountain pen. They'll never catch me."

Class 9B2 in 1945. **First row, left to right:** *Sheldon Fishman,*
George Liker, Eddie Brown, Cyrus Cohen, David Gips, Bernard Criscuolo.
Second row: *Claire Eisen, Carmelia Patalano, Bernice Lacher,*
Doris Eidlin, Rosalyn Fuchs, Arlene Rashbaum, (unidentified).
Third row: *Danny Wolfe, Stan Engelberg, Leon Trager, Red Hecht,*
Martin Boyarsky, Alex Pavlick, Philip Brody, Murray Schneider, Herbert Berkowitz.
Fourth row: *Gilbert Barr, Philip Slavin, Eugene Stein, Harvey Wechsler,*
Alvin Stamler, Maximillian Novak, Jay Brash, Gilbert Barr.
Top row: *Lenny Waldman, Sidney Titefsky, Donald Rubin, Martin Tanchuk,*
Abe Chayet, Julius Herman, Murray Schwartz.
Although maroon bowties were the hallmark of our senior class, you
can see that there were two rebels. No matter, they were girls. Our official teacher,
Miss Sanderson, whom we had harassed that morning and provoked that afternoon,
refused to be photographed with us.

"They won't catch you because you smell like that crap you have in that bottle."

"Oh, yeah? My gym locker is next to yours, Don. I catch your whiff when you change into gym shorts."

Leon, a mystery buff, suggested we wear Sherlock Holmes hats.

"Are you nuts? You can't wear a hat to school. And none of the girls or I would wear it," offered prissy Gilbert.

"My mother is tired of coming to school so often," I told them. "I don't want to do anything that will bring her there again. So, wearing something sounds like a good idea, but what?"

George responded, "How about a sharp tie?"

Donny, always ready with an insult, replied, "I see you in the lunchroom George. Everything you eat will be on that tie the first day you wear it. How about a bow tie? Everyone in the class will wear a bowtie!"

"Yeah! Yeah! Yeah! We'll check with the class tomorrow."

So, it was unanimously agreed. But, where would we get bow ties, and how much would they cost? Don said there was a store near the Leff's Freeman on Southern Boulevard that made ties and bow ties. He asked me to accompany him there on Saturday. The meeting was adjourned.

The tie maker agreed to make thirty-seven maroon bow ties for 20 cents apiece. He said he needed a $3 deposit. On Monday we told the class we needed $3 to place the order. Names were recorded as classmates each placed 20 cents in an envelope. For the rest of the term, the boys and girls of 9B2 wore their ties proudly. Teachers were on the alert for any misstep by the class with the maroon bow ties.

At graduation ceremonies, the senior class, including our class in bow ties, entertained the audience by singing *Ballad for Americans*—not without incident. At the beginning of the program, Norman Zimmerman, carrying the American flag, tripped on the top step and sprawled out on top of it while the school band kept on playing *Pomp and Circumstance*.

I moved on to James Monroe High School for my next adventure in academia. Don and Red Hecht went to a vocational high school for a short period. When they turned sixteen, they lied about their age and, with the approval of their parents, joined the army.

The Drugstore

It never was "the drugstore"; it was "Adoff's." If I was down with a cough from a chest cold, Ma would say, "So you'll go to Adoff, and you'll get me mustard for a mustard plester." She placed the mustard powder in a bowl and then added hot water to make a paste. This horror was transferred to a wide cotton gauze sac and applied to my chest. Its acidic fumes filtered through the gauze, sped directly up my nose, and drained my tear ducts. I could inhale through my nose again, but did it help the cough? Who knows?

The drugstore was on the street level of an apartment building on the corner of Seabury Place and East 172nd Street. Two large curved glass urns, filled with a light blue liquid, sat at each end of the window on Seabury Place. These stately vessels framed a monthly over-the-counter drug promotion. Dummy nonprescription drugs were scattered between the urns, interspersed with ads extolling the benefits of Ex-Lax or heartburn medications such as Feen-a-Mint, Bisodol, or Sal Hepatica. Evening in Paris perfume was the permanent feature in the window on East 172nd Street. A large pale blue photograph, the length of the window, displayed a slightly out of focus, beautiful, dreamy woman in a reclining position waiting for her lover to home in on the tantalizing scent of the perfume.

The drugstore was an aid station, a place where prescriptions were filled, a supply source for our medicine cabinet, and an adjunct to the phone booths at the nearby candy store. If a few rubs with a dirty finger didn't dislodge a cinder in the eye, a shout of "Let's go to Adoff!" was heard. The victim, surrounded by the boys, marched off to the drugstore.

"Adoff, I can't see. There's something in my eye."

Adoff would step out from behind his dimly lit counter and usher the victim to the bright light flooding the doorway.

"Keep your head up, and don't move."

We watched in awe as Adoff raised his arms and pushed back his sleeves. If the cinder was in the upper lid, without washing his hands, he placed one hand on the patient's forehead and the thumb of his other hand on the patient's eyelashes. Next he asked the patient to blink. This lifted and inverted the lid. Finally, like a maestro with his baton, he swooped a Q-tip over the inverted lid to dislodge the cinder. Viewing this medical miracle, I was convinced that Adoff should have been a surgeon. His gray-tinted, rimless octagonal lenses, his meticulously pressed gray cotton jacket, and his serious countenance assured me we were dealing with a professional.

As we were about to leave, Tsoots stepped in.

"Adoff, I'm *fahrshtupped* [constipated]. You have maybe a *fihzik* for me?"

Adoff suggested Ex-Lax, with a warning: she should see her doctor if she had no relief after three days.

"Three days? You want me to wait three more days? I have *shtayner* [rocks] in my *kishkes* [insides], and you want me to wait three days? Maybe a *feldz* [boulder] will come out!"

"OK, don't take Ex-Lax. Go see Dr. Kulock," Adoff counseled.

Our medicine cabinet contained aspirin, iodine, peroxide, Mercurochrome, Milk of Magnesia, alcohol, some gauze, and a roll of tape. Should one of us have an intestinal logjam, our laxatives were fruits and vegetables supplemented by Milk of Magnesia.

"Rose, I had a corn muffin in the Automat this afternoon, and now I have heartboinin' in mine chest," moaned Pa.

"I just bought Ex-Lax."

"No, no, that's for constipation and your Feen-a-Mint helps me like a *toiten bahnkess* [like a dead man is helped by cupping—an old fashioned remedy for bringing blood to the surface of the skin]. Get me please a tablespoon and the bottle of Milk of Magnesia."

I stood by, absorbing the medical knowledge whenever it was dispensed in our apartment.

In 1940, an A&P supermarket was built to the left of my apartment building. Housewives purchasing their groceries could get their first aid supplies there cheaper than at Adoff's. Many tenants, like my mother, remained loyal to their professional, Adoff.

At Adoff's I made the rare phone call for my parents. The store's number was the one we gave to our relatives in Montreal. The candy store also had phone booths, but Adoff could be relied on to send a messenger to us, because business at his drugstore was less hectic.

I was sitting in a phone booth at Adoff's waiting for him to fill a prescription when I saw Flat Anne through a window of the folding door. Her slender shape nearly dissolved in the dim light. She nervously waited until Farrell (nicknamed that by Sol Pearl because he claimed he knew every policeman on the beat) left. Then, stealthily, she made her way to Adoff, who was in the rear, filling my prescription. She whispered something to him. He came out, went to a shelf behind the counter and quickly slipped a box into a large paper bag. Menstruation was a topic not to be mentioned in public places. Condoms were squirreled into a secret drawer near the register. At the mumble of "Sheiks," Adoff opened the drawer, wrapped his hand around a small, tin container, and then quickly transferred the tin to his edgy customer. A man's legitimate or illegitimate sexual activity was not a topic for public discussion.

Brodsky the Butcher, Pinsky the Vegetable Man, Litroff the Baker, Jack the Candy Store Owner, Jake the Pickle Man, and Adoff the Druggist knew everyone in the neighborhood. They knew the joys, aspirations, and disappointments of their customers. But as progress brought the supermarket to the neighborhood, all the services of these mini-enterprises were incorporated into the A&P. Who were the clerks? Who was the manager? Who knew? The manager could have asked, "Who are the patrons?" None had a relationship with the others. When I waited to pay for the rolls at his bakery, it was nice to be quizzed by Litroff, "No challah? Your mother was baking this week?" A sincere "hello" greeted me when I opened the door and stepped into Adoff's. Even the pickle man's insults let me know he was aware that I existed. The A&P supermarket contributed to their demise. These small businessmen didn't answer to a board of directors. Their directors were their customers. Local tradesmen contributed to making our rough cement streets and asphalt gutters a lively neighborhood.

The Candy Store

No matter how they tried, the three frosted bulbs emitting a dull yellow glow above the candy store window could not compete with the light pouring from the surrounding tenements. The impotent candy store lights could attract neither insects nor new customers. All the residents knew where the candy store was, so its bulbs and even the flickering red neon sign in the front window reading "Breyer's" surrounded by a green serrated leaf were not going to generate new revenue.

Every neighborhood had a candy store. Ours was tucked between a four-story and a three-story tenement in the middle of 172nd Street between Seabury Place and Minford Place. Rising from the sidewalk in front of the store like an irregularly shaped brown malignancy stood the newspaper stand, its aged wood weathered, splintered, desiccated, and polished by rear ends resting on it. It might have been identified as an artifact unearthed in an archaeological dig. Pressure-treated lumber was decades in the future. Why hadn't this organic monster decayed into dust over the years? Its collapse was prevented by a brace of enameled metal signs squeezing it together like a tourniquet. "Pepsi Cola Hits the Spot" was announced on one side of the stand, countered on the other by a smiling young lady holding the classic curved bottle and declaring, "Coca-Cola: The Pause That Refreshes!" A grinning, white-mustached face advised, "Model: Smoke It. You'll Like It" adjacent to a GI who swore, "I'd Walk a Mile for a Camel." Mr. Peanut, rejoicing on his skinny legs and brandishing top hat and cane, announced, "The World Goes Nuts with Planter's Peanuts," and the distinguished Prince Albert, dressed in his cutaway, stood tall and proud on the front of the red pipe tobacco can. Together they all hid and held together the wooden decay behind them.

An adjunct to the stand was the wood-framed glass door plastered with colorful stickers: Mentholated Spuds cigarettes, Double Duck soda by

Hammer, Keep Kool with Kools, Lucky Strike Green Has Gone to War! and Sir Walter Raleigh, his visage emerging from a ruff collar, offering valuable coupons in a pack of cigarettes.

Dark, dismal Depression decor greeted us upon opening the door. Stepping over the threshold it was difficult to avoid bruising a hip on the two small, circular, marble-veined ice-cream parlor tables to the left. Each sported two chairs with round, dark brown plywood seats set into their circular metal frames; their curved legs and backs seemed to be constructed from thick, twisted, uninsulated telephone cable. On the right, a six-foot-long faded red Formica counter, yellowing and frayed at the edges, displayed the penny sweets and sours: Fleer's bubble gum, Just Born chocolates, sesame seed squares, shoe leather (dried mashed apricot), solid rectangles of Hooton chocolates, red wax lips, clay bubble pipes, Baloney bubble gum, red and black licorice twists, brown tubular licorice, squares of Joyva chocolate-covered raspberry jelly or halvah, Tootsie Rolls, little wax bottles filled with sweet red liquid, colorful candy dots attached to bright white paper strips, and chewy, nutty, white Mary Janes. Each of these enamel-wrecking sweets could be rolling on your tongue and overwhelming your taste buds for a penny or two. Buzzing flies tested every uncovered delicacy. Apparently delighted, they returned for more. In broad daylight, a roach occasionally promenaded across the sticky counter. Sanitation in this store was merely a word that followed "Department of." Behind the counter, out of reach, on each side of an ornate cast-iron cash register, the 5-cent candy was terraced in open boxes. Walnettos, Planter's Jumbo Blocks, Dreams, Mounds, Hersheys, Nestles, Bazzini nuts, Good and Plenty, Jujubes, Chuckles, Sen-Sen, and Black Crows composed a small part of this pricey confectionery. At a right angle to this display, running the length of the front window, five shiny chromium lids topped clear octagonal jars containing syrups that reflected the colors of the spectrum when the sun's rays lit them.

It was late afternoon. The boys had just finished a Stickball game and were hanging out in the candy store. A click from the door handle, followed by a feeble push on the door, and an unkempt, bedraggled body shuffled in. Jerry stage-whispered to me, "It's Gravel Gertrude!"

We didn't know her baptismal name. She was christened Gravel Gertie after an untidy wizened character in the "Dick Tracy" comic strip. Gertie and her husband were the janitors of 1524 Seabury Place. Prunelike, dry, wrinkled skin highlighted an alcohol-induced, mottled cherry and blue complexion fading to gray as it reached her lips and hirsute chin. She was a sight that chased the most vicious dogs from her alley. When she reached such a state of sobriety that she could elevate herself to a vertical position and reel into the candy store, she shouted to Peanzy or Sol, who worked the counter, "One up on the dope!" which translated to a double Alka-Seltzer. This remedy would alter her body chemistry so that it could once again accept more cheap whiskey. In spite of her macabre appearance, she was completely harmless. Gert got her fix for the day and left. With the end of that brief episode, we were left silently looking at one another.

"Let's outstare the Painter!' shouted Lunchee. This call summoned us to the street. The Painter was a quiet gentleman who lived on the second floor of an apartment house directly opposite the candy store. He had the awesome ability to stand at his window, hands in pockets, and stare out for what seemed like hours without twitching a muscle. As in a team photograph, we gathered in a tight cluster across the street from his window and stared at him without blinking an eye. The moment he showed any sign of movement, a roar of "Yay!" resounded throughout the neighborhood. Until the day he moved away, he had no clue about the entertainment he provided the boys when they took a break from the candy store.

Mrs. Kalish, who lived in the same building, closely watched the comings and goings at the candy store. Now, in she walked to make a phone call. Hidden in the shadows at the left rear of the store were two phone booths with brown embossed-tin walls, a wooden seat wedged into a corner, and a folding glass door for privacy. Since very few residents could afford a phone, all their incoming and outgoing calls were transacted within these booths. Barely catching her breath, she announced loudly enough for us to hear, "Hello, Sophie.... Yes, we'll go to Brighton Beach this Sunday. But this time you bring the sandwiches, no mayonnaise, and tell your Murray not to make any wisecracks about my bathing suit. Just a minute, I'll close the door. All the *yentes* [gossips] in the store are listening."

Up to the age of nine, my friends and I were messengers who called residents to the phone. The usual gratuity was one or two empty milk or soda deposit bottles that we redeemed at the candy or grocery store for 2 cents apiece.

The phone rang. It was my turn. Mrs. Winter who lived in the New House was wanted on the phone. When she didn't have any milk bottles or soda bottles she would give a generous 5-cent tip. As I was about to make the turn toward Mrs. Winter's house, I saw Coaltown and Citation heading for the candy store. We named these two frail, slight Orthodox Jewish men in their eighties Coaltown and Citation after the legendary Kentucky Derby winners. They could barely walk: with the support of their canes and one another, they took measured steps, like little windup toys. Arm in arm they tottered out three times daily to services at a nearby storefront synagogue. Coaltown always appeared in a black, tight-fitting overcoat with wide lapels and a velvet collar; a black derby was pulled down to his white eyebrows. Citation made his fashion statement in a loose-fitting gray overcoat with a black Persian lamb collar wending its way around his neck and down to the first button; a black derby also topped his head. I knew at a glance why they were hobbling toward the candy store: they didn't have a *minyan*—the ten men needed for prayers, as prescribed by Jewish law—this evening and were coming to recruit the boys. I quickly returned to the candy store. "Coaltown and Citation are coming!" I shouted. This precipitated a sacrilegious mad dash for the nearest hallway to avoid conscription. My good deed accomplished, I proceeded to Mrs. Winter's apartment.

The tantalizing syrups in the octagonal jars displayed in the front window were used to mix sodas at the fountain. The ingredients for the secret formulae used to make egg creams, lime rickeys, and cherry Cokes were drawn from these vessels. Tsoots, an elderly neighborhood widow with a wry sense of humor, walked into the candy store and ordered, "Give me a *glozel tserry vasser* [glass of cherry soda]." After emptying more than half the glass, she put it down and asked, "Maybe you made this for a cut? Dis is *tserry vasser*? Feh. Dis is Mercurochrome. I'll bring it to Adoff's drugstore." In appreciation for the laughs she elicited, she pinched our cheeks as she left the store without paying for the soda.

Owning a candy store was a marathon of labor—seven-day-a-week drudgery. The day started at 6:00 am when the newspapers arrived and ended about 10:00 pm. Only the High Holy Days and the first two days of Passover bolted the lock. The hours toiled divided into the week's purchases produced a pathetic income.

Steve the Greek was one owner of our candy store who didn't work endless hours. He was a widower living with his nine-year-old daughter, Stephanie, in a cubicle at the rear of the store. When he anticipated the arrival of the Bull (who taunted him), he would announce, "Uh-oh, I better close up before the Bull comes!" Regardless of the hour, out went the lights, and the door was shut behind us.

The next entrepreneur after Steve was Morris, Sol and Peanzy's father. Morris bought the store thinking it would supplement his income as a cabdriver. Jerry ordered an egg cream on Morris's opening day. From the deep recess of a ceramic cup near the soda dispenser, Peanzy lifted a long stirring spoon coated with congealed syrup; a roach dangled from its end. Without a comment, Jerry quickly changed his order to a chocolate Mello-Roll.

Peanzy spent as much time sampling the merchandise as selling it. This led to a substantial gain in weight and his demise as an exceptional athlete. After a year and a half, Morris raised the white flag. He sold the store to Refugee Jack. Refugee Jack was a Holocaust survivor. At the end of World War II, he was married in a Displaced Persons Camp in Germany and then came to the Golden Land only to find this tarnished candy store. Why should we have treated him any differently from his predecessors? When we found a weakness, like all successful parasites we exploited it.

Jack's eyes glistened and his mouth salivated whenever a young lady crossed the store's threshold. We dedicated this ditty to his lust:

> *Refugee Jack*
> (sung to the tune of "Gentleman Jack")
> Refugee Jack's
> A sex maniac
> There's no such thing
> As a piece of *dreck*

To Jack, Jack,
The Sex Maniac.
(repeat)

The lighting in the store may have been dim, but the characters who frequented it made it glow like a beacon. At home, comedy by Eddie Cantor, Bob Hope, George Burns and Gracie Allen, Jack Benny, Fred Allen, Fibber McGee and Molly vibrated from our Emerson radio, but these comedians could not compete with the humor generated during an evening at the candy store. It would have sent all the professionals to join our fathers on the unemployment line.

Sex was rarely discussed in the candy store and never by the boys. We wouldn't have known what to do with a willing partner if we had found one. But one day two elderly citizens, Beep-Da-Da-Brook, a retired furrier, and Silver, the proprietor of the Minford Place grocery, were in the candy store sipping on seltzers when a sexy young lady came in for a pack of cigarettes. Soon after she left, Silver, panting breathlessly, stammered, "*Oy!* Vott I could do *mitt* her."

"You could do notting *mitt* her," replied Beep-Da-Da-Brook.

"So, *nu*, big shot," replied Silver. "Vott ken you do?"

"She could get me so eggsited, I could kerry a pail *mitt* it! End vot ken you do?"

"She could get me so eggsited, I could put fifteen pennies on it!"

"Yeh, vun on top uhv di odder!" replied Beep-Da-Da-Brook.

We would have been rolling on the floor had it been swept.

No one laughed harder than Pinyeh, although we doubted that the dialogue had penetrated his thick skull. He was the owner of the largest head ever supported by a human neck, according to Sol Pearl. Tight, dirty blond curls carpeted this head. Below this mat was a cranium that rocketed off the Mohs scale of hardness. Peb, who was to become a chemist, claimed it was an amalgam of igneous rock and kryptonite. Anyone who tested his knuckles on that skull would have confirmed this.

We were well aware of the physical differences between male and female, especially when this mystery woman came into the store. No one knew her name or much about her, but we knew she lived in the neighborhood. There was no husband, but there was a child.

"So, what do you want, Arthur?" she asked her four-year old son.

"I want that bag over there."

"You mean a bag of potato chips?" asked Sol.

"Yeah, I want a bag of tomato chips and also maybe a moishey bar."

"Hey, Sol! Give the kid a bag of tomato chips and a moishey bar," said Jerry.

"Stupid!" commented the mother. While bending over to lift Arthur, she exposed a few yards of cleavage.

"*Oy,*" said Silver, whose eyes were bulging out of their sockets. "*A leben aff doss kind*" (God bless that child). The child was no longer Arthur. The next time he came into the store he was *A leben aff dos kind.*

Both Fat Anne and Flat Anne were frequent visitors to the candy store. With her shoulder blades as an anchor, two massive breasts sailed forth upon Fat Anne's chest, while Flat Anne was impatiently waiting for breasts to bud—anywhere. It was a warm evening when Alvin noted that Flat Anne, self-conscious of her shortfall, was wearing a sweatshirt.

"Why a sweatshirt in this heat?" asked Alvin. "Are you waiting in the bullpen to be called in to relieve?"

She knew what he was referring to. Up and out she went, another patron pierced by a barb from one of the regulars.

On the surface we were rough teenagers, but inside we were as sensitive as those we attacked. Prepared for some kind of abuse when we stepped into the candy store, we were armed with nothing but our wit to retaliate. After a high school football practice, I went to the candy store for a large seltzer. Foolishly, I had the idea that my football helmet had temporarily removed some of my hair during the season.

"You'll be ahl bahld before yerr ahld," shouted Sol in a phony Irish accent.

"You're already bahld and yerr not ahld," I replied.

After this forecast, I tried massaging my scalp daily. This was followed by a daily measurement of the distance between my hairline and my eyebrows. Slowly, I was convinced I was a doomed passenger on the road to baldness. I survived, as did the others battered by the wicked voices in this harsh but humorous environment.

No impending hair loss threatened David Leff. A dense black mass of extremely kinky tresses flourished on his head. The older guys used his hair as resin to dry their sweaty hands while playing Stickball; hence, David became Resinhead.

The Creep's name for Sol was Big Head or, sometimes, Noiviss (Nervous). So, why not soften that barb by hurling one at another patron? When redheaded Marilyn stepped into the store for a pint of cherry-vanilla ice cream, Sol called out, "Hey, Red, got any hair there yet?" She slammed the door as she left. Another customer lost to Sol's insensitivity.

Whenever there was a possibility of turning a coin, Willie the Weasel made his entrance. Jake the Snake, his adjutant, accompanied Willie one evening carrying two boxes of sweaters that had been accidentally separated from the men's department at Ohrbach's. Willie's promotion for the sweaters was "Five berries and they're yours. But put a lock on these powder blues or your father will steal one and give it to his girlfriend."

His pitch fell on deaf ears. Since the sweaters had generated no interest, he dropped a pair of dice on the floor. "Let's go. Roll them, and rake in the bills."

Suspecting doctored dice, no one picked them up, no one rolled them, and no one raked in the bills.

A few weeks later, the Painter came into the candy store with a shrunken powder blue, pilled rag the size of a washcloth. He was looking for an absent Willie.

Monty the Lecker shared his time between the poolroom and the candy store. By basking under the poolroom lights and inhaling the dust-laden nicotinic air, he developed a yellow-green complexion that complemented his dirty blond hair. The candy store was the showroom for his girl of the week. It appeared as if these girls had joined Monty in the pool room's "tanning salon" to develop their sallow complexions. Comb, brush, soap, and shampoo were not in their inventory. They were essentially preoccupied with the lower portion of their face, the part that accommodated a cigarette. They appeared bored with life despite their vital age. It was said that

Monty dealt in drugs. I never saw a transaction, but I did see him being frisked by detectives on the day I returned home from the army.

The Sheriff looked as if he had spent an exhausting day driving herds over the East Bronx range from sunup to sundown. His rugged appearance would have made him an excellent candidate for the Marlboro Man. We called him the Sheriff because he might have been six-foot-two but was so bowlegged that his rear end could have swept the floor as he tied his horse to a hitching post and moseyed into the candy store to wet his whistle on a foaming stein of seltzer. This quiet gentleman was Monty's father. We couldn't fathom how he and his lovely wife could have produced a Monty.

Tall, dark, and handsome Windy was the best-dressed man in our neighborhood. When a garment showed signs of wear or fell out of style, he would go "shopping" at S. Klein department store, on 14th Street in Manhattan. After carefully selecting his garments, he would carry them to the fitting room, where he would remove their tags, leave his worn clothing on a hanger, and then step out of S. Klein on the cutting edge of fashion.

Gums was the janitor from the tenement across the street from the candy store. He made an occasional visit to the store to buy a pack of cigarettes for his wife. Gums had no teeth. His face appeared to have imploded at the mouth. His tongue was not visible. It seemed like a vestigial organ whose only purpose now was as a conduit for a glob of saliva that he launch from his mouth. Our hearts missed a beat at the sight of it. But Gums had a back that could easily accommodate a concert piano and a pair of arms that could easily lift one.

The only thing predictable about him was his blood-to-alcohol ratio. Sometimes he would run into the cellar to recover the ball for us. At other times his glare would immobilize us. His wife, whom we called the Mask, from the movie *The Mask of Demetrius,* was an unsightly mess. She, like Gums, was black, but a surrealistic landscape of pink and white keloids made circuitous trails down her face, merging at her jaw into a delta of rivulets running down her neck. Could you blame Gums for having a passionate affair with alcohol?

What was the source of these peculiar names? Lenny Blum, aka Lunchee, was a major contributor. He was christened Lunchee when we discovered that he requested free school lunch. To eat this unkosher food was unheard of in our immigrant community. So, the name Lunchee became his Scarlet Letter.

The names were not generated by malice. They referred to an event or physical characteristic unique to the individual. Some nicknames were created for special occasions and drifted away as the event that produced them became forgotten. Others, like Lunchee, became such a permanent part of the individual that we had to stop and think when asked for his given name.

Lunchee produced his most memorable name for a neighborhood character the day Mutt returned from the barber with a haircut that would have been standard operating procedure at a monastery. It looked like a hairy pancake on the top of his head. Lunchee, startled by the coif, called out, "Hey, Mutt! What did Willie use to shape your hairdo? It looks like an iron pot." That was it. Mutt was Iron Pot until his next haircut.

A kid whom we loved to hate was Pimple Ear. He had an obvious protuberance on the upper arc of his right ear. We felt we could take liberties nicknaming him because he wasn't an athlete and he was smaller than most of us.

"Give me a cherry Coke," he said to Peanzy, "and no one in the store is going to call me Pimple Ear."

That was the red flag.

"Why can't I call you Pimple Ear?" asked Rock.

With that, Pimple Ear scooted out of the candy store leaving his drink on the counter. We stepped outside prepared for the next round. He was on his way to report to his father that he had been called Pimple Ear. His father, a tall, nearsighted, uncoordinated, and unattractive man, came lumbering toward us. We fled. He was a testimonial for endurance long before the fitness craze. Maintaining his plodding pace for ten blocks was no challenge to him. In spite of his tenacity, he never caught us. I believe he enjoyed the chase as much as we did.

Sally had an abnormally long stride. When she walked up the hill from Minford Place toward the candy store it seemed as if she was walking up Mount Kilimanjaro. Each measured step seemed to hang in the air before gravity pulled it toward the cement. An outstanding Norwegian long-distance runner at the time, also with a very long stride, was Gunder Haag. He was the talk of the sports world. Hence Sally lost her given name and became Gunder. She eventually married the Rail, who, Sol claimed, was the narrowest human in the Bronx.

Monty (no relation to the Monty from the pool room) was a new member of our crowd and therefore a welcome patron at the candy store. He soon learned that he had to cry out "Safety!" whenever he farted, otherwise he would be pummeled over the head until he fully recited

> Baley, Baley, a bundle of straw
> Farting is against the law
> Hit me now, hit me then
> Hit me when I fart again
> Safety, amen.

He was baptized when we had our weekly club meeting at his apartment. The farting began before we sat down and continued unabated. Monty, gasping for air shouted, "From now on, anyone who farts will be fined a dime.

"Oh, yeah? What if it's a silencer, and we don't know who farted?" asked Jerry.

"You go around and you smell the asses," replied Monty.

"Yeah, who is going to do that?" asked Krebs.

"I'll do it!" replied Monty.

From that moment, he was Have-a-Whiff Monty.

The farting was not confined to Monty's apartment. Henny Landau was the undisputed champ of the Charlotte Street candy store owned by Lee the Gee. A serious contender for the brown tiara was Alvin Lakind, representing our 172nd Street candy store. He seemed to be propelled by a continuous discharge of proteinaceous effluence from his rear; therefore he felt that the umber laurel should be resting upon his head. Was it the decibels of the vacuum released by Landau or was it the day in and day out consistency of Alvin's emissions that would garner nomination to the Swill of Fame? Talmudic scholars could wrestle with this question for centuries.

The candy store's acoustics made it a perfect place to determine the champion. Since the two contenders never had a fart-off, however, the question remains unresolved.

The Oscar-winning movie *The Yearling* featured a young boy, Fodderwing, who was totally dedicated to horses. After seeing the movie, Julie decided it was time to provide a home for and feed pigeons. He spent hours on the roof of his apartment house with the same devotion to the pigeons (in Lunchee Blum's opinion) as Fodderwing gave to the horses. Therefore, Lunchee christened Julie with the name Fodderwing.

Herbert Dicker and his mother had barely escaped Nazi Germany in 1939. They settled in our neighborhood. When Herbert's mother called him Habart, Lunchee Blum, the world-renowned name giver, added Lübengruber to complete the Germanic tone.

Due to the population density of the neighborhood, the names were legion. U.T.S. for Up-Turned Shoes. Whatever shoes he wore, the toe boxes were always elevated at a thirty-degree angle. Gals (always in quest of females), Flippy (giant ears like flippers), the Nose, the Rail, the Bull, Zudick (big rear end), Miserable, Needlenose, Wimpy, Gitchee, Nootch (the bookie), Pebblebee, Big Red, Mootch, Puggy, the Web, Shnippie, the Kid, and Freddie the Hock. Georgie Kaufman called me Geneva Canadian because I visited my relatives in Canada. This was followed by Dud because I once made a firecracker from match heads that had great promise for producing a resounding explosion but fizzled and died.

Another character was something of a mystery. Where he came from nobody knew, but he stepped into the neighborhood with the alias Rahchmuniss. He frequently appeared bearing rumors of baseball trades. Someone discovered that he had been given a job with Bert Lee, who re-created baseball games on a radio broadcast called *Today's Baseball*. The rumor was that Bert Lee had hired him as a gofer out of pity, because his parents had died. Hence the name Rahchmuniss, which means "pity" in Yiddish.

The atmosphere that permeated the smoke, dust, and gossip of the candy store was not an intellectual one. Harassment of the owner was one of our prime activities. One winter, Seymour and Ely, the last proprietors, barred me from the store. I had to stand in the frigid doorway of the adjacent empty store waiting for a friend to step out and tell me what was going on inside. To this day, I have no idea what precipitated my expulsion.

Although unusual characters abounded in the neighborhood, 99 percent of the citizens were hard-working, middle-class folks with lower-class bank accounts. They raised their children to do their best in school and be law-abiding citizens. They struggled; they denied themselves simple pleasures throughout the Depression to rear children who then could own cars, buy homes, travel to places their parents had never heard of. But the closeness, the warmth of family, the humor—where have they gone?

Whenever the boys have a reunion, we review our memories of the candy store. Whether it's a search for youth or an infatuation with a poor, congested, happy, and peaceful era is irrelevant. The nostalgic effect it has on us is an ingredient in the glue that has kept us together throughout the years.

Today, a pharmacy is a candy store, a supermarket is a candy store, a Seven-Eleven is a candy store, but there was really only one candy store, the neighborhood candy store. Like the shtetl of Eastern Europe, it has been assigned to the brittle and yellowing pages of history.

Shrolleh on the Receiving End

During the summer of 1943, my brother bussed tables at Wingdale Country Club somewhere in the Catskill Mountains. From his guests' gratuities he rewarded himself with a trip to Hollywood, a popular young man's clothing store on Prospect Avenue in the Bronx. Two weeks later he returned with a box holding his tailor-made suit, a zoot suit on the cutting edge of fashion among Blacks and Hispanics.

A zoot suit was an extreme expression of style. It had its origin in the Mexican-American community of Southern California. Shoulder pads about the size worn by a defensive lineman in the National Football League were sewn into it. The double-breasted jacket was tapered so that it fit snugly around the midsection and flared out like a skirt as it draped down to the knees. The lapels were broad but narrowed to a sharp point resembling the end of a scimitar. The pants ballooned outward at the knees but tapered to narrow cuffs that were pegged so tightly they almost stopped the blood flow at the ankles. This remarkable garment rested in my brother's box.

Shrolleh, who usually retired very early, had been sleeping for about an hour. My brother knocked on his door.

"Vot iz it?"

"I want you to try on a suit."

"Vot suit? I'm sleepink."

"Come on and get up. It's important!"

Partially asleep, Shrolleh emerged from his room, eyes at half-mast. He struggled with the narrow aperture at the cuffs, but in a few seconds he successfully pulled the pants over his bare feet. The jacket hung loosely over his torso and down to his knees. His hands were lost somewhere in the sleeves. The lower parts of the pants formed a puddle of fabric at his feet. His faced glowed like a red balloon above the jacket. The total effect had us in convulsions.

Within a few months, Shrolleh realized that my brother was not going to wear this outrageous suit. The skirtlike flare of the jacket was beyond alteration, but he had my father deflate the ballooning pants around the knees so that he could wear them. He sported the fashionable six-inch peg as he strutted to work with his Thermos and two sandwiches in his hand.

Shrolleh was absolutely terrified of any insect or rodent. I was fourteen years old when I found a spool of extremely thin, iridescent maroon-colored copper wire. While unreeling the wire, I pressed it together and fashioned a copper mouse from it. To this mouse, I attached a very thin thread.

Our apartment had a long, narrow hall. Shrolleh's bedroom was immediately on the left near the front door (my brother was in the army then, so Shrolleh had the room to himself). I slept in the living room, at the far end of the hallway.

I placed the mouse at the entrance door, shut the light, and crept into bed. Within fifteen minutes I could hear Shrolleh's key probing the slot in the lock. The door opened, and he flipped on the light switch. Thread in hand, I slowly pulled the mouse toward me. Did he see it? The sound of his footsteps abruptly came to a halt. After a brief silence I heard, *"Finster iz mir meineh yohrren!"* (dark are my years). Fortunately, the pillow muffled my laughter.

The following day, in my Spanish class, during a boring translation, I recalled my uncle's reaction to the mouse and exploded in laughter.

Miss Ziegler would have none of this. "Wolfe, step outside the room, and wait for me at the end of the period."

The bell rang. She demanded to know what had happened and who was my accomplice. Yes, Shrolleh was my accomplice, but how could I explain an event such as this to someone who didn't know him? She asked that my mother come see her the next day.

When I told my parents what had happened, both of them burst into laughter. The following day my mother tried to explain that we had a peculiar boarder in our apartment who did funny things. I guess she got the message across.

Pa's Club Chair

When it was in the kitchen, it was a kitchen chair. Why not? It matched the three other chipped brown kitchen chairs. Carry it into the living room, and it became Pa's club chair or, on the rare occasions when we had dinner in the living room, a dining room chair.

After dinner, Pa would settle onto this stark, brown, painted chair, turn on our Gothic Emerson table radio, and listen to Gabriel Heatter announce the news with his trademark "Ah, yes, there's good news tonight ..."

At the end of the evening, the chair was transported to his bedroom, where Pa emptied his pockets onto its seat and then draped his pants and shirt over its back.

For five days a week, eight hours a day now, Pa worked as a finisher on women's coats. He guided his needle through dense wool fabrics or the pelts of fur-bearing animals. The lady wrapped in a warm, fashionable coat had no idea how this man had labored to finish the garment.

At the end of the workday, he relaxed by leaning against a nearby passenger in the crammed rush-hour subway car. When he finally arrived at the East 174th Street subway station in the Bronx, the sharp downward angle of the subway steps was not user friendly to a pair of legs untested by exercise throughout his years of pushing a needle.

He wobbled down and dragged himself home. The man was in dire need of a respite. His easy chair was stiff unpadded wood. This could not go on. Ma canvassed our neighbors for help to find Pa a comfortable chair. In a few days, Mrs. Suslow from apartment 3 rang our bell.

"Mrs. Wolfe, there's a sale on chairs at Macy's. For $25, your Morris could be on a comfortable chair."

"Oy," groaned Ma. "If he knew I paid $25, he wouldn't be so comfortable."

Ma rushed down to Macy's and found a small, simple upholstered chair covered in a dark blue fabric decorated with small woven blue triangles. Each raised triangle had a woven yellow dot at its center. Within a week, a red-and-black Macy's delivery truck brought the upholstered chair. The far-right corner of the living room welcomed Pa home. What a transition! From hardwood, with chipped layers of brown enamel paint, to a soft cushioned seat, back, and armrests. Pa looked at it as if a stranger had barged into our house.

"Rose! Where did this blue chair come from?"

"It came for you from Macy's."

"Did I ask for it? Do I need it?"

Ma was annoyed. She replied angrily, "In prison those bums have a better place to sit than on that chair of yours."

Pa was never one to argue with Ma. He slipped into this strange, upholstered piece of furniture. A smile erased the fatigue he had accumulated over the years. No longer did he wrinkle his pants on the seat of that Spartan kitchen chair. Back to the kitchen it went, where it belonged.

When Pa came home from work, he removed his coat, washed his hands, and deposited himself into his new chair, accompanied by an "Ahh." Ma placed the radio on a small table next to the chair, so that he could shout back at the commentator giving the depressing news of the day. After dinner, Pa returned to his comfortable chair for a thorough review of his newspaper.

This became his routine over the next years. Eventually, when he collapsed into his club chair after dinner, like an amoeba, he softly filled a pothole that had developed in the seat. The fabric's damask triangles no longer protruded; they had eroded to the level of the surrounding material. At the worn, oily headrest, Ma coordinated the navy blue chair with a light blue terry washcloth. The chair was no longer a pretty face in the living room, but it still earned its place from the comfort it gave to a very good man.

One day I sank into Pa's club chair to read the newspaper. The chair swayed as if I were on the *Lusitania*. This was a chair not long for this world. I knew Pa would sit on it until he and the chair collapsed onto the linoleum floor.

"Pa," I called out to the kitchen, "this chair is moving from side to side when I sit in it. It's falling apart."

"Ah, it's nuttin' *mitt* nuttin'," he replied.

"Ma, what do you think?"

"If he wants to sit on the floor, I'm not going to pick him up."

I saw that I wasn't getting anywhere. What could I do? I recalled Mr. Rosenthal, our science teacher, showing us photos of different bridges. He then asked which geometric shape in the photo gave the greatest support to the bridge. Philip Brody, the nerd, gave the right answer: a triangle. That rat always had the right answer.

At the end of the day, I went to Jennings Street Market to find some means of supporting the chair. There, at the side of Miller's fruit stand, waiting to be adopted, was a three-inch-wide wooden slat.

I brought the board home, but how could I cut it to size? This posed quite a problem for a fifteen-year-old whose tool inventory, kept in the junk drawer, was a hammer, a screwdriver, and some nails in a red Swee-Touch-Nee tea can. The solution was in miserable Mr. Muller's third period woodshop. I could have asked to borrow a saw, but I feared this man. After deliberately mispronouncing Sol Shmulewitz's name, he had called Sol a "fat saboteur." He had pointed to my apartment house, across the street from the school, and denigrated "those immigrants" who hung their clothes on a clothesline to dry.

I unbuttoned the second and third buttons of my shirt and slipped a jig-saw inside it. For the rest of the period I stayed bent over to avoid showing any bulges. My pounding heart could have catapulted the saw out of my shirt. At last, the bell signaling the end of the period rang. I ran out of the woodshop to homeroom for dismissal. I slipped the jigsaw into my loose-leaf notebook, but its fat handle protruded. Tucking the handle under my arm, I left the room at the sound of the bell.

As soon as I was home, I turned over Pa's chair. The thin gauzy fabric at the bottom, intended to disguise its innards, was in shreds, but the wooden frame showed great potential. I rested the slat over the frame and marked the length. It was quite difficult to cut along my pencil line using the blade of a jigsaw, but my jagged cuts followed somewhat the line I had drawn.

Pa seated on his club chair, and Ma seated on Pa's old "club chair," 1940.

The hammer and nails waiting in the junk drawer for years for a call to active duty were put to work. I nailed down the board diagonally on the frame, creating two triangles! By late afternoon the chair was as steady as the day the Macy's truck had delivered it.

Monday arrived. I nervously slipped the saw into my loose-leaf notebook and delivered it unnoticed to my third period woodshop without incident.

Kitchen chairs remained in the kitchen. They knew their boundary. My father continued to ease himself into his trusty blue club chair for three more years, but then its end was nigh. Ma couldn't bear the demise of our fragile blue tenant. A sympathetic cousin directed her to Vanleigh Furniture in Manhattan to buy a replacement. Pa's old club chair was taken to the edge of the sidewalk, waiting to be claimed by the Department of Sanitation or someone desperate for a club chair no matter how old. Within two weeks, Pa was ensconced in a lime-green, nylon-looped club chair and began to work on the pothole he had lost with his blue buddy. Complaining that the material was too slippery and the nylon made him sweat, our leader gradually adjusted to his new nest.

The Walking Wounded

Just as Robert Oppenheimer was able to split the atom, just as Jonas Salk was able to create the polio vaccine, just as Henri Matisse was able to produce incredible colors, Alvin Lakind also had a gift. He and only he was blessed with a wonderful sense of humor and the ability to identify and befriend every mentally challenged personality in our neighborhood. As an innocent victim of this talent I relate this experience.

The name Doovidl is a loving Yiddish diminutive of David. In spite of being a grown man of about twenty-five years, Doovidl Simon had the mentality of a five-year-old. Below his shock of dark red hair lingered a giddy smile. English was secondary; Yiddish was his primary language. During the day he frolicked with his eight- and nine-year-old friends. Alvin was able to examine him under a microscope because Doovidl lived in an apartment building directly opposite Alvin's private house.

One pleasant summer evening, I walked two blocks from my apartment to Charlotte Street for a visit with Alvin. In the distance I saw him busily engaged in a conversation with Doovidl. When I arrived, Doovidl drew me to him, pointed to Alvin's house and said, "*Ah du voint ahn Alvin Lakind*" (an Alvin Lakind lives there).

Alvin followed this by putting his arm around me and pointing to Doovidl's apartment window, saying, "*Ah du voint a roiter meshugener*" (a red-headed crazy man lives there). To which I nodded and said, "Hm, is that so?"

Doovidl, thinking I was laughing at him, punched me in the arm. With that, Alvin smiled and assured me that Doovidl was harmless. It was just a friendly gesture. That was the way he played, Alvin said.

But Doovidl did not let up. I backed away; he followed. With Doovidl on my tail, I ran a block down Charlotte Street, through the Jennings Street Market, and toward Wilkins Avenue, until I finally lost him as I approached the Freeman Street elevated subway station. On my return, Alvin, convulsed with laughter, said, "You should have stopped running. Doovidl is harmless." The lump on my upper arm did not confirm this.

On the same street there lived another mentally challenged but sweet character named Buhmmie. His speech was slow and garbled.

One day, some of the boys were at Lee the Gee's candy store listening to the World Series between the New York Giants and the Detroit Tigers. Buhmmie said he'd bet anyone an ice cream on the game. Alvin asked, "Who do you like?"

"Cho-co-late," he mumbled.

When the laughter died down, Beak Levy followed up with another wager. Beak was another friend of Alvin's. (Alvin had anointed him Beak because his nose was shaped like a hook.) Beak bet anyone a quarter that he could keep his tongue in a glass full of Evervess (a highly carbonated seltzer manufactured by the Pepsi Cola Company) longer than anyone else in the store. Nootch the Bookie had a watch with a second hand. He said he would do the timing. Lee opened the Evervess, and Beak poured it into a glass. Without fanfare, he plunged his tongue into it. It took about five seconds for him to remove a swollen, maroon tongue. "Well," he said with tears in his eyes "who can beat that?" No one answered the call.

Alex was another unfortunate case brought to my attention by the ever-vigilant Alvin. He was a victim of Down syndrome. At approximately thirty years of age, he had no communicative skills. Hunched over on his tiptoes, he could be seen either dangling a white handkerchief from his hand or flipping a small club as he walked through the neighborhood. One day in October 1944, during the presidential campaign, a parade carrying President Roosevelt in a convertible came along Boston Road, adjacent to my apartment house. In spite of the cold, drizzly day, the streets were crowded with residents eager to see the man whose "fireside chats" had them glued to the radio. We could hear the band approaching. Leading the parade, ahead of the main body, was Alex on his tiptoes, with his handkerchief dangling from his rear pocket and a club flipping in the air. In spite of Alex, or maybe because of him, Roosevelt was elected for a fourth term.

Alex led President Roosevelt's limo down this section of Boston Road.
Hermann Ridder Junior High school can be seen in the rear.

Alvin told me I had to catch a performance by another of his discoveries, Laybel. This star's theater was the sidewalk, his stage a milk box, in front of the Romanian Restaurant on Wilkins Avenue.

"Go see him," Alvin said. "He's always sitting on a milk box playing a harmonica."

On Friday afternoon, I went to Jake the Pickle Man's stand. After purchasing pickles and witnessing Jake's performance, I walked half a block farther to audition Alvin's new talent find. I saw a neatly dressed thirty-five-or forty-year-old man, with gray worsted pants clinging tightly to his bulging abdomen and substantial rear. Upon seeing me, with the attitude of a concert artist, he began tapping a foot; then he puffed into his harmonica. He continued tapping as dissonant sounds escaped from the instrument. That evening I went to report to Alvin.

"He wasn't sitting on a milk box?" Alvin asked. "How long did you stand there?"

"About five minutes," I replied.

"His feet couldn't support that *boych un tuches* [belly and ass] for five minutes!"

"Then maybe there was a milk box and he sat on it," I replied.

The Parrot was still another eccentric who dashed around the neighborhood. She was a rouged, slight woman, about twenty-five years old, whose nose was also contoured like half of a U-turn. Our neighborhood couldn't support two Beaks, so the combination of the rouge and the nose inspired Alvin to call her the Parrot. I suspect she lived on Charlotte Street (where Alvin lived) because it was a nest for most of these unfortunate characters. In the summer, as she passed the candy store, I squawked at her like a parrot. She charged toward me, with her little pocketbook swinging wildly, and spewed a deluge of four-letter words with the ease of water rushing from a nearby hydrant.

But four-letter words were not exclusively the Parrot's domain. A slightly built, very short, and agitated man, possibly forty years old, rapidly wandered the streets declaiming a repertoire of expletives that would have placed the Parrot in a class for slow learners. In warm weather, when the boys were hanging out in front of the candy store, he would break his stride, walk up to one of us, and dish out his well-stocked inventory. Our response, impotent compared to his firepower, seemed to give him an orgasmic charge. With his mission accomplished and a smile on his face, he gritted his teeth and harmlessly walked off to his next recital.

We were sitting on the curb between games of Pitching In when a short, chubby, unattractive girl walked by Nick the Shoemaker's shop.

"Ask her for the price of Gold Dust soap flakes," said Alvin.

"Why should I ask her? Who cares about soap flakes?" I asked.

"Just ask her," he said.

She approached, and I asked. She not only gave me the price of Gold Dust soap flakes but the prices of Rinso and Lux and which of the brands were on sale.

Were there more characters populating the streets of our neighborhood? Of course there were, and Alvin discovered them all.

"You've never seen anything like this," he said. "When Mr. Lattner comes by, look at his feet."

"Who is he? Have I ever seen him?" I asked.

"You can't miss him," he replied.

Early Sunday morning, I took my usual seat with the *Sunday News* on the steps at the side of Adoff's drugstore. A man came plodding by. To negotiate each step, he lifted a foot as if it was at the end of a barbell and then, to move forward, he crashed it flat onto the sidewalk. Agony contorted his face. He owned the flattest feet I had ever seen. Of course, it had to be the one, the only, Mr. Lattner.

Some slipped by Alvin. The Squirrel, a man perhaps in his sixties, was a nightly visitor to the Minford Place Laundry, our alternative to the candy store for hanging out. Joe, the only evening employee, was happy to have the boys as his guests. He was especially happy when the Squirrel made his entrance. The Squirrel was slight, about four-foot-ten, with pointy ears and gray hair, and wore an oversized navy-blue coat. He truly resembled a squirrel. Joe, with a few words from a sacrament, baptized him the Squirrel. As soon as the Squirrel passed the entrance and entered the laundry, Joe would always play out the same scene. He would get his magazine of nude girls and place it on the counter.

With bulging eyes, the salivating Squirrel would shout, "Hey! Verr you get it?"

No matter how Joe tried to distract him, the Squirrel spent the entire evening glued to the magazine.

Rain, snow, or shine, another local human oddity was always seen parading through our neighborhood with a crutch wedged into her left armpit. We never knew her real name, and she was yet to be nicknamed by Alvin or Lenny Blum. The crutch could never keep pace with her determined gait. Lodged under her arm, it dragged behind her, offering no support, if she needed any.

One stormy day as she came cruising by the candy store using her crutch as a rudder, Sol, behind the counter, said he would give a pint of ice cream to anyone who would lick the sponge on the crutch that was jammed against her armpit. A collective "Ugh!" resounded throughout the candy store. A few of the boys stood at the door viewing her approach. Drenched from head to foot, with water cascading down her forehead and into her mouth, she came to a halt and bubbled, "Nasty weather, isn't it?" How could anyone be cruel to this harmless soul?

Just as Alvin provided entertainment and laughs for these unfortunates, he did not deprive the boys of his gift. As soloist of a synagogue choir during preadolescence, he brought his lyrical talent and choral history into the candy store and developed a new musical concept. He became the creator, arranger, and choirmaster of the Pricksters. This choral group consisted of Winkler (he dropped out; he was too cool), Moish aka Zudick, Jerry aka Trench Feet, Bob Jacobson, and myself aka Dud. Our repertoire ran the gamut from the contemporaries to musical comedy to the golden oldies. Rehearsals were minimal. The lyrics were identical regardless of the selection: rapidly, we would sing, "prick-pu-prick-pu-prick-pu-prick" to any tune in our vast repertoire. The music lovers in the candy store begged for more.

At the drop of a gap in conversation, a lone note escaping from Alvin's throat was quickly chaperoned by the Pricksters into a full song, filling the smoke-filled air with the sound of music.

Alvin was a calm and gentle person, but he was a demanding choral master. Auditions were held in the candy store whenever a prospective Prickster felt he had the gift to join the virtuosos. Our signature piece, *Misirlou*, if sung properly, demonstrated all the requirements for an aspiring Prickster.

We couldn't fault him for trying, but Krebs was the perennial washout. It was the same old story. Alvin asked him to prick to *Misirlou*. Critically listening to the struggle, Alvin would sadly say, "I'm sorry Krebs. Twice you pricked when you should have pued. Go back, practice. Maybe in a few years …"

My pièce de résistance was the solo for *Roger Young*. It was a somber song about Roger Young, a marine who was posthumously awarded the Congressional Medal for valor on the island of New Georgia in the South Pacific. I would sadly recite the words, "On an Island in New Georgia in the Solomons," while the Pricksters mournfully hummed and pu-pricked in the background. I spoke the words with such pathos that Alvin was able to generate a flow of real tears.

At the end of our final concert, we felt that the Pricksters' repertoire should not be buried under the candy store's linoleum floor. We went to a booth in a penny arcade on Broadway to etch everyone's favorite, *Misirlou*, followed by James Monroe High School's alma mater, *Beyond the City's Noise and Clamor.*

Moish gave the intro: "And now, directly from Broadway, the Pricksters give you *Misirlou!*"

We knew this was the final curtain. We pricked our little hearts out. Somewhere there is a thin six-inch plastic record that should have been dipped in platinum.

Alvin's creative talent went beyond his musicianship. He choreographed a maneuver that had everyone in the neighborhood scratching their heads. Usually in the evening (hardly anyone did homework), during a quiet moment in the candy store, Alvin would yell out, "Iwo Jima positions, take!"

We scrambled to the glowing light pole outside the candy store. With our bodies at an angle, some on top of one another, we grasped the pole just as the marines supported the American flag in Joe Rosenthal's classic World War II Iwo Jima photo. After a few minutes, we collapsed into a human heap and then returned to headquarters. The Painter viewing this nonsense from his window stood emotionless. Damon Runyon would have worn out his pen nibs had he been witness to the scenes played out inside and outside our candy store.

I rarely spoke to Henny Landau, Peanzy's older cousin. He and his friends, Wimpy, Gitchee, Bucky, Yoysel, Chink, Pinyeh, Henny's brother Bernie, and the dwarf, Louis the Pimp, held court at Lee the Gee's, our sister candy store on Charlotte Street. I rarely went to Lee the Gee's, and the probability of my sitting next to Henny on Lee's newspaper stand was off the books. But there I was one evening, sitting on the stand between Henny and redheaded Grace's father. Without forewarning, Henny lifted himself from his sitting position and was suspended in air for a moment. There was nothing but space between the wooden stand and his rear when, like a soprano belting out a high note, he emitted a shrill sound from his rear end. A downward pitch toward tenor-baritone followed. As it nose-dived to bass, it exploded into a booming thunder. I couldn't believe a

Seabury Place and Charlotte Street in 2004, former location of Lee the Gee's candy store. His newspaper stand stood tall until its timbers trembled under Henny Landau's vibrations.

human could generate a sound of such length and decibels. Grace's father sat there mesmerized; he turned blue-gray and appeared to be in a state of shock. I escaped, after shaking off the vibrations from the slats beneath me, with the hope that I would recover in time to accurately relate this notable event to the boys at the 172nd Street candy store. The following day, unfortunately, Grace's father had a heart attack and died.

Alvin often referred to the consistency of his flatulence with pride. But, like Phil Rizzuto, who had not yet been voted into the Baseball Hall of Fame, he felt unfairly rejected by his peers. Henny Landau wore the brown crown.

I related to Alvin a quote from the baseball great Ralph Kiner: "Home run hitters drive Cadillacs; singles hitters drive Fords."

"But you can depend on me for day in and day out consistency," replied Alvin.

Recalling the traumatic evening on the newspaper stand, I quietly asked, "But Alvin, did you ever kill anyone?"

He stuck to his position as tightly as his briefs stuck to his rear.

Was every neighborhood in the East Bronx like this, or did we have exclusive rights to these anomalies?

Stickball

Combine a broomstick, a pink "spauldeen" (a high-bounce rubber ball made by the Spalding company), and a minimum of five players on each side and you have the basic elements of a New York City institution, the Stickball game.

In the late 1940s, a 15-cent investment in that classic pink ball was the catalyst for choosing sides and getting up a game. Every neighborhood had a team. Every neighborhood team thought it was the best. This was resolved by playing a home and an away game for a dime a man. Of course, we really *were* the best: we had the Creep, the Joe DiMaggio of Stickball. With his long legs, simian arms, and hands the size of a baseball mitt, he covered the entire field. An error was not in his repertoire, and he mercilessly berated anyone who committed one, simultaneously bestowing a humiliating nickname. For example, when the Creep played shortstop in a game of Off the Curb, he went after every ball that was hit to the right or left side of the infield. Consequently, Jerry, playing third base, had no opportunity to field a single ball. Finally, near the end of the game, a ball was hit to Jerry's right, and the Creep couldn't reach it. The ball bounced past Jerry and into the outfield for a base hit.

"I put da kid on toid base, and he stands dehr like he got trench feet!"

On the spot, Jerry was no longer Jerry—he was Trench Feet.

The Creep's brother, Herman, was nicknamed after he tried to catch a game-ending fly ball with one hand and then dropped it.

"Ketch da ball wid two hands! Look at ya. Ya swat at da ball like a one-armed bandit!" cried the Creep, as the winning run crossed home plate. It was baptism by fire: Herman was anointed the Bandit.

It was a rare treat for us to watch the national pastime in Yankee Stadium. But we had our own pastime, no charge. Considering the economics involved, Stickball was a rational pastime. The bat was a broomstick.

"A stick, a glove, a pink Spalding, and the Creep."
That was all the boys in the 'hood wished for.

Where did we get one? A housewife did not part with her broom readily. An investment in a broom was an investment for life. But not if Abe was in the area. Had she made the mistake of airing out her broom on the fire escape, Abe's hawk eye would spot it.

"Get me to the ladder, and no goosing," he would say.

We lifted him until he could grasp the ladder dangling from the first-floor fire escape. Stealthily, he made his way up the iron steps toward the target. With booty in hand, he then tiptoed down the steps to the ladder. Dropping the broom to us, he was able to dangle from the ladder and fall gently to the sidewalk. With this résumé, Abe went on to become mayor of Herman Ridder Junior High School.

Nick the Shoemaker was the next major player in the operation. As soon as he saw the broom heading toward the store, his wide, sharp-nosed pliers was on the counter.

"If you guys gave me enough work, I wouldn't have time for your stinking brooms" was his good-natured complaint whenever we asked for his pliers.

With the pliers, we removed a nail that anchored a silver coil of wire holding the corn bristles of the broom together. The wire unwound easily. Then we shook the loosened corn bristles into the mouth of the corner sewer. Voilà! a genuine broomstick—the Powerized Louisville Slugger of Stickball.

When we had no other choice, we settled for a mop handle. It had a narrower diameter than the broomstick. There were two types attached to mops. The one made of hardwood was our first substitute for a broomstick. Desperate conditions forced us to use the other, a porous pinewood mop stick. The ball had no respect for this stick. It frequently cracked the stick when a batter made a hit.

Mop sticks were too long to be used as bats. But who owned a saw? A hammer, a screwdriver, and some nails were the only tools in our kitchen "junk drawer." We found a solution. We inserted the mop stick into one of the holes of a sewer lid, lowered the stick to the desired length, and then walked round and round the lid, pressing the stick against the lip of the hole. Eventually the excess piece of the mop handle separated and fell into the dark pit of the sewer.

The police considered stickball sticks illegal weapons. When they drove by and caught us with them, they would take the sticks, giving us a crack on the back to boot. We assigned Stanley, one of the younger kids in the neighborhood, to the street corner as our lookout for any patrol car. If he saw one coming he would yell, "Chickee, the cops!" We quickly gathered our sticks and ran into a nearby tenement building. If the police were too close, we dropped the sticks through the sewer lid holes, and they fell about twenty-five feet to the bottom. After the police drove by, out we came, and a few boys would plunge their fingers into the sewer lid holes to lift the lid. Since I was one of the smallest kids, I was then "volunteered" to descend into the sewer. The cylindrical cavern exposed a sewage pipe at the bottom with a fermenting puddle sitting on either side. As I climbed down the ladder on the side, my palms collected the rusty flakes coating each rung. Rats scrambled, and the taste and smell of the obnoxious ferment trapped in the warmth and humidity enveloped my entire being. By the time I reached the sticks, my palms resembled the skin of an ugly brown reptile. The sticks were partially rinsed by the disgusting water pooled alongside the sewer pipe. There was no way I was going to step into those puddles. With one hand clutching a rung and one foot on the sewer pipe I gathered the two sticks from the putrid water and ascended in record time. To the relief of the boys, I deposited the slightly wet and filthy jewels at ground level, the sewer lid was set back in place, Stanley returned to his perch, and the game continued.

The tenement architecture and the rare car that might be parked on the field determined the ground rules for Stickball. Stoops, fire escapes, cellars, spiked fences, gates, doorways, and parked cars were in play—that is, if the ball was caught off any of them without a bounce, the batter was out. A line drive caught off a gossiping woman who had the nerve to sit on our field of play was also an out. These complex ground rules were refined throughout the years and passed on to the next generation.

The stick we used for Stickball was also used for Pitching In. Again, a sewer lid was home plate. The pitcher threw the ball to a batter standing alongside the plate. Behind the catcher was the umpire calling the balls and strikes. An outfielder covered the area behind the pitcher. The batter didn't run around the bases; instead, the distance the ball was hit determined the type of base hit. The rules were clearly defined. A ground ball caught in front of the pitcher's mound or a fly ball caught before it bounced was an out. A two-base hit traveled past the pitcher's mound and bounced before it was caught. At a farther designated distance, the fly ball was a triple, and farther still, a home run.

Once I pitched a blazing fastball to Moish. He smacked a blistering line drive that went directly into my mouth. Since the ball did not bounce but remained lodged between my teeth, he was out. Whenever the boys meet, I am reminded of this embarrassment.

One brisk autumn day, during a heated debate with claims and counter-claims, we decided that there was only one way to resolve the issue of who was best at Pitching In: on the playing field. The usual quarter a man ante was upped to fifty cents—this was serious business.

On the short walk to the field, I wanted assurance that this would be a complete game. "Rock, how many times, in the middle of a game when you were losing, have you said your mother was calling you? No one heard her. And, I don't like the way you dig your fingers into the ball before you throw it. You can't do that with a baseball," I said.

"First of all, my mother never called me in the middle of a game."

"So, you quit in the middle of a game when you were losing, that's it," I replied.

"And," Rock continued, "this isn't baseball, so I can throw the ball any way I want to."

The dispute continued until we reached the field in front of Nick's shoe repair store. The hydrant in front of Nick's was the canine firing range. Every passing dog zeroed in and fired for effect at its base. Knowing the baptismal history of the hydrant, we draped our jackets over its top.

Jerry went behind the sewer lid, which was home plate. He was my catcher in special games such as this. Soon the score was tied one to one. We went into extra innings. There was one out when Alvin came to bat. On my next pitch, Alvin hit a fly ball toward Adoff's drugstore. Meyer, who was Nootch the Bookie's assistant, came ambling by the drugstore pushing his newborn daughter in her carriage. Krebs ran to catch the ball. To avoid crashing into the carriage, he skidded to a stop, but the ball landed directly inside.

"It's a two-base hit!" yelled Alvin.

"It's an out!" screamed Krebs. "I would have caught it if this lousy carriage wasn't in the way."

"Since the ball wasn't caught, it's a ground-rule double!" barked Mutt.

"It's an out. I could have caught the ball," shouted Krebs.

"What about a do-over?" suggested Moish.

The fact that the ball had landed in a carriage with an infant inside was of no concern. Was it a base hit or an out—this was the issue. Fortunately, the child was not hit. Meyer enjoyed the argument, and the game came to an end without resolution. After the jousting was over, Meyer, always ready for business, asked if we wanted any action on the Sunday Giants' game at the Polo Grounds. We were too excited for such nonsense, so he went on his way. Upon our return to the playing field, we found the hydrant bare— no jackets. We ran into Nick's.

"Nick, did you see our jackets?"

He said, "The I Cash Clothes Man passed by a few minutes ago. Maybe he took them."

The rag man was nowhere in sight. Like poisoned mice we scurried around the neighborhood trying to find his horse and wagon. As we turned up Charlotte Street, aha! There he was, with bells jingling and his horse shlepping him and his spoils. We ran alongside pleading with him to stop. The wagon came to a halt. He knew why we were there. From a grimy canvas sac, he grudgingly removed our jackets.

"Here. Take your *shmatehs* [rags]. I couldn't get a dime for them anyway."

The next generation had no need for Abe, our broom snatcher, or Nick, the Shoemaker. Shiny, colorful Stickball sticks were sold in candy stores. Those unfortunate kids didn't know that hitting the ball with the stick was only a part of the game. Acquiring the broomstick, going to Nick for the pliers, removing the wire that freed the corn bristles, shaking the bristles down the sewer were all the preamble to the event, and the arguments after were the dessert.

Shoe repair became almost as costly as a new pair of shoes. Nick shut his door. Muggings at night and stolen pocketbooks during the day made our neighborhood dangerous. Some residents found apartments in other parts of the Bronx. Those who remained became prisoners in their homes.

Stickball and Pitching In are still played in some Bronx neighborhoods. Not in my old one. Seabury Place now boasts private ranch homes "where never is heard a discouraging word" and no pink Spalding is in play. If perchance a ball does roll in the street, it is stamped with an outrageous price for our once 15-cent treasure.

It Wasn't on the Calendar

To every thing there is a season, and a time to every purpose under the heaven.

Ecclesiastes 3:1

Seabury Place was polka-dotted with pink. Spaldings were bouncing off buildings, streaking through the air, and disrupting the gossip of women sitting on fruit boxes in front of their apartment houses. We knew the major leaguers were returning from spring training. Yankee Stadium, the Polo Grounds, and Ebbets Field were green and ready for a new season. Hot, humid summer was in the wings, scheming to torture us. It came, it did, and it passed. Then there was a nip in the air. Falling leaves wove their way into the mesh of Crotona Park's cyclone fences and bundled themselves at the base of the wire walls. The Sweet Potato Man returned, pushing his charcoal embers through the streets of the East Bronx. This was our wake-up call for football practice. We crawled home proudly, wearing the dirt and bruises of a real man's game. The Giants football team celebrated Sundays at the Polo Grounds.

But what were the signs for marble season, for yo-yo, Hi-Li, street hockey, tops, and pickboard season? The calendar didn't show those. There was no panel convened to schedule the dates. They just happened.

In the fall, a decrease in the atmosphere's ultraviolet rays stimulates birds' gonads for their southern migration. Perhaps these same rays stimulated our glands for the outbreak of marble season. On an undesignated autumn afternoon, the boys filled their pockets with realies (clear marbles) and immies (ordinary marbles), ready to launch them on their maiden spin.

I went to Mr. Beer, my mother's dairy grocer, to get a wooden Breakstone cream cheese box. In those days cream cheese came in a large brick that filled a twelve-inch-long wooden box. I took the box to my junior high school woodshop class, where I cut three holes in one wide side of it. One hole was just slightly wider than the diameter of a marble. The next hole was a bit wider than that, and the third hole was about an inch wide. Above the smallest hole, I wrote "25," the next "15," and the widest "5." At a designated distance, perhaps twelve feet, the player attempted to roll his marble through one of the holes in the box. The figure above the hole indicated the number of marbles the player would win if he succeeded. If he failed, I kept his marble.

Mutt always rushed to the street with his box as soon as he came home from school. He was a fierce competitor, so I always tried to get there before he did.

"I won't be here tomorrow. I have to go to Jake for pickles. What time are you coming down with your box?" Mutt asked.

I knew he was trying to con me into coming down late, so that he could get all the action. "Yeah, I'll also be late. I have to get a haircut."

There were no pickles bought; there were no hairs cut. We were in the street with our boxes as usual, immediately after school.

At the beginning of the season, both of us did quite well in our enterprise. But prosperity turned to despair when construction trucks left fine sand granules on the asphalt: they prevented the boys from directing their marbles toward our boxes.

The most popular marble game required at least two players.

"I'll choose you for who goes first," Jerry said. "Odds."

On a count of three, he put out two ink-stained fingers (he was a lefty), products of a day at school, and I put out two. That was "evens," so I went first. I rolled my marble along the dark gray walls of the curb and into an iridescent puddle from yesterday's rain, slick with grease excreted by the occasional car visiting Seabury Place. Jerry easily rolled his marble into the floating rainbow. The distance between the two marbles was close enough to span with his thumb and pinky finger. He took my marble.

"Oh, here comes Mutt with his pickboard. I wonder whether he stuffed some losers into it."

Mutt's pickboard offered a game of chance. This three-by-five-inch board was made of layers of thin cardboard pressed tightly together into a half-inch-thick mat. It had a colorful lithographed top layer illustrating the theme of the board and designating the winning picks. Immediately below was a grid of narrow holes, ten across and twelve down. A thin tissue between the upper and lower layers covered the holes. In the holes, between the tissue and the bottom layer, were tightly folded papers indicating "Fumble," "Stuck in the Mud," "Left at Post," all losers. "Touchdown," "Home Run," "Knockout," "Win," "Place," and "Show" were winners. A win was 3 cents, a nickel, or a rare dime.

With a small metal key, the player punctured the tissue covering a hole and out came the folded paper. If the theme was baseball, "Strike Out" or "Left on Base" were losers. There was only one "Home Run," but it earned you 10 cents. Most of the picks were losers, of course. Enterprising Richie kept a folded winning pick in his hand while he quickly stuck the key into an empty hole. Then he brazenly showed his "winning pick." Mutt soon wised up to him. That was the end of Richie's picks on the board.

We knew only one source for the pickboards. They were sold at a hobby shop owned by a very short, hunchbacked entrepreneur we called the Hunch. His gray cotton utility jacket hanging a distance from his back profoundly emphasized his deformity. One day, a teenager came in to buy a pickboard. He innocently asked, "Are you the Hunch? I want to buy a …"

Livid, the proprietor grabbed a model airplane from a display and threw it wildly, yelling, "I'm not the Hunch! My name is Louis Ross!"

We were amused, but we ran for the door before he had a chance to launch another airplane.

Other unannounced, spontaneous sporting events during autumn involved yo-yos, Hi-Li paddles, and tops. Red-and-black wooden Duncan yo-yos were sleeping and spinning on strings. Little red sponge balls were tapping off the faces of wooden Hi-Li paddles.

To promote sales, the companies sent demonstrators to candy stores in the neighborhood to perform tricks. How did they continuously hit the ball off the thin edge of the paddle? How did they get the yo-yo to "walk" down the looping paths of string? We tried in vain to duplicate these tricks but had to be content with keeping the little red ball bouncing off the face of the paddle and the yo-yo spinning up and down at the end of its string.

Infrequent visitors during this season were the tops. Most were inch-and-a-half-wide, cone-shaped, brightly painted, solid wooden knobs with sharp or rounded metal tips at the point end. We wound a string around the top, starting at the point. There was usually a button or a knot at the end of the string that we placed between two fingers. The idea was to toss the top forward. As the string unwound, it caused the top to spin rapidly. When the top touched the ground, it spun until it lost momentum. The top that spun the longest was the winner.

Yo-yos, marbles, tops, and Hi-Li paddles were purchased or replaced at the candy store. Thus, this venerable establishment provided another essential part of our entertainment.

Eventually, the snows came. We folded up the streets and settled into the candy store to await the Boys of Summer and other events not on the calendar.

October Winds

Summertime, the time for baseball, had passed. It was autumn, the time for roller hockey. October winds sent discarded newspapers and handbills racing along the gray ridges that bordered our neighborhood sidewalks. October winds sent me to the rear of our hall closet, making my way through camphorated fumes, with my head between a dress and an overcoat whose pockets were filled with little white mothballs. I lifted the dog-eared flaps of an aging cardboard box to search through the chaos inside. Entangled among the never-to-be-used curtain rods, mangled wire hangers, and assorted clothing hooks were my roller skates. They could have been disengaged in an organized manner, but in my frantic attempt to free them quickly from the bottom of the box, I sent rods, hangers, and hooks flying in all directions.

I had a pair of Union Hardware roller skates, a legacy from my older brother. My friends who had a choice opted for streamlined Chicago Racers. Although the Union Hardwares were more maneuverable, the Racers were sleeker, faster skates, and their wheels did not box to slow a skater down.

We met at the candy store. The owner, Steve the Greek, had 25-cent hockey sticks waiting to be claimed by the boys whose sticks had not survived the previous season.

Peanzy inspected his 10-cent narrow curved field hockey stick. "This looks like a piece of dried spaghetti. I'm sick of it. I'm getting a real stick," he announced. He passed 25 cents over the counter for a brand new, genuine big guy's hockey stick.

"We need energy," said Milty. He passed around a Mr. Goodbar to share with the boys. When the bar finally returned to him, he looked down at a few lonely peanuts gathered in the folds of the wrapper. "What is this? OK. You guys will pay for this at the end of the game."

Woolen knit caps were drawn over ears, jackets were buttoned, and collars were pulled up. With skates dangling over our twelve-year-old shoulders, we opened the door, immediately eliciting a scream from Steve, "Close da God demm door! It's freezing in here!"

We left the warmth of the candy store to challenge the brisk October winds. My horsehide mackinaw had reached senility. It didn't remember how to keep me warm or how to fall apart. At the beginning of autumn, I relieved its confusion by depositing it into one of Mr. Tekula's trash cans. My brother's pliant navy wool felt jacket allowed me a flexibility I had never experienced wearing my leather body armor.

It was opening day, the first game of the season. The street was ours. There were no cars parked on the field, and it was too cold for gossiping women to sit on the sidewalk and harass us. Skate keys were passed to those waiting to clamp their skates to the outer edges of their shoe soles. Meanwhile the litany of opening-day complaints was filed and blown away by the freezing air.

"My wheels are rusty! They don't move! I should have oiled them last year."

"I can't get any speed from my wheels. They're boxed. I'll get new wheels tomorrow at Jack Adams on Boston Road."

"He charges an arm and a leg. It's half the price at Dollinger's on Tremont Avenue."

"My strap broke! It's like cardboard! Does anyone have a rope?"

"What are you, crazy? Who carries rope? Steve the Greek ties his old newspapers with rope. Get it from him."

"Lend me your key—my skates are too short!"

"Does anyone have an extra pair of gloves? My fingers are freezing."

"Where's Jerry?" asked Krebs. "He said he would be here."

"He'll be here. He's always here. He said he's bringing goals his father made."

"Who has the puck?"

To make a puck we went to a Jennings Street grocer for an empty wooden Breakstone's cream cheese box. We removed the half-inch-thick, dovetailed ends of the box and nailed them together. The result was a four-inch square puck with projecting "teeth" (the dovetails) eager to take a bite out of the goalie's shins at every attempt to stop the puck.

The grumbling ended when sides were chosen. Abe, who was partially paralyzed from polio, dropped the puck, and the game began. At first the skating was tentative, cautious. Anticipating a fall, we skated in a squat with legs far apart. As the game progressed, knees straightened, skates edged closer, and legs became more familiar with one another. Everyone was in motion, whether they controlled the direction they were traveling in or not. Bodies were bumped, thumped, and dumped. The wheels of the skates engraved abstract thin white parallel arcs on the smooth black surface of the Seabury Place asphalt. Ankles were turned, shins were scraped, pants were torn, but everyone was having a good time.

We were taller, our shoe sizes were larger, and our skates were rustier than the previous year. But there was one perennial constant: "Did the puck pass through the goalie and over the sewer lid for a goal?" This was the grist for the inevitable arguments following every shot on goal. Unless we saw the puck pass clearly over the sewer, we could not take the word of the dishonest goalie or a cheating nearby player to call the goal. Of course, the game always ended in an argument. Most games ended in an argument.

"There he is! There's Jerry," shouted Mutt.

Jerry came marching down the street, proud and tall, struggling with two goals, one in each hand. Convinced that they would put a halt to the disputes, Jerry's father, an upholsterer, had built these goals. Each one was covered with heavy, green-and-white-banded upholstery fabric. They resembled the window awnings on the fancy high-rent New House on the corner. The goals' dimensions were based on a complete lack of knowledge of the game. They were knee high, not about five feet tall. Although they weren't regulation, now we could determine whether a goal had been scored.

Draped in his omnipresent trench coat, 220-pound Bull was the goalie at one end of the street. At the other end, Jerry was defending his father's contrivance. Within a few minutes, Peanzy had scooped up the puck at the face-off. All alone, he skated toward Bull. To fake the goalie out, Peanzy made a sharp turn to the right but then fell to the ground, watching his skate dangle below his stockinged right foot. The stress of the turn had ripped the sole off his shoe, and the sole was all that was still connected to the skate clamps. Peanzy dragged himself off the field, but, of course, the game went on.

Milty picked up the puck and fired it at Bull. It caromed off his leg. The assault continued. Another shot followed, then another, followed by the inevitable pileup at the mouth of the goal. Bull was at the top of the heap. Beneath him lay the puck and on top of that the goal, which was now a crumpled rag and a few splinters. No goal! Krebs picked the puck from under the mass of humanity and passed it toward the other end, where Jerry was prepared to face the impending onslaught. The skaters raced toward the loose puck. Jerry was in position, hunched over and focused, ready to thwart a score, but he was totally unaware of the tragedy that had befallen just behind him. A gust of October wind had found the pocket of the goal and scooped it up. When last seen, it was bouncing along lower Seabury Place, tumbling toward Lee the Gee's candy store on Charlotte Street. We retired to our candy store for protection from the chaos of street hockey and the October winds.

Jerry's father's goals survived a slim fraction of a single game, but this was our moment in Camelot.

Seabury Place

> In short, there's simply not
> A more congenial spot
> For happily-ever-aftering
> Than here in Camelot.

An Alert and Scheming Mind

In the early 1900s, advocates of organized play for children, in an attempt to ease the entrance of immigrant youngsters into the American mainstream, encouraged them to use athletic facilities. It was an ideal place to develop courage, respect for authority, cooperation, unselfishness, and fair play. With this impetus, basketball became a "Jewish sport" in New York City, according to Peter Levine's history *Ellis Island*.

Levine chronicles Paul Gallico, a respected sportswriter for the *New York Daily News*, explaining the intimate connection between Jews and basketball this way: "Curiously, above all others, the game appeals to the temperament of the Jews. While a good Jewish football player is a rarity, Jews flock to basketball by the thousands," he asserted, because it placed "a premium on an alert and scheming mind, flashy trickiness, artful dodging and general smart-aleckness," traits naturally appealing to, "the Hebrew and his Oriental background."

Perhaps our particular Jewish umbilical cords did not extend all the way to the basketball courts of Crotona Park in the Bronx. We rarely wandered far from our placenta, the candy store and its adjoining streets, the source of our physical and psychological nourishment. We were neither schemers, tricksters, artful dodgers, nor smart alecks. Consequently, the game of basketball never caught on with our gang.

Street games dominated our preteen and adolescent years. Every neighborhood had a team for Stickball, the street version of baseball. Street football we played with a rolled up newspaper tied with string.

But basketball? It required two hoops and a backboard. How could we clear our congested street for a court? No, basketball did not catch on until Peanzy was given a basketball for his fifteenth birthday. We marched to the Esso gas station on Boston Road, inflated the ball, and then trekked to the basketball courts in the P.S. 61 school yard.

How could we create competitive teams if we'd never played the game? The two players who could dribble a basketball without looking down on it selected their teammates on the basis of their Stickball skills—a reasonable decision, since reflexes required for one game usually transfer to another.

The ball was passed onto the court, and the game began. If there is a Jewish gene that coordinates the skills and "scheming minds" for basketball, our gang had been shortchanged; our DNA was AWOL. Shins were bruised, eyes were blackened, and fingers were hyperextended. Every turnover was preceded by a push, a jab, or a kick by the gladiators. It was not pretty.

With the onset of darkness, a truce was declared. Hobbling home, massaging our bruises, we were determined to come out with improved dexterity for round two.

The game kept repeating in my mind all week like the persistent fried onions in my mother's horrible hamburgers.

I'm faster than Jerry. Why can't I dribble around him?

Why can't I approach the basket gently on a breakaway when Irv yells "Float!"

Why can't I dribble the ball as I run without looking down at it?

Sunday arrived without a single answer to these gnawing questions. This time there was no choosing for sides. It was the "big guys" against us kids. Abe brought his girlfriend, Judy, an excellent athlete, to observe and critique the brawl. Big Red, the Bandit, Eppie, Banarer, and Abe were at least a head taller than we were. The only height we had was short-tempered Irving Winkler.

The mayhem began. There wasn't a scintilla of improvement in our game. Winkler continued to yell "Float!" as I tried a layup but drilled the ball into the backboard. Jerry refused to shoot for fear of a verbal barrage from Winkler. Alvin, completely ignoring Winkler, continued to shoot from the outside and miss. The "big guys" took most of the rebounds. We hardly got our hands on the ball. Finally, Alvin got the ball and brought it up court, looking to pass to our big man, Winkler. Where was he? Where was Winkler? Since we had passed the ball to him only once when we had it, Winkler had removed himself from the game and sat on the sideline muttering about our inept play.

The "big guys" were as clumsy as we were, but they dominated with their height. They had more shots at the basket and won because the law of probability was in their court.

It was twilight; time to go home. We discovered that the spiteful school custodian had padlocked the gates leading to Boston Road while we were still playing. The barbed wire running along the top of the fence stared down at us. There was no way we were we going to climb over that rusty coil. Abe noticed a hole near the top of the fence adjacent to the locked gate; it was large enough to crawl through. Like gymnasts, Abe, with Judy at his heels, climbed up, wriggled through the hole, and then slipped down to a cement ledge six feet from the ground. From there, they dropped to the street. While this was going on, Winkler drifted toward the Charlotte Street gate at the far end of the field. It was also padlocked.

We were considering our climb when Winkler returned to issue the following decree: "Tell my mother to make four chicken sandwiches and bring a bottle of Pepsi. I'm not coming home until tomorrow, when the school opens."

We stayed a while encouraging him to leave. Our message finally reached him. Cautiously, he grabbed the wires of the cyclone fence and began his ascent toward the hole near the top. Then he looked down and panicked. Awkwardly, he slid back down the fence, landing where he had begun his climb. He was imprisoned in the yard. With no alternative, the rest of us climbed up, eased through the hole, and then left. No one went to Winkler's parents to inform them of their son's problem. To this day, neither Jerry nor Alvin nor I can recall how he finally came home. Irv himself has passed on, so we'll never know.

The winter rains came; the cold and the snow chased us off the streets. The candy store was still our headquarters, but we had a new, albeit unreliable, friend, basketball.

P.S. 61 had opened its doors one night a week for shuffleboard, checkers, chess, Nok-Hockey, and basketball. We had the basketball court to ourselves. It was not a popular game among the "alert and scheming minds" in our neighborhood, which turned to other diversions such as homework.

Although the court was in an elementary school, the baskets were set at regulation height, ten feet. But directly behind one backboard was a slatted, flexible, wooden wall. Whenever a player was slammed into it, it bent and, as if in agony, cut loose with a groan that resonated throughout the low-ceilinged room. Immediately behind the other basket were swinging doors leading to the marble-floored vestibule. A fall on the marble brought a dark contusion as a souvenir. Whatever skills we had brought to the first game in the school yard degenerated to total chaos. Twisted ankles and swollen lips were acceptable damage and no excuse for a time-out. Let's go—on with the show!

One evening, a thin, curly brown-haired, delicate Woody Allen type was sitting on the bench waiting to get into the game. The combat was over. It was his turn to fire for effect.

"Hey!" yelled Alvin. "You're next!"

"Me next?" he asked.

He stood, zipped up his jacket, and then dashed toward the exit doors, growling, "I'm getting out of here. This is a game of *brute force!*"

Oh, if only those social reformers of the early 1900s had been spectators to our interpretation of the game. They would have hurried back to their textbooks to find a different method of nudging immigrant children into the American mainstream, and Paul Gallico would have had serious indigestion from eating his words.

Dessert

The gray basalt curb on East 172nd Street rounded toward Seabury Place. This curb had probably been set into place by Italian immigrants in the mid-nineteenth century. As the years passed, a two-foot angular chip appeared in the center of the curb. Perhaps the chip had been caused by the heat from the fires we made adjacent to this curb to roast the potatoes we called "mickies." Or maybe by the heat from the fire we set to the stack of wooden fruit boxes we named "Hitler's House" and burned alongside this curb.

Whatever the cause, an imaginative mind discovered that a hard rubber ball, accurately thrown against this portion of the curb, would go sailing past the four corners of the intersection. As a result, the game Off the Curb—another variation of baseball—was born.

Our playing field was the ten-yard square formed by the intersecting streets; each corner was a base. There was neither a pitcher nor a catcher nor a shortstop, just a left fielder and a right fielder.

The batter ran up to the angular chip in the curb, threw the ball against it as hard he could, and then ran to first base. If the ball struck the vertical portion of the curb, it would bounce into the intersection as a ground ball, usually resulting in an out. If the ball struck the angle of the chip, it would fly toward the outfield.

Sometimes it would carom off Adoff's drugstore window, sometimes it was a long fly out, sometimes it would bounce into the open cellar adjacent to Adoff's, where Schmidt's vicious German shepherd ruled. His mouth was overpopulated by rows of spiked teeth. The wet undulating tongue dangling from the side of his mouth flapped like the bedsheets hanging from the nearby tenement windows. There were no heroes on either team; nobody ever attempted to recover a ball that bounced into that open pit.

After a canapé of early morning softball followed by an entrée of Stickball and a Coke to quench our thirst, sides were chosen for dessert: Off the Curb.

Our game was rarely disrupted by traffic. No one on those streets owned car, and gas rationing reduced driving to a minimum. But Sunday strollers trying to escape from the heat in their apartments often interrupted our game.

It was a warm summer Sunday afternoon at the end of June. Since television sets were out of most neighbors' price range, many of the older residents in the neighborhood found our games a pleasant distraction. They knew our names and how well we performed.

This Off the Curb game began with a two-base hit by Abe. The next out moved him to third. This was followed by a fly ball hit to me in the outfield. Abe, on third base, was poised, ready to tag up and score.

I had a very strong throwing arm. As soon as I caught the ball, I let loose with a throw that might have nailed him at home. Unaware there was a game going on, a casually dressed middle-aged couple came strolling by. The husband was in the line of fire of my throw, and the ball struck him in the head. He collapsed onto the sidewalk.

As he sprawled there, unconscious, his wife in tears dropped her pocketbook, fell to the ground beside him, and begged him to get up. A passerby looked him over, stared into the wife's eyes, and said, "He's dead!"

This announcement amplified the shrieks from the wife. A chorus of screaming neighborhood women who had gathered at the scene accompanied her. "Call a cop!" one of the women hollered.

"The *trombeniks* [bums]! They should go to the park if they want to play ball!" a woman yelled.

"They should be in the army instead of on the streets!" shouted another.

My friends scattered in all directions. I was left alone in the outfield. Immobilized by terror I stood there, pelted by the eyeballs of the gathering crowd. Where could I hide? I couldn't move. What had I done to him? What would they do to me?

Meanwhile, Abe was trying to score on my throw. A driver stopped his car directly on the base path to view the tragedy. Abe, not to be denied by this catastrophe, jumped on the front left fender of the car, ran over the hood, leapt off the right fender, and touched home to score; then he quickly disappeared into the crowd and became an interested onlooker.

The driver of the auto thought he recognized Abe. He walked over to him and asked if he'd seen anyone run across his car. Abe said he did see

In 2004, I point to the place where we played Off the Curb. Here,
a passerby was felled by the ball and declared dead by a bystander.

someone go across the car's hood and run toward Charlotte Street. The driver returned to his car and took off for Charlotte Street with Abe's sneaker prints on his hood and fenders.

Perhaps it was the screaming. Maybe he was only temporarily dazed. Whatever the reason, the corpse miraculously came to life, stood still for a while to stabilize himself, and then walked away with his wife at his side.

The other boys surfaced from their hideaways and came back to the curb. An argument immediately ensued. Not whether we should have run to Adoff's drugstore for help, not whether we should have called an ambulance for the unconscious man, but whether Abe's score should count in light of the disturbance.

The game continued. I felt hugely relieved. The corpse had revived, pardoning me from life imprisonment. To celebrate being freed from incarceration I bought myself a delicious chocolate Mello-Roll when the game ended.

And so I stumbled my way through adolescence, bouncing off obstacle after obstacle like the pink rubber ball we used in playing Off the Curb.

There's a War On

For months, newspapers, magazines, posters, and the radio had reminded us of the tapering triangular tower, the *Trylon,* and its mate, the globular *Perisphere,* symbols of the 1939 World's Fair in New York City. Finally, on April 30, 1939, the gates opened to the "World of Tomorrow." It was the focus of our daily conversations. It competed with the turmoil in Europe for space in the newspapers. On September 1, 1939, Germany invaded Poland. From that date until its conclusion, World War II completely consumed our lives.

Congress, anticipating our eventual involvement in the war, enacted the nation's first peacetime draft on September 14, 1940. The air corps trained with flour sacks for strategic bombing. The army trained with wooden guns. General Billy Mitchell was in the process of being court-martialed for proposing that the United States build a modern air force. The nation was still wallowing in the Great Depression. Unemployment reached record levels. Citizens lost their homes, farms were abandoned, and malnutrition was rampant in the South and Southwest. Confronted by these catastrophes, our government had to determine its financial priorities. At this point, the military was not a pressing concern, but, faced with an impending entanglement in another world war, it soon engaged in an intense acceleration, manufacturing weapons of war and training our armed forces.

What was war to me? I was nine years old. I knew that the Nazis were bad. Newsreels showed the frightful German army goose-stepping across the screen and Stuka bombers, in a screaming dive, dropping their bombs on Polish civilians. The bombing of Coventry followed the fiery London blitz. Air raid wardens, culled from the aging population in Great Britain, played a prominent role in preventing panic by safely directing residents toward shelters and helping to evacuate casualties. We were not yet at war, but the New York City Department of Civilian Defense, in preparation for such a disaster, called for volunteers to become air raid wardens.

On the afternoon of December 7, 1941, I was home listening to a Giants' football game from the Polo Grounds. The game was temporarily halted. An announcer said that the Japanese had bombed Pearl Harbor. Where was Pearl Harbor? Were *we* going to be bombed? Were we at war? Two years of newspaper photos, newsreels, no news from our family in Lithuania, and my father yelling at the radio commentators to tell them how to stop the onslaught had taught me what war was.

Civic-minded members of our neighborhood who were beyond draft age (fifty or older) or physically unacceptable for military service volunteered as air raid wardens. An empty store adjacent to my apartment building became their headquarters.

The New York Department of Civil Defense seemed to have a rod divining the most inappropriate characters for the job. Mr. Lapin, for example, was known to be a charitable soul. He collected annually for the Red Cross and made sure each contributor was given a little white button imprinted with a red cross. He distributed a miniature red plastic Cross of Lorraine lapel pin to each person who gave to the tuberculosis drive. When volunteers were recruited as air raid wardens, Mr. Lapin was there. This man had the flattest feet that ever pivoted from a human ankle. Every step he took contorted his face into a hideous expression of agony. By the time he reached an area in need of evacuation, the all-clear signal would have sounded. In spite of this, he answered the call and was accepted. Pimple Ear's father, who needed a remedial class in turning on and off his flashlight, was also prowling the streets during air raid drills.

The sirens wailed, the lights went out; it was an air raid drill, a blackout! I watched from my ground floor window. The air raid wardens, carrying their veiled flashlights, toddled toward their assigned stations. It was a scene stolen from the Keystone Kops. The warden across the street kept spotting his unveiled flashlight into his apartment window letting his family know where their hero was. Another found an orange crate, sat down, lit a cigarette (which could be seen for miles from the air), and waited for the all-clear signal to end the slapstick. Those who were serious wore blue twill one-piece overalls with an embroidered orange-and-blue (New York City colors) triangular Civil Defense patch on their left shoulder. A white plastic helmet with the Civil Defense logo completed their wardrobe. My eleven-year-old's instincts told me I would have to depend upon my own wits if there was an air raid.

The wardens' headquarters decor was eclectic pre-Jurassic primitive. Three abandoned chairs with chromium legs supporting torn blue marble-patterned plastic seats were coordinated with an upholstered couch that surrendered its batting to anyone who sat on it. The desk was a collapsible bridge table whose legs quivered under the weight of a paper clip. Directly outside the store, waiting to be collected and recycled for weapons of war, was a huge pile of scrap metal and rubber objects contributed by patriotic residents. Like a malignancy, it grew in place, metastasized horizontally in a northerly direction toward Boston Road, and then rose upward toward the roof of the one-story building.

The schools responded to the call for an active home front. All students were given a plastic ID necklace. It was a thin, circular, off-white one-and-a-half-inch disc with the student's name and address inscribed in thin blue script. Masking tape covered the classroom windows to prevent flying shards during an air raid. Once a week we were ushered into the halls, as gongs, in cycles of three, tore at our eardrums. If the threat was immediate, we curled ourselves under our desks.

A plot of land in nearby Crotona Park was assigned to our school. This area, enclosed by a snow fence, was to be our school's Victory Garden. Each class had a section in which it was to grow vegetables. Jerome, who was in Jerry's class, was an overenthusiastic gardener. He could be seen foraging with a giant metal ladle on Boston Road, scooping up dung deposited by plodding horses pulling fruit and vegetable carts or milk wagons. He brought his booty to school in a large, brown paper bag and placed it in the coat closet to await the class's trip to its garden patch. The odor, permeating the students' clothing, brought their parents to the principal, demanding an explanation for the scent that accompanied their children home. Jerome was asked to retire his ladle. His radishes, incidentally, were no larger than our dung-deprived ones.

We featured radishes in our Victory Garden.

Sugar, gasoline, and meat were rationed. Stamps for sugar and meat were distributed on the basis of family size. With chicken on Friday, pot roast on Sunday, and meatballs on Wednesday, we hardly depleted our allowance. Gasoline was issued on the basis of an essential occupation. I can't think of a soul in the neighborhood who suffered from this edict. No one owned a car, and no one had an essential occupation. When we saw a car parked on our street, it usually belonged to Dr. Kulock, who was making a house call. Those who complained about the shortages were greeted with, "There's a war on, moron!"

Sugar was an infrequent item on the grocery shelves. The large, one-story complex adjacent to my apartment building that housed the air raid wardens' headquarters also housed an A&P supermarket. All the neighbors raised their antennae to detect the arrival of rationed sugar. Mrs. Feuer, who lived on the ground floor of my building, was our neighborhood watch. Her window facing the delivery entrance to the A&P was always open. While she kept one eye on her disabled husband, sitting on a folding chair on the sidewalk beneath her window, her other eye watched for the delivery truck. As soon as she spotted sugar on the multi-wheeled conveyor belt leading into the store, she worked the apartment bells like a corporate typist, simultaneously shouting, "Sugar in the A&P! Sugar in the A&P!" This eighty-year-old woman showed the energy of an adolescent. She should have been awarded a medal for community service at the end of the war.

Rubber was needed for the war, so ersatz rubber visited our home in the form of shoe soles and heels. They added a design feature to our linoleum floor. Whenever we pivoted or slid, a black streak appeared. By the end of the week a section of the multicolored linoleum could have been framed and hung in the Impressionist section of the Metropolitan Museum of Art.

As the war approached closure, residents who had endured five years of tension were looking for release. Block parties blossomed everywhere. A self-appointed group began a collection for a huge banner to celebrate our heroes who had gone off to war. Money was contributed for kegs of beer and pretzels for a street party. A portable phonograph provided music. After a boring speech by a substitute teacher (who was later accused of pocketing some of the money), the banner was raised, and beer flowed from kegs.

It was a beautiful red, white, and blue banner, approximately fifty by thirty feet. A blue star represented each man from the neighborhood who was in the service, a gold star those who would never return. "We Honor Our Boys" was emblazoned across the top in bold blue sewn letters. The banner's cables extended from an apartment building at the south end of Seabury Place across the intersection on East 172nd Street—about 150 feet. Reinforced holes and flaps were sewn into it, so it could withstand the force of high winds. In spite of this, it eventually tore, leaving nothing but the supporting cables and a few threads dangling from them.

The boys came home; apartment doors flew open to welcome them. Partying continued for days. But there was no rejoicing for the longshoreman and his wife who lived on the third floor in my building. Their son was in a POW camp after being shot down over Germany. His mother was apprehensive about his treatment, because he was Jewish. She would ask me to read her son's letters aloud; she suspected that her husband, who could read, was deceiving her. The letters seemed to be dictated by a propaganda minister. The handwriting was so perfect it could have been the work of a scribe. It took a while, but eventually her son did come home, fragile and a bit confused. He spent a year as an outpatient getting treatment from a veterans' rehabilitation hospital.

The huge mound of metal and rubber recyclables in front of the air raid wardens' headquarters remained unclaimed throughout the war. Finally, the Department of Sanitation moved in. They spent three days clearing the sidewalk of these essential war materials.

The war was over. With the hope of a prosperous and peaceful future, some veterans married, some returned to their jobs, some entered college. The Allies created the United Nations to avoid another catastrophe like World War II. Within five years we were involved in the Korean War.

My Final Hand-Me-Down

In 1943 the United States was involved on two fronts, the invasion of Italy and attacking the Japanese-occupied islands we had lost in the Pacific. We were not doing well in either zone. My brother, Harold, had older friends who had joined the New York State Guard. He lied about his age to join them. In a few months their unit was activated and absorbed into the U.S. army. My distraught parents appealed to their cousin Louis Shereff, an attorney, to help get Harold discharged because he was only sixteen and a half years old.

Meanwhile Harold had been sent to Camp Polk in Louisiana for basic training. My parents grew apprehensive. There was no news about his discharge. Six months passed. Harold finished basic training and was given orders for a two-week delay en-route (two weeks at home) before reporting to Fort Devens, Massachusetts, the camp from which the GIs embarked for Europe.

He came home, opened the door, and dropped his duffel bag. I saw a handsome GI, standing tall and tan from the Louisiana sun and wiry from basic training. I was thrilled to see him. I couldn't connect him with the bombs, guns, and bullets I saw in the newsreels.

"What time did you have to get up? What did you eat? Is your gun in your duffel bag? And your helmet? What was it like? Did you use real bullets and grenades?"

Ma ran in from the kitchen, kissed him, and then turned to me and shouted, "Leave him alone—don't you see he wants to eat?"

Harold paid no attention to her. He was as eager to tell me as I was to listen. Ma retreated to the kitchen to prepare dinner.

"They woke us up at five in the morning," he said. "You wouldn't believe the crap they put on our trays. The flies ate most of it."

From the kitchen we were interrupted by Ma's testimony to herself. "Did you think the army would give you what *I* give you? Did you ever see a fly in my kitchen? Did a fly ever swim in your chicken soup? Here you get good food on clean plates."

Harold smiled and continued, "An hour after breakfast we went to the field for calisthenics under a blazing sun. By the time we were through, we looked like we'd been pulled out of Crotona Park Lake."

We heard the doorknob turn. Pa came in, gave Harold a nervous hug, and told him he looked good. Pa knew there was an impending invasion of France.

Harold saw the troubled look on Pa's face. He went to his duffel bag and pulled out his dirty laundry; then he held up a pair of pants. "Pa, these are the first pants you didn't have to alter for me."

"Yes," Pa replied. "But look what you had to go through to get a pair of pants that fit."

There was silence. Harold went to the bedroom to take a nap in the privacy of our parents' bed. When he was home, he slept on a collapsible bed in Uncle Shrolleh's bedroom. In his barracks he was sharing the space with forty men.

In two weeks Harold left for Fort Devens. Our apartment was shrouded in a pall of silence. Ma's eyes were waterlogged; Pa wouldn't listen to the news or read his newspaper. My uncle wouldn't tell his crazy stories about the shtetl.

Harold had forgotten to take his army-issued OD (olive drab) wool knit cap, the cap that is worn under a helmet. It was the same kind of OD wool cap that Radar wore in the television series *M.A.S.H.* Now it was mine, and I wore it proudly. I had never felt this way toward any of his previous hand-me-downs. With my feet encased in a polished pair of army boots, given to my father by a friend, and the OD cap on my head, I strutted into Hermann Ridder Junior High School; the boots hardly touched the ground.

I couldn't wait for winter to arrive. I pictured the OD hat hugging my head as I glided by the skaters on Crotona Park Lake. Finally, it came. My

Harold in 1943, before he went overseas. He was sixteen and a half years old.

friend Lenny offered me his pair of racers. "Here," he said, "I could never get the hang of these."

This upgraded me from the 25-cent, turn-of-the-century, Third Avenue secondhand shop figure skates I'd always struggled with to a pair of long thin blades that could easily bite into the ice. It was a splendid feeling, effortlessly gliding on these blades with my precious OD wool cap on my head. Usually, I wore the hat with its bottom folded up. When the weather was cold, I'd lower the sides below my ears. After a two-hour session on the lake, I returned home with a cap soaked in sweat. My mother introduced me to Gold Dust soap flakes. I washed the cap, rinsed it, squeezed it, and hung it to dry from a faucet handle in the shower. The following morning it was dry, refreshed, and looking like new.

It was one of the rare days when I went to school without my cap. I sat through my classes impatiently waiting for the bell to ring. Finally, school was out. I raced home to get my cap and skates and run off to Crotona Park Lake. But where was my cap?

"Ma, did you see Harold's cap?"

"Didn't you wear it to school?"

That was helpful. The kitchen table had nothing but a few crumbs speckled on it. I looked under my convertible bed. I found the pocketknife

I hadn't seen for months. Maybe I had forgotten to remove the hat from the shower faucet handle. No, a damp washcloth was hanging there. I couldn't waste any more time. It was winter, and darkness arrived early.

I repeated, "Ma, where's my cap? Did you see my army cap? I think I left it on the faucet handle."

She responded by quoting a sage passage from her life experiences. "You'll find it when you're not looking for it."

I wasn't going to buy that. What was I going to do—pretend I wasn't looking for it?

Where was that cap? It continued to elude me. My brother used to say that he could lose a garbage truck in our apartment. Maybe he'd come home with another cap. The only military issue items that remained to me were the boots my father's friend had given him. Somehow they just didn't look right without my OD cap. Whenever I saw them, they reminded me of my brother's cap. I placed them in a dark corner of the closet. Eventually, Ma gave them to a neighbor.

Harold was in England, training with the First Division for the invasion of France. Our cousin, who had been working on Harold's discharge since my brother had entered the army, finally succeeded. Harold returned to the United States before D-Day. When he opened the door, I saw that he had no duffel bag. Then I knew that my adventure with the OD wool knit hat finally had come to an end.

Later Teens

A New Venue

Sonny Leff had burst into the candy store with the news. "Hey, guys, the Dover Bar has a TV set!"

"What's the big deal?" asked Peanzy. "My rich uncle in New Jersey has one, too."

"Yeah. Everyone has a rich uncle in New Jersey with a TV set, while we're here on Seabury Place with a radio," grumbled Mutt.

Sonny, looking right through Mutt, pleaded, "It's facing the street. We can see the fights through the window!"

Peanzy, totally unimpressed snapped, "What are we going to do? Stand there like a bunch of schmucks and look through a bar window?"

We were too young to step into a bar, and even if we had been old enough there was nothing we wanted to drink there. But it did have that TV set. Why not take a look?

On Friday, the boys gathered outside the candy store for the three-block walk to the bar. The pace picked up as we zeroed in on the flickering red neon Dover Bar and Grill sign. In 1946, a television set was a novelty in the neighborhood. In fact, it was a novelty in most neighborhoods.

Friday Night Fights was sponsored by Gillette Blue Blades. Only the outstanding contenders in their weight class were featured. Fortunately, this was the night of the first middleweight championship fight in which Tony Zale, the Man of Steel, defended his title against Rocky Graziano. Both could be counted on for an exciting fight, a few illegal blows, and maybe a knockout. We huddled at the window, short guys in front.

"Take that stupid hat off, Krebs. I can't see the screen," shouted Jerry.

"The hat stays on. Get a pair of glasses, dummy."

"Krebs, you'll need a pair of glasses if you don't take that hat off."

As a unit, we rolled with each punch. Tony Zale was knocked down in the third round. It appeared to be all over. Uh-oh, here came all 350 pounds of Tiny, the bartender, barreling toward us. The apron resting on his massive chest and colossal waistline resembled a postage stamp. He politely asked, "Are you guys able to see the fight?"

He seemed friendly. Why not try for an invitation indoors?

"Yeah, but we can't hear it," said Mutt.

"What do you want me to do, bring out the TV and some chairs for you?" He returned to the bar shaking his head.

Tony Zale made an amazing comeback and knocked out Graziano in the sixth round.

On Saturday, Dick Young and Jimmy Powers provided their comments on the fight in the sports section of the *Daily News*. Before long, we knew the strengths, weaknesses, and peculiarities of all the contenders for each title. This was the first sport to be truly integrated. Joe Louis was fading but still the heavyweight champ. Kid Gavilan, a black fighter, had just come to the United States. He featured a "bolo punch," which he claimed was a legacy from cutting sugar cane in the fields of Cuba. Rocky Graziano, a boxer with a criminal record as a civilian and court-martials in the military, was a rough middleweight with an inventory of illegal blows and holds. A light heavyweight fighter named Murphy soaked his hands in brine to toughen them. Marcel Cerdan, the French middleweight, and Edith Piaf were lovers. The Ray Robinson–Jake LaMotta fights were classics. Willie Pep was king of the featherweight division, until Sandy Saddler took the championship, and then Sandy lost it to Pep the following year.

But all good things must come to an end. Cold weather had us jumping up and down and fogging the bar window. This could not go on.

One day I joined Mutt when he went to buy a comb at Woolworth's. On our way home, we stepped into a candy store on Wilkins Avenue. Unlike our candy store, this was not a hangout. Staring down at us was a TV sitting on a wooden shelf beamed toward three round ice cream parlor tables with chairs.

"Give me a package of Walnettos," said Mutt. The purchase of this 5-cent candy, he felt, was his ticket to watch TV on Friday night. The proprietor said that, as long as we bought something, we would be welcome.

For a 10-cent malted or a nickel hot chocolate, the boys watched *and* heard *Friday Night Fights* from the minor discomfort of ice cream parlor chairs. We could listen at leisure to the familiar Gillette commercial, "To look sharp, da-da-da, da-da, to feel sharp, da-da-da, da-da ..."

In 1949, Jerry became the first of the boys to have a television set. Jerry's sister, Marylin married her boyfriend Bob after he was discharged from the army. Housing was at a premium, so the newlyweds moved into Jerry and his mother's apartment. Jerry's mother slept in one bedroom, Marylin and her husband slept in another, and Jerry slept in the living room. Bob bought a sixteen-inch Zenith TV set with a round screen set into a tall wooden cabinet. It was placed at the edge of the living room carpet next to a wall. We watched *Friday Night Fights,* with Bob joining in our rowdiness. Marylin came in occasionally to offer her comments. Jerry's mother couldn't understand how anyone could watch "two young men punching each other in the head." She made her statement and disappeared.

It was standing room only in Jerry's apartment in 1950 when the NIT (National Invitation Tournament) college basketball championship game between CCNY and the University of Kentucky was televised from Madison Square Garden. The City College team was composed of poor white and black New York kids. Adolph Rupp, a basketball legend and a bigot, led Kentucky's number-one-rated lily-white team into Madison Square Garden. Before the tip-off, the usual handshake between opponents was denied to the black CCNY players. The boos of the crowd in the Garden was deafening. This intensified our rooting for City College. I was sitting cross-legged on the floor in front of Krebs, who was in a chair directly behind me. As the game approached the final buzzer and the lead kept changing hands, his trembling knees kept denting my back. The game was too intense for me to ask him to stop. Everyone was focused on the score. City College, which had not been favored to win by anyone, beat the University of Kentucky in the last minute of play. Our cheers joined the roars bursting out of nearby windows.

Television, a new mode in entertainment, crept into its new venue—the living rooms of our neighborhood.

Haute Cuisine

Oh, they try; they really try; but it's futile. Today's kosher delis have tables with matching chairs. A neatly dressed waiter hands you a five-page glossy menu with inserts in plastic pockets featuring the day's specials. It's strictly business. You order corned beef or pastrami on rye, you eat, you go home. Where is the old-fashioned neighborhood kosher deli, where the menu was what you saw broiling on a grill behind the window or resting on a wooden counter behind a glass panel? Where the special of the day was a fatter, juicier, more flavorful frankfurter? Where swollen pastrami made club sandwiches wider than the aperture of our mouths? Where have you gone kosher deli? New York's senior citizens turn their salivating tongues to you.

In the 1940s, within three blocks of my apartment were three kosher delis: Annie's, on Boston Road near Wilkins Avenue; Mintz's, on Boston Road adjacent to P.S. 61; and Misek's, on Boston Road directly across the street from Hermann Ridder Junior High School. At any of these eateries, for a dime you could have a hot dog with mustard and sauerkraut rinsed down with a bottle of Frank's Orange or a Coke. Although they sold the same merchandise, each store had its unique character.

Annie knew the problems and joys of all her customers. They knew that a visit to Annie's called for thorough preparation, because they would personally get uninhibited grilling along with her frankfurters. It began with her penciled eyebrows escalating toward her scalp. "I didn't see you in the last two weeks. Are you still living with your wife? How's your blood pressure?"

Annie had a booming voice that was augmented by her shimmering dyed red hair, slightly rustier than the dried ketchup clinging to the caps of her greasy Heinz bottles. Once, before I could even order, her cross-examination began: "Did you see? Yoneh Shimmel was caught selling *treyf* [unkosher] corned beef?"

"Who squealed on him?" I asked.

"Squeal? One look, and Alex [a neighborhood boy with Down syndrome] could tell it was *treyf* corned beef. Squeal? Shouldn't that bastard be reported? Never mind that; maybe you know a man, a relative, an *alrightnik* [successful man] for me?"

When Mrs. Hirsch came in, Annie inquired, "Are the kids doing better in school? I don't think they do their homework. I see them in the street all the time."

Her deli was situated below Bernie Heitner's apartment building. Bernie was tall, dark, and handsome; he had a big appetite and the money to support it. A visit by Bernie was an experience not to be missed. Annie's way of expressing love for Bernie was to mound meat on a slice of rye bread to a point where it collapsed before the other slice of rye could cover it. While slicing the pastrami, she blasted her celebrated aria to an elderly employee waiting at the rear of the store, "A portion French for Boinard!"

"For Boinard!" were the code words to heap the fries until they were overflowing the dish. With booty in hand, Bernie walked to his table, leaving a trail of fries and strips of pastrami on the floor tiles behind him.

Annie's was a classic neighborhood deli. The counter was a small area where the customer ordered and paid for the food. The floor was covered in white, one-inch octagonal tiles hiding under a few handfuls of sawdust. Plastic-covered chromium chairs were pushed under tan Formica-topped four-foot-square tables. In a tiny room at the rear of the store, an elderly employee with a charred cast-iron pot partially filled with oil and a strainer sat at a primitive stove waiting for the call to fry potatoes.

Menu? What menu? Her entire inventory was spread out before you. Peering through the window you beheld frankfurters sizzling on the grill. Immediately to the right, the counter continued behind two glass panels through which you could see salami, bologna, frankfurters, and rolled beef, adding to the intoxicating aroma. On top of the counter, on a small dish, one-inch chunks of knoblewurst (a garlic sausage) rested below a sign, A Nickel a *Shtikl* (piece). Behind these delicacies, against a wall, a gas-heated stainless steel vat filled with boiling water held a hunk of pastrami waiting to be sliced. Could this have been the source of high blood pressure and off-the-chart cholesterol readings in the East Bronx?

Make a left when leaving Annie's, walk no more than a city block along Boston Road, pass Leff's candy store and P.S. 61, and you arrive at Mintz's Deli. In sharp contrast to Annie's, the store was neat, the store was quiet. A reserved and gentle couple, Mr. and Mrs. Mintz were unable to generate the energy that electrified Annie's. They knew little about their customers' lives. What they did know came from no inquisition. It was the type of deli where you ordered and usually took out. The take-out frankfurter, topped with mustard and sauerkraut, was wrapped in a large sheet of white paper and accompanied by a Frank's Orange. I ran home with my treasure, unwrapped the mustard-stained paper, scooped up the loose strands of sauerkraut clinging to it, and was ready for the warm and delicious treat nestled inside the bun.

Make a left outside Mintz's, walk the block length of Hermann Ridder Junior High School, and you arrived at Misek's Deli. Mr. Misek was a slight, fragile man. His wife was the waitress, French fry cook, and busboy. Although his store was closer to Seabury Place than Annie's, it was magnetic Annie who drew us to her.

Eventually, when we were teenagers, the Miseks sold to the Gitelsons. This deli was to support Mr. and Mrs. Gitelson, their married son, Murray, and their son-in-law, Gene. With a couple of coins now jingling in our pockets, our trips to the deli were more frequent.

"I want a pastrami sandwich—lean. The last time I had one, the pastrami slid down my throat," said Irv.

"Sit down, and you'll take what I give you."

In spite of the angry reply, Irv munched on a lean pastrami sandwich trimmed nicely by Mr. Gitelson.

After a weekend Stickball game, Gitelson's was the place to review the highlights over a pastrami-on-club sandwich with French fries. Independent Jerry had his usual Romanian steak smothered with fried onions. Gene, Mr. Gitelson's son-in-law, an addictive talker, usually barged in with unsolicited comments.

Soon there was a classy kid in the deli family: nearby Bucknoff's. All his tables and chairs matched. He had a menu, plus daily specials, and a waiter. The store was neat and clean. The clientele were upscale compared to those at our delis. For a month, Bucknoff's was our place for a weekend nosh. It wasn't long before we returned to familiar Gitelson's, where we could step in with T-shirts sweaty from a Stickball or softball game, argue to our heart's content, and listen to the pearls of wisdom rolling off Gene's tongue.

Eventually, the neighborhood changed, the stores changed, the signs changed. Bright yellow, green, and red signs replaced the understated deli and grocery signs. Today there are bodegas instead of delis. I'm sure their customers will have stories to share with their children. Annie is gone, Mintz, Misek, and Gitelson are gone, the blue and red neon Hebrew National sign is gone, but never the memories.

Burgers as I Knew Them

Sleep doesn't come easily to me. How many different positions must I assume before I am fast asleep? One night, while tossing in bed, I searched through the files of my adolescence and found the meals that had passed over our blue-and-white enameled kitchen table. One meal was memorable—not because of its outstanding flavor, not because of its tantalizing aroma, not because of its artistic presentation, but solely because I couldn't figure out why Ma bothered to make it.

She called it *hockfleish*; we called it hamburger.

She connected her cast-iron meat grinder to a kitchen chair, fed cubes of meat into its trumpet-shaped opening, and, while turning the handle, lectured: "Someone told me Brodsky adds a lot of fat to his ground meat. I once bought it and made *hockfleish*. I watched them cooking. Before my eyes they shrank to the size of walnuts. We don't need that. Who knows what else he puts in there? I buy chuck; I trim it and grind it myself."

After grinding the meat twice, she placed it in a large glass bowl, mixed it with salt, pepper, an egg, and chopped onions, and shaped portions between her cupped hands to form large, oval teardrops. Then she placed them into a frying pan partially filled with simmering water. As they cooked, they absorbed some water while surrendering their blood, fat, and flavor to the surrounding puddle. When she thought they were ready, Ma tested one for taste and color. If its texture was like vulcanized rubber, its color ashen gray, and its consistency like a World War II hand grenade, it was ready to eat.

I tried to spear the burger, but my fork was completely outclassed. I expected the tines to gently pierce and break the meatball, but its surface merely bent and bounced back to its original shape. With enough pressure, my fork penetrated and my knife was able to carve out a segment. I burrowed the fragment into the mashed potatoes beside it and then plunged it into a puddle of ketchup. This red condiment was the magic potion that made the meal, turning an inedible into an edible. My family never ate out. In our house, this was the hamburger I knew.

Without dissent, my digestive system successfully processed whatever went from my plate to my mouth. But as I approached adolescence, Ma's burger and its onions dropped the gauntlet. Its challenge was "I dare you to digest me." My enzymes attacked the burger. Then they brought in their heavy weapon, hydrochloric acid. This concoction flowed into my stomach and up my esophagus once the hamburger arrived. I began to experience a burning sensation. I joined my father when he complained about "heart-boinin'." When I told Ma, she said, "Ask Pa. He'll give you Bisodol." This was the antacid he had nearly choked on.

Where had she gotten this awful recipe? I'm sure *she* didn't think it was awful. Pa gnawed on the grenades without comment; my brother, Harold, usually left a half burger but ate everything else on his plate; and Uncle Shrolleh assaulted them with his usual gusto. We munched on these missiles and did not complain. But if any meal merited a grumble, this one was it. Did Ma apportion herself a burger? No, she was the waitress during our meal. Her share of most of the meals was the leftovers.

My image of the hamburger was soon to change. In ninth grade I worked as a weekend messenger for the Carnegie Hall Pharmacy, on the corner directly below Carnegie Hall. My first assignment was to locate and remove cat excrement from the cellar. My nose quickly located the source of the aroma. The fumes were so bad that my ears could hear the fragrance diffusing around the room. With a shovel I removed the waste and sprayed the area with an aerosol can. Mr. Fisher, the owner, was so impressed with my work that he led me upstairs to the grill and said to the cook, "Sam, give the kid whatever he wants."

I leafed through the menu. From one of the colored illustrations I saw a hamburger, French fries, and a Coke. A hamburger? This didn't look like Ma's hamburger. I decided to try it. Sam placed a flat disc of ground meat directly onto the grill, no simmering water. His spatula removed the meat from the grill when it had a brown crust on both sides. Then he slipped it into a bun and set it on a plate alongside a mound of French fried potatoes. Dare I douse the burger with ketchup? I wondered. A dab couldn't hurt. It was delicious! Could Brodsky's meat ever taste like this?

After a few deliveries, I went home. Upon opening the door to my apartment I was greeted with, "I forgot to give you a bialy sandwich. Did you have anything to eat? You must be starving."

"I had a hamburger."

"A hamburger in a drugstore? I never heard of it. Adoff doesn't have hamburgers."

"It's a very big store, Ma. They serve hamburgers, hot dogs, and even steaks."

"Again with the *treyf* [unkosher] meat? Yes. Remember what happened when you ate that hot dog at the Crotona Pool? You couldn't get off the toilet seat. Go to the bathroom and take two tablespoons of Milk of Magnesia. Maybe it will get it out of your system."

The following week, after a *hockfleish* dinner, I told Ma that the burger I'd had at the pharmacy was flat like a potato *latke* (pancake).

"Sure it's flat," she said. "It's flat because they save money. How much meat goes into a flat *latke*?"

"But it tastes good when they make it on a hot grill."

"I made you the same *hockfleish* since you were able to eat meat. All of a sudden you don't like it?"

"No, I like it, but this was different."

"In this house we are healthy. We don't need different."

Consequently, the gray grenades continued to emerge from that soggy puddle for nineteen more years.

In 1962, I married Sheila. On one of our weekly visits to Seabury Place we were served Ma's version of a burger. It lay unmolested on Sheila's plate.

"You didn't touch the *hockfleish*, Sheila. You didn't even taste it," Ma said. "I knew I should have made a chicken."

"No, I just don't eat very much," replied Sheila.

Today, we are cautioned that hamburgers are a danger to our health. Their saturated fat is converted to plaque, which blocks the flow of blood through the arteries. It turns out that Ma was ahead of her time. In our home in the thirties, forties, and fifties, she fished her burgers out of the pan and poured the islands of fat down the drain. She must have known something about its threat without counsel from a dietitian. But, in spite of her wisdom, the *hockfleish* saga came to an end the day Sheila refused to eat one.

Pa's War

The I Cash Clothes Man drove by our street on his horse and wagon. Whatever clothing outlived its usefulness was sold to him for 25 or 50 cents. Not a garment of ours was found in his sacks.

Our old clothes were washed, ironed, and placed in a cardboard box adjacent to my parents' brown-stained plywood clothing closet. When Pa determined he had the right quantity and assortment of clothing, with thick thread, he sewed four white canvas panels together into a large sack. We helped him place all the clothing into it, and then he stitched it closed. He melted a stick of red wax over the stitching for further security. The round sack with its red stitching resembled a giant baseball.

Then it was my turn. I proudly addressed the bundle and filled out the customs declaration for its destination, the shtetl in Lithuania where the rest of my family lived.

Suddenly, the cardboard box for the clothing was gone, and I no longer was asked to address bundles or customs declarations. It was early 1940, and the war was not going well for the allies. Germany's murdering Wehrmacht efficiently completed its military mission of murder. Rumors of the atrocities stunned the Jewish world. Poland fell in three days. Protest meetings held in New York City and throughout the United States fell upon deaf ears. President Roosevelt refused to admit a shipload of Jewish refugees into the United States. Throughout the day radio bulletins informed us of Allied losses. In the evening, our family sat by our Emerson table radio listening to Gabriel Heatter and Johannes Steele reporting on and analyzing the news. William Shirer was reporting from Berlin, Edward R. Murrow from London, and Walter Cronkite in the United States.

"Bomb the bestids where the live!" shouted Pa.

"Morris, he can't hear you," said my mother.

"I don't care," said Pa. "We're losing the war!"

Pa saved his choicest blasts for Father Coughlin, a priest from Detroit who delivered virulent anti-Semitic sermons on the radio on Sundays.

As the United States began mobilizing for war, my father's coat factory was contracted to produce woolen overcoats for the WAACS (Women's Auxiliary Army Corps). He started to work five days a week, sometimes even overtime. I remember the joy in our house when he dragged himself home with $100 for one week's work.

Unconfirmed rumors about the fate of the Jewish population in the conquered European communities left my family in despair. When the war finally came to an end, the figures we had heard turned out to be a mere fraction of the actual bestiality inflicted upon the entire European population. The tiny shtetl my parents came from was left *judenrein* (clean of Jews) by its zealous Lithuanian friends and neighbors. The dream of a family reunion after the war went up in the smoke escaping from Buchenwald and Auschwitz and in the ashes that were buried in the soil there.

My uncle Morris, my mother's brother, brought two shtetl survivors to Montreal. Another survivor, Israel Gantovnik, settled in Israel, where he wrote the saga of the shtetl under German occupation in the Yiskor Book, a book to commemorate the Holocaust.

The Boys' Night Out

Mel Allen's smooth southern drawl was steeping in the humidity of a New York August evening in 1946. The boys gathered closely around the candy store radio to listen to the top of the eighth inning of a Yankee-Cleveland game. The count was three balls and one strike on Tommy Henrich. There was a man on first. The Yankees were losing two to one. At this critical moment, Krebs ordered a malted. The machine was set in motion. Like shotgun pellets, cracks of static pierced Mel Allen's animated delivery. From beside the radio came, "Hey, Jack, shut off the damn malted machine. We can't hear the game."

"Shut off the malted machine? This is a business. The malted machine makes money for me. The radio makes noise."

Mel Allen interjected, "It's a Ballantine Blast! The Yankees lead, three to two!"

The embossed tin walls of the ceiling vibrated with our approval. It poured through the open door and onto the street.

Tsoots struggled into the store on her arthritic legs. Startled by the noise, she asked, "Vot heppened? Did Stalin die?"

"No, Tommy Henrich hit a homer."

"Who did he hit?" she asked.

The next batter struck out to end the inning. Anticipating a commercial extolling the virtues of golden Ballantine Ale, Herman decided that this was the appropriate time to make his announcement.

"I have a date this Saturday."

"So what?" asked Peanzy.

What does one do on a date? I thought.

Whatever it was, Herman was not going to do it alone—he had asked his date to recruit five of her friends as dates for us, to act as a buffer against any uncomfortable situation that might arise.

"Listen, guys, don't embarrass me with your outfits this Saturday," he pleaded.

The oppressively warm evening did not sweeten our disposition toward his critique. "Why? Are you the last word in fashion? Those rust-colored pants and that chartreuse shirt belong in a circus, not in our candy store."

"OK, OK, Danny, but no sneakers, no T-shirts, no dungarees."

Jerry, sitting in the open phone booth, couldn't wait to plunge his dagger in.

"Is a suit, a tie, and a vest suitable for the occasion?"

"Crap. I'm sorry I got you guys dates. Now I know the Moonlight Ride up the Hudson is going to be an embarrassment."

Peanzy, whose father was a part-time, mostly unemployed cabdriver, was furious. "Up the Hudson? That costs $6 for two! I can't ask my father for that. Do you think home relief checks are trolley transfers?"

The older boys, "the Big Fellas" as we called them, gathered around and sharpened their lances. "Is it worth $6 to grab a feel on a boat ride? Fat Anne will give you one for nothing," said Big Red.

This brought a few laughs from the older boys.

Refugee Jack, owner of the candy store, had season tickets to these comedy events; he would have abandoned his penny-profit business if he had been denied a front row center seat for them.

When Saturday night arrived, we climbed onto the crosstown bus carrying us to the more affluent West Bronx. At the back of the bus, Rock edged over to Krebs and stage-whispered, "What if yours is a dog and mine is a piece?"

"Hey, I never thought of that!"

"What would you do?"

Hunched over in our seats, we were trying to solve the dilemma when Jerry suggested we get off at the next stop and go home.

"Great idea!" shouted Krebs.

He was supported by assenting nods and smiles from all except Herman. "What are you trying to do to me? I get you guys dates, and now you want to go home? You're a bunch of rat finks!"

We tore into Herman like a pack of carnivores. "Since when are you such a hero?" asked Peanzy. "Who needs this? The candy store is more fun!"

"We can get our own girls," added Krebs.

"If we wanted a dog, we'd go to the ASPCA. Who are you, anyway? A Romeo all of a sudden?"

"These are friends?" Herman threw back. "You're sixteen years old. Do you want to be babies all your life?"

This barb smarted. Reluctantly we agreed to endure whatever ordeal awaited us. Passengers came on; passengers got off. We continued in silence. Finally, a furious Herman announced, "This is our stop. You have their names and addresses. They live on Aqueduct Avenue. And don't forget to say hello to their parents."

We stepped off the bus and scattered to search for each date's apartment house. Oh, no! I thought, an elevator building! I hope my outfit is OK for these classy people. I reluctantly approached the lobby, opened the door, and pressed the elevator call button. Once I was inside the elevator, a scissor gate formed a fence in front of me. I'm surrounded, I thought. What am I doing here? I don't know her. She doesn't know me. I'm no lady-killer, but I'll bet she's a dog. What will we talk about? I should leave.

Fifth floor. I pulled the gate open. The 5D on her apartment door glared at me. Halfheartedly, I squeezed the buzzer. The door opened. I was stunned. My date was lovely and slim, with long black hair draping a very pretty face. I couldn't wait to return to my friends to find a brace for my insecurity.

"Hi, I'm Della."

I stood there frozen. My name did not pass my lips.

"Wouldn't you like to meet my parents?" she asked.

No, I'd rather not, I said to myself. But was this an option?

"Mom, Pop, I'd like you to meet …?"

Della looked at me as I mumbled "Danny."

Her parents were sitting on a velvet green couch. At either side of it, lamps on end tables projected a warm, soft glow throughout the room. At home, the beacon from our torchiere lamp flooded the living room. With its glare reflecting off the white ceiling and our shiny linoleum flooring, it could easily have illuminated a squadron of *Luftwaffe* on a bombing run over London. The carpet in Della's living room absorbed any sound from the taps nailed onto my Cat's Paw heels and soles.

"Did you have trouble finding our building?" asked her mother.

"No, the bus stop was nearby," I muttered.

"Would you like a Coke, Danny? Have some cashews," her father offered.

Unlike my immigrant parents who spoke a broken English, her parents spoke without a trace of an accent. The seconds seemed like hours. I couldn't wait to get out of there. Della kissed her parents good night, and the adventure began.

On our walk to the elevated subway station, I felt as if my tongue had inflated and engorged my mouth cavity. Not a word escaped. I raced up the two flights of elevated subway steps. Della plodded behind me as if she were climbing a vertical wall.

This girl is in very bad shape, I thought. I stood at the top of the stairway, wondering if she would survive the ascent. With an extended hand, I helped her to the top of the landing. She was wheezing as if she had just completed a marathon. When the train arrived, she sank into a stiff yellow woven-bamboo seat, exhausted from the aerobics.

Our destination was the Day Line dock on the Hudson River in Manhattan. When we arrived, a small crowd was gathered around the ticket booth for the Moonlight Ride. I noticed Krebs trying to squeeze in front of the line while tugging on his embarrassed date. Oh, no. Am I going to spend the night with that? What a *putz!* I knew I should have stayed home. Or, better yet, taken refuge in our candy store.

Jerry, Rock, and Peanzy finally arrived, accompanied by their dates. We waited for a while. Della took the initiative to introduce herself to the others. Had Herman lost his way? He'd instigated this whole thing—where was he?

The boat began taking on passengers. As they were boarding, I noticed that most of the couples were much older than we were. This convinced me that I should have stayed home. I'd have plenty of time later to do what older people did.

Finally, Herman came running up with his date, and we all boarded the boat. The band was tuning up at the rear of the lower deck. Since none of us could dance, we cleverly ushered the girls to the opposite end of the upper deck. This left us with the option of making conversation. How long can one sustain a discussion about high school and the injustices meted out by our miserable teachers, or whether the Yankees had a chance of winning the pennant?

What was I to do? From the moment the boat left the dock, the older folks were on the floor dancing. As I saw the older men crushed against their dates' secondary sexual characteristics, all I could do was watch with envy from the upper deck. Since I didn't know how to dance, the exotic, carnal sensuousness of female flesh was as foreign to me as the touch of Braille.

To relieve my awkwardness, I leaned over the railing and watched the lights winking at me from the shoreline. To my surprise, Della came close by. Uh-oh, a change of position was necessary. Timidly I said, "Let's sit down."

I meant for each of us to occupy a deck chair. No sooner had I made contact with the canvas when Della boldly deposited herself onto my lap. I sat there, immobilized.

What was I to do? What could I touch? What couldn't I touch? Was there something sophisticated I could say? How about, "Do you know that the Hudson River is an estuary?"

No, that would be stupid. Terror paralyzed my tongue. My heart pounded, my legs trembled, my fingers shrank into my palms.

Since both of us were of the same species, I had expected a small, firm rear like mine. After all, she was a thin girl. Instead, what I felt on my lap was a flaccid, mushy mass that expanded on and overflowed my lap far beyond my expectations.

This is a sick girl, I decided. How could a healthy girl have so soft an ass and one that expands so quickly? And remember the difficulty she had climbing up the subway steps?

I excused myself and summoned my friends to the restroom for a critical debriefing. Peanzy was there powdering his sweaty neck and navy blue sport shirt with white talcum. He shouted, "Hey, guys! This stuff is great!"

A booming voice crashed from behind one of the toilet stall doors.

"And yer not payin' fur it, are ya?"

It was the voice of the attendant, who was attending to personal business behind the doors. We hastily left for more friendly surroundings. Krebs was first to report.

"Can you believe it? My date doesn't know that the Giants play in the Polo Grounds."

"I can believe it," said Peanzy. "She looks like she never threw a ball in her life. If I were married to her, I would do what my uncle did."

"What did he do?"

"Go out for a pack of cigarettes."

"What brand?" asked Krebs.

"It's not the brand, stupid. He took off, because he couldn't stand his wife. He went out for cigarettes and never came back."

Herman was positive. "Mine isn't bad. I think I'll call her again, if any of you will go with me."

"Not me. My date must be in a two class. I don't think she knows she's on a boat," said Jerry.

Rock chimed in, "Mine is a real dog. I would have had more fun with a guy."

"Mine has a soft ass and is totally out of shape. I don't need this," I added.

After a thorough assessment of our experiences, we reached a consensus. None of these girls merited further attention from such suave guys.

It was well past our bedtime when the boat circled to return to the dock. I fell into a canvas seat without the nuzzle of a stranger's floppy rear on my lap.

By the time the boat docked, we were exhausted. We supported each other while sleepwalking to the subway station. When our train finally arrived, we rushed for the bamboo seats, which now felt like pillows.

After accompanying the girls home, we agreed on an assembly area to further evaluate the evening.

This was my first date alone with a girl. That "Have a seat" incident on the boat kept taking encores as the weeks passed on. I'm sure Della was not impressed with me. Why should she be? I was yet to awaken from my arrested maturity.

High Rollers

Al hit the pink Spalding onto a third-floor fire escape. Was it worth chipping in for another ball with the Stickball game going into the last inning? With this unanticipated finale, we decided to retire for sodas at our clubhouse, the candy store.

Sol, our friend and the owner's son, was snapping off Coke bottle caps at the fountain. Fat Anne, in her Betty Boop bob, was licking the cone of her chocolate Mello-Roll. Harry the Rail, who was as narrow as he was wide, was nibbling on sunflower seeds; the wet shells clung to his cuffs and the candy wrappers scattered around his penny loafers. Our bulletin board, nailed to the side of the phone booth, reported that Sonny Leff had "vomited" on the counter the night before.

Suddenly and without any warning, Sol in his sparkling white starched apron hurdled the counter and landed at the feet of Fat Anne. He nimbly curled a leg around her and, with a tight embrace, pleaded, "Let's go to it, Anne!"

Anne drew back, smiled, and continued licking her chocolate Mello-Roll.

Pearl reluctantly stepped in the door, wearing her school-day brown-and-white saddle shoes and pleated skirt. We weren't there as far she was concerned. She knew she was pretty, but happily her confidence waned as she cautiously entered enemy territory. She anticipated; Sol obliged.

"What'll you have, Strictly?"

Sol knew she detested the name Strictly. He had christened her this after listening to her talking in the candy store phone booth one day: "Did you hear about Errol Flynn? I knew he was a fag. Give me Clark Gable: he's strictly a man.... Strictly speaking, I hate those new nylons. They make my legs itch.... What? Flame-Glo lipstick? I bought it at Woolworth's. It's strictly for the birds."

When her mother, who was in the store, heard Sol call Pearl Strictly, she said, "Sure, she's strictly, she's strictly kosher!"

"Strictly kosher my ass," said Sol. "She's strictly bullshit."

Upon hearing the nickname, Pearl slammed the door behind her, swearing never to return. To Sol, her rage was worth a lost customer. He enjoyed performing for the boys, who were deriving their last burps from the few drops left in their Coke bottles.

It was a day like any other day in the candy store. We expected laughs; we were never disappointed. After a while, we had had our ration of fun and were about to call it quits when two infrequent visitors made their appearance. Jake the Snake and Willie the Weasel, two permanent residents of Pop's pool hall. Willie was holding two oranges, and Jake had a pathetic overcoat drooping over his arm. Without a salutation, Willie dropped the gauntlet. "I'm wagering this cashmere my rich uncle gave me against cash that my man Jake can throw this orange farther than anyone in this store."

What were sixteen-year-olds going to do with this ratty excuse for a cashmere overcoat?

Monty, who was Jake and Willie's sidekick, smelling a fast buck, raced across the street and up to his apartment. He dashed back down with two of his older brother's suits to up the ante for the shabby coat. The suits were pre-war vintage, and who would wear that droopy cashmere? Why would anyone even think of an overcoat? It was summer—the only thought we had about clothing was shedding it. But we had been given a challenge to our athletic ability that could not be dismissed. We emptied our pockets and came up with $12. Willie, the promoter, said it wasn't enough for two suits and a new cashmere. Sol could not miss this event. He removed $3 from the till to make it $15.

There was no haggling. Whoever threw the orange farther than Jake took the cash and the rags. Sol, knowing Willie's financial antics in the past, suggested that the money be left at the candy store for the winner.

The boys huddled to determine who was going to throw the orange. They agreed that I had the strongest arm. Since Jake was tainted with a yellow-green poolroom complexion, and no one had ever seen him play ball, we couldn't picture him throwing an orange half a block. Was this going to be a laugher (no contest)?

Outside the candy store, Willie draped the two suits and the cashmere coat over the newspaper stand. We crowded around the sewer lid in the middle of the street, opposite the candy store, which was to be the throwing point. The coin toss indicated that I was to go first. I wasn't going to disappoint the boys. With the orange squeezed tightly in my left hand, I ran toward the sewer lid and then released it. The orange sailed down East 172nd Street, past the intersection at Minford Place, then hit the second floor fire escape of the first building on the left, where it splattered on the cast-iron bars. Surely it would have gone farther without that obstacle.

Now it was Jake's turn. He ran up to the sewer lid and threw his orange. To everyone's surprise, it soared through the air, crossed the Minford Place intersection, and landed in the middle of the street, directly opposite the point where my orange had made contact with the fire escape. A quick measurement was followed by the usual argument.

"Anyone with eyes can see that the orange on the fire escape is behind Jake's blast in the middle the street," argued Willie.

"What are you, blind?" asked Alvin. "The fire escape didn't move. I can see that the splatter on the fire escape is far ahead of Jake's orange on the street."

As the squabbling went on, Willie quickly dashed up the hill to the newsstand. He grabbed his cashmere, while Monty, trailing behind him, gathered the suits.

From the open window of the candy store Sol shouted, "Hey, guys, wait! Where are you going? Let's do it again. Let's get a winner."

The garments would have to wait for another scheme; Willie and Jake declined a tiebreaker. But the curtains were not drawn on their performance. With the folded cashmere over his arm, Willie announced he had a delicious dessert for tonight.

"I imported some vanilla trade from Java. Slip me five, and you're guaranteed to see rockets!" Translation: I have some lightly pigmented girls for you. Give me $5 and I guarantee you'll have a great time.

"None of that crap," said Mutt. "My brother was in the Navy. He told me what VD could do to you."

How could we struggle with our homework when a new show opened daily in our candy store? There would be a different script tomorrow. Which players would be in the wings waiting for their cue to *Enter Laughing?* Did it matter? The show would go on.

Aunt Dora and the 42nd Precinct

Dora, the now-aged aunt with whom Ma had lived when she arrived in Canada, had remarried and gone to live with her husband in his son's house in Peekskill, New York. Dora and her husband had occupied an upstairs bedroom throughout the years of their marriage, but, when her husband died, his son told Dora to plan on leaving the house. He made life miserable for her. He ignored her. He wouldn't take her shopping. He kept the thermostat at 65 degrees in the winter.

When Ma became aware of Dora's situation, she found an apartment for Dora on our street in the Bronx. At this point Dora was unable to care for herself. Ma cleaned her apartment and did her laundry. What Ma could not do was prevent Dora from wandering the streets. She would leave her apartment and set out on a trip to the bank to make sure her meager savings weren't being tampered with. Frequently a police car would pick her up. A phone call would tell me to retrieve her at the 42nd precinct police station on Simpson Street.

One time, Dora's wanderings got me into hot water. In our living room, Pa's fragile, swaying, upholstered club chair was held together by a board I had nailed to its base. My friend, Bob Jacobson, six foot four and well over 240 pounds, was not permitted to sit in this chair. Ma brought a sturdy wooden chair for Bob from the kitchen. Early monastic period, it could easily support a freight car. She moved this chair into the living room whenever she anticipated Bob's arrival.

Now that we had TV sets, my friends and I rotated homes for watching weekend sporting events. The Giants were playing the Green Bay Packers one Sunday, and at my house we arranged ourselves around the TV awaiting the kickoff. Bob hadn't arrived yet. The phone rang. Anticipating Bob's call, I picked up the phone and said, "You know you can't sit on the upholstered chair. The wooden chair is waiting for you."

"Who is this?" asked the angry voice at the other end of the line.

"Dan Wolfe. Isn't this Bob?"

"How old are you? What is this with the chair? We just picked up a confused, elderly lady who has your phone number and address in her pocketbook. Come down to the 42nd precinct to pick her up."

I rushed to the station. Trying to avoid the piercing eyes of the desk sergeant, I headed straight over to Aunt Dora, but the sergeant stepped out from behind the desk to warn me, "I don't want to see you here again."

Our future attempts to put a stop to Dora's excursions were useless, so I became a frequent visitor to the 42nd precinct on Simpson Street.

Boys Will Be Boys

He would stand for hours at the gate leading to the entrance of his cellar apartment. Only the breeze that fluttered his shirtsleeves indicated that this was not a statue but a live human being. He leaned slightly forward, with his right boot on the top step, his left on the lower, and his folded arms resting on his right knee. After a while, to restore circulation, he would stand erect and place his right palm against the wall of his building as if to support it. His gold-rimmed frames blended beautifully with his shiny black creased skin. We knew him as Glenn Gould, the janitor of 1520 Seabury Place, the apartment building that housed our candy store.

Glenn had a choice spot at the top of the steps overlooking the street, a box seat to watch our Stickball games. An avid weekend fan, he knew the weaknesses and strengths of all the ballplayers. During one of our competitive inter-neighborhood games, we were losing by one run going into the final inning. Glenn could see our dejected faces as we came in for our last attempts to win the game. Moish, our best hitter, was scheduled to bat third.

"Don't worry, boys," said Glenn. "The Bambino [Moish] is coming up."

He was right on target. Moish hit a homer over the outfielder's head to tie the game. We won it in extra innings.

Lenny Blum was the catalyst that energized Glenn. Lenny was the only one he knew by name, although he said it "Boon." At the sight of Lenny, his smile revealed a mass of teeth tarnished by tobacco and framed in gold.

"Boon! What nasty things are you going to do today?"

Lenny just laughed, gave him a big hello, and asked him what nasty things he had done last night. Glenn loved that. It seemed to awaken the manhood in this aging, lonely man.

When he was in the mood for conversation, Glenn told of his dangerous military operations in the South Pacific, which had brought about his "severe asthmatic condition." He claimed that the doctors at the Veterans Administration had said it could be remedied only by "a bottle of grapes" (cheap wine). He would take 50 cents from his pocket, look over our gang, select the messenger, and say, "Go get me some grapes for my (cough, cough) asthmatic condition, which I got in the military service."

This was the signal to run to the liquor store near the East 174th Street subway station and buy him a pint of Thunderbird.

He had two sons and a daughter. The oldest was Carl, next came Billy, and the youngest was Brenda. Carl was a handsome, talented dancer and singer. He won all the talent shows at Hermann Ridder Junior High School. We thought Hollywood was his next stop after high school. We predicted that Billy, too, would make headlines one day, in very different endeavors. It was a rare day when he wasn't chauffeured home in a police car or engaged in a street fight with a kid in the neighborhood. Brenda was the recipient of the same fragments of DNA that made Billy. But she was not yet old enough to fully interpret their message.

After we saw Carl's mother—all 270 pounds of her—maul another woman, she was given a clear path to return to her apartment or wherever she wanted to go.

During football season, we convinced Carl to be a running back for our team. When his mother got wind of it, she rumbled into the park and pulled him off the field. Pummeling him all the way home, she screamed, "You ain't gonna ruin your dancing career with this garbage!"

Glenn was above all this. When Brenda got into hair-pullers in the neighborhood, he referred the protesting mothers to "the Mrs." Whenever Billy came home with a police escort, he observed, "Boys will be boys!"

It wasn't long before that fateful day came when Billy fulfilled our predictions. He made the headlines in the *New York Post:* "Youth Pushed in Front of Oncoming Train!" Yes, Billy had pushed a little boy in front of a subway train. A memorable line about Billy from the *Post* was, "in spite of his mischief, he always had the ability to make people laugh."

Billy was remanded to the Bronx House of Detention to await trial. Glenn still appeared on his perch at the top of his basement stairs.

"Hey, Glenn, what happened to Billy?" I asked.

"Boys will be boys," he replied.

After that, the Gould family quietly moved from the neighborhood, never to be heard from again.

The Boys of Autumn

Football practice on a little triangle of greenery enclosed by a cyclone fence in Crotona Park was a refreshing respite from the chill and grayness of autumn. Yes, autumn was in the air, and football was on the ground. Our team was peeling and stomping while scraping the mud and leaves from our shirts and pants. Earthworms couldn't have been more intimate with the ground than our boys of autumn.

Every football team must have a coach. Sonny Leff, who took himself very seriously, was ours. Two outstanding features in his résumé qualified him for the job: (1) He was seventeen, two years older than we were, and (2) he was the only one who applied for the position.

The equipment we brought to practice closely resembled the equipment we wore after school: a flannel shirt, a pair of dungarees, and sneakers. No one owned shoulder pads. There was only one helmet for the entire team. It was made of thin split cowhide painted a grainy red and blue. Inside this alleged head protector was a quarter inch of compressed cotton batting pretending to shield the wearer from a blow to the head. For further security, there was a web suspension to absorb a blast to the top of the head. After three practices, this helmet could be folded and tucked into the rear pocket of a pair of dungarees.

No more than three or four games were scheduled for the season. In spite of this, we practiced twice a week. Mooney was our quarterback, Peanzy and I were the running backs, and Moish was the fullback. The number of players who showed up determined the number of linemen. Abe was our center. Although he was handicapped by polio, he played an aggressive and fearless game. Puggy and Rock were our guards; Mutt and Krebs were our unreliable tackles; Donny and Jerry were at end. Donny was younger than we were and was yet to develop coordination, but we found a place for him in the starting lineup because he was the owner of the only helmet. Jerry was a reliable end, provided Mooney was able to throw accurately to him. René, whose family had recently emigrated from Franco's Spain, was our kicker and punter. Before his kick, he would announce, "Kicking formation, please."

We rehearsed our plays to make our offense a well-tuned and well-lubricated vehicle. Whoever was the ball carrier wore the helmet. Because my head was too big for the helmet, I was part of a trick play we cleverly used a few times during games. To deceive our opponents, the blocking back wore the helmet. Our opponents, thinking he was carrying the ball, chased him, while the bareheaded running back, Peanzy or I, ran ahead for a substantial gain.

Despite the lack of helmets, we had only one injury of note. A game was scheduled with the neighboring Suburban Place team at Crotona Park's athletic field. Without uniforms and with only nine men on each team, we didn't qualify for the regular football field. We found a rectangular space somewhat resembling a football field immediately to the left of the regulation field. Its left boundary was a rough-surfaced cement wall about fifteen feet high.

Suburban Place's running back was Sonny. He was about six foot two, while most of us were aspiring toward or just reached five feet. In response to Sonny's height and weight, we recruited Max as punt returner. He was very thin but very fast.

The game began with a kickoff to Peanzy. Wearing the helmet, he deceptively lateraled the ball to bareheaded Max. Max sped off to the left, running parallel to the cement wall. He carried the ball quite a distance, but when he was hit he collided with and then caromed off the abrasive wall. Max valiantly held onto the ball. Stunned and scraped, he picked himself up, to the cheers of our boys. We told him only a tough guy could have held on to the ball the way he had. With his face and arms bleeding, he looked as if he'd been dragged over a large sheet of coarse sandpaper. Max went home to tend to his injuries knowing he was our hero. That was the opening play of the game.

Soon the score was 12 to 6 in favor of the Suburbanites. Sonny, a bruising runner, was battering our linemen. Frequently he ran through our line as if the boys just weren't there. Late in the game, he broke through our line and ran toward me. I stopped him with my shoulder and then grabbed his foot. He flew up and then flipped over me, landing on his head. Dazed, he couldn't continue. His team walked off the field. The game was over. We won by a forfeit!

Another game of note occurred after we had beaten a team of our contemporaries from nearby Charlotte Street. Seething from their loss, they asked for a rematch.

"You were lucky you beat us. Most of our team was at Herman's brother's bar mitzvah. How about another game in two weeks?"

"What time?"

"Same time, same place."

There weren't many teams in the neighborhood, so why not?

Although we lacked protective equipment, our coach, Sonny Leff, arrived for the rematch in an outfit appropriate for his role: a wide brimmed, dark brown fedora and a navy blue overcoat with shoulders so broad that he appeared to be the only one from our team with shoulder pads.

An entirely different team from Charlotte Street was waiting for us. They were the older brothers, World War II vets recently discharged from the service. We could have embarrassed ourselves and gone home. That would have been the intelligent thing to do, since this was going to be a contest of teens against men. But that wasn't our way of thinking.

For this game, I sported a novel piece of equipment, although I don't recall how it ended up in my hands. It was a soft black helmet in a style that might have been state of the art during Jim Thorpe's 1920s era. Each section was joined but separate like the appendages of a lobster. Its uncertain protection was further enhanced by the lack of a chinstrap. Before the game, I had sought a remedy for this defect.

"Ma, do you have something that will keep this helmet on my head?"

"You wear that on your head? What is that thing? It looks like my old pocketbook."

"It can fall off my head when I'm playing a football game."

"So, don't wear it," she replied.

When I persisted, Ma offered a small roll of quarter-inch-wide white elastic that she used to replace the stretched elastic in her panties. Sure that this wouldn't be able to withstand a power tackle, I doubled the elastic. Now I had a helmet with a chinstrap.

The game began. We kicked off; the vets received. They scored on their first possession. After chasing our jitters, we began to give a good account of ourselves. The vets scored again but against a more confident team.

Then it was our turn. Peanzy carried the ball around the end, outrunning the entire defense. We scored! We made the extra point, and the score was 13 to 7 in favor of the vets at the end of the half.

At the beginning of the second half, I carried the ball. I broke through the defensive line and into the backfield but then one of the linebackers drilled his shoulder into my chest. He hit me so hard that my helmet was knocked straight up over my head. The elastic around my chin did not abandon me, however; it bit into my chin as the helmet gained its peak altitude and then rocketed back down onto the top of my head. The tackle and the descending helmet combined stunned me. I lay on the ground, but Coach Sonny was there to ease me back into the game. He ran onto the field and, with his penknife, cut the elastic under my chin; then he adjusted my helmet. With no substitute to take my place, I woozily returned to the game. We lost 13 to 7, but we were very proud of our effort.

My next football experience was for the James Monroe High School varsity, wearing genuine football equipment and having a doctor present at each game.

James Monroe Football

It was the last week of May 1947. One of the few noteworthy announcements coming over the public address system at James Monroe High School was, "Tomorrow, after the eighth period, Doc Wiedman will be holding tryouts for the football team in the boys' gymnasium."

I was a junior and weighed in at 127 pounds, but Doc was known to have lightweight teams. Could I make it? Why not try? This was the second year of the return of high school football to New York City; it had been suspended for the duration of World War II.

The following day, at the end of eighth period, I dashed to the gym. Doc stood on a platform barking instructions for stretching exercises. Then we were divided into groups of four to learn the fundamentals of blocking from the previous year's veterans. The backfield candidates were running short sprints. The floors vibrated from pounding sneakers.

T-shirts were damp with sweat; overtaxed respiratory systems had us gasping for air. An occasional groan could be heard when a well-placed shoulder hit a solar plexus. Doc Wiedman paraded around the gym in his classic white shirt and bow tie, carefully scrutinizing the mayhem.

Within a week we moved outdoors. Doc divided the candidates into groups of five. The fastest of the group in the forty-yard dash were placed in the backfield, the taller boys were made ends, and the rest became guards. The slower and usually heavier players were assigned to tackle or center.

I came home with a parental consent form, fully confident that my parents would give me permission to play.

"What's this?" asked my father.

"You have to sign this paper to allow me to play football."

"You play ball in the street. I don't have to sign a paper. What is this?"

James Monroe High School.

Ma chimed in. "What is this? You're signing for him to become a cripple, that's what it is."

At this time we did not own a TV set. How Ma knew about football was a mystery to me. Finally, they agreed, and I turned in the form to Doc Wiedman.

I finished my junior year. Football practice ended in June. I was still on the team. Doc told us to get plenty of sleep, eat well, and run in the sand whenever possible, to strengthen our legs during summer vacation.

While I was waiting my turn to bat in our Sunday softball game, Irv turned to me, "Are you really on the Monroe football team? You're smaller than the cheerleaders."

"So what? You're twice my size, and you didn't have the guts to try out."

"My mother wouldn't let me try out. Anyway, De Witt Clinton will kill you. All of them are twice Monroe's size."

"They may be big and they may be heavy, but we nearly beat them last year, and we'll beat them this year."

It was Irv's turn to bat, but he didn't leave it alone. As he stepped up to the plate, he turned and said, "Don't forget who told you."

With the arrival of September, I returned to school without a thought of academics. Football was on my mind. Uniforms were distributed at the field house. The veterans selected the choice equipment; the rest of us were left with the pre-war remainders. The only new equipment we newcomers were given were jocks and sweat socks. Our helmets had probably been stiff at the time of their manufacture, but now they were as soft as berets. Our thick wool maroon jerseys were more appropriate for an Antarctic expedition with Admiral Byrd than a game of football. The final insult was the shoulder pads and hip guards. They might have been serviceable for a Pop Warner Little League football team. We wore them; did we have a choice?

Practice began with stretching exercises. Once our muscles, tendons, and ligaments were limber, we began the torturous duck walks and squat jumps. Finally, we graduated to grass drills; they were the ultimate agony. If we did them properly, every muscle throbbed with pain. We would double-time in place, and then Doc would shout "Forward fall!"

We dove forward onto our chest, abdomen, and legs without using our hands to break the fall. Then he would shout "Backward fall!"

We lifted ourselves off the ground and then hit it again with our backsides. After many repetitions, he shouted "Up and double-time!"

While we were abusing ourselves in the dirt, Murray Leak stood up, holding the strap of his helmet.

"Leak! You're not going to market. That helmet is not a basket. Get it on your head."

"I'm nauseous, Doc."

"This is a big field. Pick out a spot, empty yourself, and double-time back when you're done."

Murray turned in his uniform at the end of practice. Maybe we weren't the best high school football team in New York City, but I'm sure we were the best bruised and best conditioned.

Our football field was yellow clay. Like the Mojave Desert, it was dry and dusty: a clump of grass here, another clump there, amid a liberal distribution of clay dotted with rocks. It was a landscaping failure created by the

WPA during the Great Depression. When I came home and blew my nose, part of the field ended up in my handkerchief.

Grass grew very nicely under the bleachers. Since Doc didn't allow us to drink during practice, when he wasn't looking we gathered clumps of grass from there and chewed on them to draw some moisture for our parched mouths.

During the early weeks of practice, I left the field house with every muscle protesting the barbarous treatment I had given it. I would not quit. I struggled home, legs apart, walking very tenderly, like a marionette with jock itch. After I managed the mile home, it was into the shower again—perhaps more heat would ease the pain. It never did.

I learned a hard lesson after the first practice: when I reached home, I doused my torso with Sloane's Liniment, a pungent, useless irritant recommended to the team by Doc Wiedman. Completely unaware of its irritant quality, I spread it liberally over my chest. As it streamed downward it produced a stinging sensation. It meandered farther, toward the crease connecting my leg to my abdomen, and then a rivulet reached the critical impact area. It formed a delta over my scrotum—a shocking scarlet blazed from the organ. I was launched to the ceiling. I felt like stepping on Sloane's head and ripping the beard from his face one hair at a time. Eventually, shower water diluted the liniment.

During a practice, a pile of players were pressing down on my ankle when Anthony Greco, a 240-pound tackle, landed on top of them. When the boys piled off, I loosened the laces of my cleats and hopped over to Doc. He told me to sit on the bench and wait until the end of practice. My ankle swelled to the point where I had to remove my cleats. Leaning on Doc, I hobbled into the field house. He removed an Ace bandage from a locker and told me to point my toe. I pointed it away from my ankle.

"Not like that, you donkey," he shouted squeezing my foot backward toward my shin. The pain was so awful I saw galaxies soaring from the lockers. Then he began to roll the Ace bandage around my ankle. When I recovered from Doc's treatment, I hobbled home. I tried to walk in a normal gait as I entered my apartment, but it was to no avail.

"What is this new walk of yours?" asked Ma. "Pull up your pants. I want to see where they crippled you."

When she saw the Ace bandage, she shouted, "Aha! You're trying to hide it with that *shmateh*. You'll show it to Pa when he gets home."

As soon as Pa came through the door I heard, "Show him. Show him what the bums did to your foot."

"Let me sit down for a minute. Why should I see his foot?"

I pulled up my pants so he could see my wrapped ankle.

"Take that thing off. What is it? Is it a bandage? I never saw a bandage look like that. Is anything underneath it?"

Ma chimed in. "That's what it is, a bandage. He'll be in a wheelchair for graduation if he plays that *meshugener* game.

"We signed for it," said Pa.

Every morning, before leaving for school, I wound the Ace bandage around my ankle, while Ma's caustic comments crashed against my ears, sending me off to school like a battleship launched on its maiden voyage.

"This is a game you're playing? This is a pogrom by the Cossacks!"

One day, after a shower, I wearily washed my sweat socks and jockstrap; then I hung them up to dry on a towel rack. The next morning, the socks were there, but the jock was missing. I was so proud of that jock. It made me feel that I was a man! I guess it was the same sensation a female encounters when she hooks up her first bra.

"Ma, did you see my jockstrap? It was hanging next to my sweat socks on the towel rack."

"Look again. I didn't take it; it must be there."

I returned to the bathroom and checked thoroughly. "Ma, are you sure you didn't see my jockstrap?"

"I put it on, and I went downstairs to play ball," she replied. "Where I left it, I don't know."

I searched the apartment for days. Maybe Ma had hidden it to go downstairs and play another game? Could it have been her attempt to put an end to my football career?

After a while, my muscles became adjusted to the grueling practice. We looked forward to the games as an analgesic for the week's accumulation of

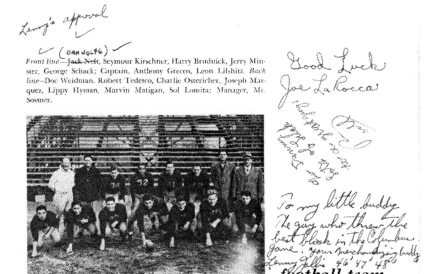

Lenny's approval

(DAN WOLFE)

Front line—Jack Neft, Seymour Kirschner, Harry Brudnick, Jerry Minster, George Schack; Captain, Anthony Grecco, Leon Lifshitz. Back line—Doc Weidman, Robert Tedesco, Charlie Ostericher, Joseph Marquez, Lippy Hyman, Marvin Matigan, Sol Lomita; Manager, Mr. Sossner.

Good Luck
Joe LaRocca

To my little buddy
The guy who threw the
best block in the Columbus
game. your merchandising buddy
Lenny Galli. 46' 47' 48'

football team

Photo of the football team seniors in my yearbook. The caption made an error
in identifying me, but my teammates' notes make it up to me.

bruises and aches. I played second string, which didn't give me frequent opportunities to justify my midweek agony.

Doc Wiedman's philosophy was to play the first team regardless of the score. My day came when we played Christopher Columbus High School on Randall's Island. I entered the game with five minutes left to play. Our boys played both defense and offense. I was on defense when Goldstein, the Columbus quarterback, threw a pass. Pete Serrone, on my right saw the play develop. He stepped in front of the receiver and intercepted the pass.

"Follow me, Pete!" I shouted.

I led him toward the goal. Goldstein, the quarterback who had passed the ball, came charging at us. I threw a block at him. Goldstein was vertical in the air, head down, feet up. His helmet met the ground. As he was carried off the field unconscious, I heard a trumpet from the James Monroe band play _Taps_. Pete didn't make it quite to the goal. He was stopped at the five-yard line. On the next play, Lippy Hyman, our halfback, carried the ball over the goal line for the winning score.

All the verbal abuse, bruises, swollen ankle, and Sloane's Liniment burning my crotch were worth it when the team mobbed me as I ran off the field.

The following Monday, as usual, our team assembled in the bleachers for a critique of Saturday's game. Doc often berated us so much in his review that we felt inadequate to win a tug-of-war with Monroe's cheerleaders.

"I want to congratulate you," said Doc. "You performed very well against Columbus." He continued, "There are some players who get little playing time. But when they do get into the game, they give it their all. Last Saturday, I sent Wolfe in." Then, smacking one hand against the other, he proclaimed "He let the quarterback have it!"

Like a Chagall character, I was floating in air. My heartbeat accelerated. I was so proud!

My Wardrobe

World War II finally came to an end. My brother completed his service in the Merchant Marine and left for Montreal to apprentice in our uncle's dress factory. Consequently, neither the clothing he had outgrown nor his GI issue dominated my wardrobe anymore.

Shirts were no problem. My father had mastered the art of turning worn collars. Long-sleeved shirts became short-sleeved shirts and, when the turned collars frayed, some evolved into pajama tops. But what about pants? How much cuff and seam could be let out from the pants of a growing teenager?

I was about to step over the threshold from the carefree pre-pubescent years into the carefree teenage years. Assisting in this transition were androgens, the new kid on the block—hormones that informed me there was an opposite sex. These chemical messengers directed me to declare an armistice with the enemy, females.

How could I attract them? The plants have an easy time of it. Their brilliant colors and wonderful scents invite insects to complete their reproductive mission. Some animals are endowed with bright colors plus tantalizing fragrances called pheromones. These seducers, which announce their availability, are synchronized with their mating season. Wouldn't it be nice if humans produced pheromones and were programmed for seasonal color displays? Unfortunately we were cursed with hormones that kept us aroused year-round. Consequently, we were not endowed with the beguiling gifts of the flora and fauna.

I thought, perhaps, my dexterity on the ice or my athletic performance on our asphalt streets would be my mating call. No response. So I focused on an updated wardrobe.

The reasonable solution was found in an innocuous storefront discovered by Alvin Lakind. It was tucked into the northwest corner of Crotona and Tremont Avenues in the Bronx. With no sign announcing the nature of the business, a window painted black was its mark of distinction.

Upon opening the door, you either hurdled, stepped on, or knocked over tightly wound rolls of fabric remnants in order to locate the proprietor. With a cigarette seemingly stapled to his lower lip, he could be found at the rear of the store bent over a humming sewing machine illuminated by the only light bulb in the store. This was the legendary Pop Meyer.

Pop's shop was a Bronx institution. People came from far and wide to mine his mammoth mound of remnants for a small roll of fabric that he could sew into a custom pair of pants for $5. First you selected the remnant. Then you apprehensively carried it to Pop to learn whether there was enough fabric for your size. A positive reply meant that he could sew a pair of pants somewhat following the outline of your lower torso. Thanks to Pop, for the first time, I owned two virgin, unaltered pairs of pants designed for me and me alone.

The summer of my junior year in high school portended a rise in my economic status. I was hired as a busboy at the Central Hotel in Ellenville, a summer resort in the Catskill Mountains. A pair of navy blue pants and a white shirt were the uniform of the day, every day. Neither my brown nor my gray pants from Pop's qualified, so I was off to see him again.

My friends—Alvin with his great sense of humor and Irv who towered over me—came along as mavens. They were frequent customers, which gave them license to give Pop a hard time. We entered the store.

"Pop," said Irv, "he needs a pair of pants."

"So, tell him what to do. I'm busy."

As I began quarrying for a navy blue fabric, I heard Alvin yell, "Iwo Jima positions take!"

He ran up a huge pile of remnants near the window, pretending it was Mount Surabachi on Iwo Jima, planted a yardstick into its peak, and then saluted.

As if it had been rehearsed specifically for the occasion, a flow of searing invectives hitched a ride on the spray of Pop's saliva. "Son nom a bitch! Bestid!" and some foreign curses ricocheted off the lonely bulb dangling in front of him. Where he picked up these choice expressions was beyond me. Irv had told me that Pop never left his store.

Finally, I found a navy blue remnant. "I need them today, Pop."

With a mouth dry from lubricating the profanity that had just spewed from it, he rasped, "In a half an hour."

He removed the twisted and wrinkled yellow cloth tape measure from around his neck, measured my inseam and waist, and then sent us away.

We returned in thirty minutes.

"Dey're done, but dey're not pressed," said Pop. "Come back in ten minutes."

We returned in ten minutes. As I opened the door, Alvin and Irv erupted with a crystal-shattering "Press the blues!"

With a throat still dry from his glossary of obscenities, Pop shouted "Drop dead—dey're pressed!"

I carried home the blues, still warm from the steam iron, draped over my arm in a vain attempt to avoid wrinkling them. Any wrinkle they developed in transit became a permanent part of the pants. Once I was home, they hung vertically in the closet, playing the role of a normal pair of pants until I was ready to embark on my adventure as a busboy.

My tender treatment of the pants was no harbinger of what was to become of them. As the days of bussing tables at the Central Hotel passed, the suppleness of the blues was replaced by a congealed veneer of comestibles oozing from my clients' plates and mouths. By summer's end the pants chronicled a sample of every meal served at the Central Hotel. They joined the leftovers from the last meal served that season—in the garbage pail.

My remaining Pop Meyer pants were not the magnet for females that I had expected them to be. The only thing they attracted was a hot iron and a wet rag to smooth out the wrinkles they accumulated whenever I wore them.

Varsity football was in its second year after World War II. After two weeks of grueling practice Doc Wiedman, our coach, called the names of the candidates who had survived the cut. I heard my name. At five foot six and 127 pounds, I was proud to have endured the punishing practices and played well when given a rare opportunity.

I thought I had earned a yellow-and-red varsity football jacket. The aches, the pains, the bruises gave me license to wear it, and, after working at the Central Hotel the past summer, I could afford the $18. But I denied myself this luxury with a series of rationalizations: It was my senior year. How long would I wear the jacket? Bright red and canary yellow were an ugly color combination. The jackets were already beginning to pill on the players who had bought them. Red clashed with my ruddy complexion. This litany of justifications convinced me that not buying the jacket was the right thing to do.

The real world awaited me, after a twelve-year journey through public education. Rolled into my 1948 high school diploma was the postwar recession. College was not a consideration. I felt obliged to reduce the financial strain on my father. For how many years had I seen this kind and gentle man overcome by fatigue, slowly hobbling down the elevated subway steps after work, and then sipping a 2-cent seltzer at the candy store adjacent to the station. So, off I went to the employment agencies in lower Manhattan.

"Make sure you wear a jacket!" my father advised.

My brother's slate blue tropical-worsted sport jacket hung in my parents' closet where he had left it before moving to Montreal. Tropical worsted was not de rigueur in the month of March, but it fit fairly well over a thick woolen sweater. Unfortunately, the sleeves were not cooperative— they meandered past my wrists and introduced themselves to my fingernails. Cleverly, I decided to bend my arms, creating an "L." This would draw the sleeves back from my fingertips to my wrists.

I left for the East 174th Street subway station. As I passed Misek's Deli, the sleeves started wandering toward my fingertips. By the time I had reached the Dover Theater, the sleeves were out of control. I began to raise my arms in hallelujah fashion to get the damn sleeves to retreat.

At last I reached the subway station and settled into a seat. With each turn of the train, the woven bamboo seat covers kept snagging my brown Pop Meyer pants, but the forty-five minute ride was a respite for my weary arms.

Numerous interviews informed me that, after twelve years of schooling, my academic diploma qualified me as a messenger boy for 50 cents an hour. I was to pay the first week's salary to the employment agency.

"What? I have to pay you a week's pay for a 50-cent-an-hour job?"

"That's right," said the secretary.

"No, that's wrong. Shove it," I replied and left.

These were depressed times, but some mood-elevating events were taking place in the world of fashion. The zipper fly made its debut. Of course, custom-made pants cried out for the zipper fly, and Pop Meyer, our custom tailor, fell into lockstep with the fashion. However, Pop's zippers, like his remnants, were determined by the idiosyncrasies of the job lots. So, if the zipper was long, the fly was long regardless of the size of the customer the pants were tailored for.

Alvin, in rust-colored tweed Pop Meyer Golden Needle Special pants had a zipper fly that must have been intended for a sleeping bag. It had teeth like a *Tyrannosaurus* and was the length of a python, resulting in a pair of pants whose waist ended under his armpits and whose crotch extending from his chest to his knees. To annoy, horrify, and amuse the women who sat on fruit boxes basking in the sun on our street, Irv would grasp Alvin's fly and twist it into a spiral while Alvin screamed and moaned.

For some of us, the Korean War offered the first pair of pants and jacket that matched and fit. The price we had to pay was that we'd been drafted into a war that had no rational cause. Unlike World War II, this was a then unpopular and now forgotten war.

Economic conditions improved, while my father's health deteriorated. He slavishly continued finishing women's overcoats in spite of a failing heart. When I was discharged from the army, I realized that a college education would provide me with opportunities that were never open to Pa. I supplemented the $110 a month I got from the GI Bill by working on a truck with Alvin, collecting fat, bones, and chicken guts from butchers in Manhattan, and I attended City College at night. I was able to finish college in four years.

My college wardrobe consisted of an Ike jacket, woolen GI pants, and a T-shirt (no logo); it earned me the name OD Kid among my classmates.

The crease in my woolen pants remained sharp for months. When it became dull, I would hone it with a damp rag and a hot iron. My Ike jacket, later to become the fashion rage of the hippies in the 1960s, fended off the biting winter winds whistling down City College's Convent Avenue in the mid-1950s.

Graduation and a real job: a high school biology teacher! This required at least two suits, a sport jacket, and a matching pair of pants.

"A suit you need? You never wore suits. Wait for a sale," my mother counseled.

"Wait for a sale? He needs it now!" my father replied.

The debate ended when Willie the Weasel sold me two high-quality suits that "fell off a truck" in the garment district.

I am now retired after thirty-five years of teaching. I am happily married. My wife and my children are the major contributors to this bliss, although tragically, I lost a dear son in 1995. The major source of friction between my wife and me is my wardrobe—the paucity and colors of my apparel, and when and where to wear which items. Pop Meyer, where are you when I need you?

Catskill Capers

It was the summer of 1947. I was seventeen years old. The country was in a postwar recession. An ex-boarder at our apartment, now a chambermaid at the Central Hotel in the Catskill Mountains, told Ma that they needed a busboy. The pay was $12 a week for a seven-day week, plus tips—not a generous salary, but unemployment was my alternative.

My navy blue Pop Meyers, accompanied by two white shirts, socks, underwear, and two towels, rested in my satchel on an overhead shelf of the bus speeding to the Central Hotel in Ellenville, a small notch in the Borscht Belt of the Catskill Mountains.

When I arrived, I was led to the shack where the waiters and busboys slept. The one available bed was a cot directly under a small hole in the roof begging for a shingle. Fresh air now, fresh rain later, I thought. My closet was a wire shelf attached to the wall directly behind my cot. I was able to balance my razor, shaving cream, and soap on it. Before squeezing my satchel under my bed, I zipped it open to hang my Pop Meyers somewhere, anywhere. I noticed some new wrinkles added to the old ones. They would remain until I deposited the pants into a trash can at the end of the season.

The kitchen staff consisted of a cook, a dishwasher, four busboys, and four waiters. I was assigned to Norman, a Columbia undergraduate student; he would be my waiter for the summer. He was very helpful in guiding me through my first week of clumsiness. Another waiter, the owner's son, Bert, said he was just waiting for his eighteenth birthday to join the Marines. The other waiters, substantially older than the busboys, merely blended into the knotty pine walls of the dining room. One busboy, Richie, was an Irish kid who was completely familiar with the kosher cuisine and knew some Yiddish words. The guests adored him.

Rarely were we served the same food as the guests. The rubbery chicken served to the waiters and busboys had never felt the blade of a *shochet's* (ritual slaughterer's) knife. Either the chicken had lived to a ripe old age and expired naturally or it had met its demise on the treadmill at a fitness center.

The meatloaf, however, resembled an illustration from a glossy coffee table cookbook. A generous serving of this savory, brown meat was embellished with a bull's-eye slice of hard-boiled egg at the center. It was delicious, and we loved it—until one of the waiters discovered that the cook, another relative of the owner's, saved the meat leftovers from the beef entrées served to the guests the previous day. She ground them to create this attractive and tasty dish. From then on, the meatloaf remained untested by the staff.

Mr. Tucker, a man in his mid-eighties, had been the original owner. Although he had passed the hotel on to his son Jack, he sat in the kitchen like a pit bull, watching for any misstep by the employees.

On my second day as busboy, I was returning from the dining room with a rectangular tray of empty juice glasses. I clipped the doorjamb with a corner of my tray. The glasses tumbled off into a heap of shards at Mr. Tucker's feet. I was about to apologize when he gently responded, "It's awright! It's awright! Don't vorry abott it. You'll be out uhv here by tomahrah."

Fortunately, I was the only dining room employee who was bilingual. I spoke Yiddish and English fluently. My departure was canceled when Mr. Tucker realized he needed my Yiddish to tickle his elderly guests.

Preparation for the Sabbath dinner began immediately after Friday's lunch. Wives were warming up in the bullpen awaiting the arrival of their husbands to relieve the sexual tension that had been building up all week. Husbands, speeding up Route 17, following the scent of the pheromones, hit the accelerator pedal another lick, as they focused on their wives and the freshly laundered bedsheets.

On Friday afternoon, busboys and waiters replaced the tablecloths, set the tables, swept the floors, and mopped the main dining room and the children's dining room. The cook, sweating profusely, screamed louder than usual at the busboys and waiters. The silver- and glass-washing man, in his usual alcoholic stupor, leaned against his deep metal sink to avoid falling on his mottled, scarlet-veined, blue-red nose.

"Get ready de dinink room fur *Shabbes* [the Sabbath]," hollered Mr. Tucker.

I was the matador's red cape and Old Man Tucker was the raging bull. The fact that I was breathing irritated every ganglion in his nervous system. Wearing short pants to counter the heat, I squeezed the mop through a wringer and glided it over the hardwood dining room floor. I looked up to see Mr. Tucker charging toward me as if a picador had just gored him.

"Dis iz vott you vehr to mop mine dinink room floor?"

I looked up and calmly asked, "Mr. Tucker, maybe I should go to Ellenville and rent a tuxedo for the occasion?"

With eyeballs bulging beyond their lids, he screamed, "*Ver geharget, mamzer* [drop dead, bastard]!"

It was two weeks prior to the big payoff, Labor Day weekend. Business was very slow. To save money, the boss sent the busboys home and told us to return for the Labor Day weekend. Not wanting to spend the extra bus fare, I asked Jack, Mr. Tucker's son, if I could stay for the two weeks and work without pay until the three-day weekend. He agreed.

Labor Day arrived. The Central Hotel was occupied beyond capacity. Instead of the usual five tables, I bussed eight. There was hardly any room to carry the trays, but that was OK—I expected more tips. In spite of my youth and good physical condition, however, I couldn't manage bussing eight tables and catering to all my guest's requests.

Everyone at the hotel was constipated. "Stewed proomes, fur da balance" (stewed prunes for the bowels) was the most common demand by the elderly guests.

"Tell da cook next time she should put more salt in da tsopped liver."

"OK, I'll do that."

The highlight of the evening was entertainment—secured, no doubt, from the best backyards and street corners of Brooklyn and the Bronx. Dinner was being served. Waiters' trays of chopped liver glided over the guests' heads as the busboys were removing juice glasses. Parsley decorated the chicken breasts next to stuffed derma and glazed sweet potatoes. Baked prunes and apricots nestled alongside the breasts. Soon the accumulating dishes to be bussed overwhelmed me. How could I clear the tables quickly so that my guests wouldn't be looking at their leftovers during the entertainment?

Behind one of my tables stood an upright piano for the evening's gala. Behind and above the sheet music were two sliding doors. Surreptitiously, I scraped off the leftovers and placed them and the cutlery onto my tray. Then I slid open the doors of the piano, placed some of my bussed dishes inside, and slid the doors closed. Dessert was served, and dinner was over. The sated guests awaited the final course, the floor show.

The smiling troubadours trotted in, waving and blowing kisses to the applause of the guests. The pianist, with a network of dyed, coal-black hair webbing his smooth pink pate, sat down, slid his bench closer to the keys, and waited for his cue. Draping one hand over the piano, the vocalist assumed her position. She nodded, and the pianist plunged his fingers onto the keys. Not a note escaped from the piano. He tried again. Silence. I looked toward the kitchen doors. The left porthole resembled a church's illuminated stained glass window as it reflected Old Man Tucker's red and purple apoplectic face. With his eyebrows somewhere in the middle of his scalp, his mustache quivering like a flag in the wind, he came charging at me with slaughter in his eyes. He flung the music sheets aside and violently slid the upright doors open, and pulled out some of the dishes. This was the opening act. It couldn't have drawn more laughs if Neil Simon had written it. The old man had a limited English repertoire, but "Bestid! Bestid!" surfed toward me on a shower of his saliva.

All's well that ends well. The pianist and I removed the rest of the dishes to the laughter of our amused guests. The show went on, accompanied by a tinkling piano.

On the following day, before I left for home, I went to collect my $4.50 for the holiday weekend.

Mr. Tucker glared at me. "You vahnt money fur your show lest night? Gerradahere!" That was my payoff.

A few weeks after I had returned home, I related this experience to my mother's cousin, who was a lawyer. Between bursts of laughter, he advised me to tell the story about not being paid to the Labor Board at Center

Street in Manhattan. A board employee took Tucker's name and address and told me that an employee could not legally agree to work without a salary—it was against the labor law. Therefore, the Tuckers owed me for the three Labor Day weekend days and the two weeks preceding them. Wow! It came to $28.50!

I knew the Tuckers had received their notice when I was called to answer the phone at the candy store. As soon as I took the receiver and said "Hello," I heard, "What the hell are you doing? Do you want to ruin me? Tell them it's a mistake!"

It was Old Man Tucker's son, Jack, potentially ruined by my $28.50. Without a response, I hung up. By the end of the week, the check was in the mail. Thus ended the summer of 1947. I went on to my senior year at James Monroe High School.

An Honest Day's Pay

The swirling white flakes seemed reluctant to make their descent. A downward plunge, a horizontal slide, and then an upward curl—anywhere but onto the dirty gray sidewalks where they would melt, in the winter of 1948.

Resting on a crocheted doily, turning its back on all this activity, our gothic Emerson table radio announced "Heavy snow today. No sign of letup for the next two days."

"Ma, the weatherman said the snow is going to come down for the next two days."

"The weatherman? What does he know with his fancy instruments? My arthritis is a better weatherman."

Her arthritis threw her a curveball. The following morning, I was unable to distinguish the streets from the sidewalk. Across the road, Hermann Ridder Junior High School's art deco dome, piled high with snowflakes, resembled a giant wedding cake. An occasional lump in the street indicated the presence of a fire hydrant. Traffic lights were superfluous. Cars were immobilized by the storm.

Most of the stores on our street were shut. The unrelenting downfall had paralyzed the entire city. I could hear our janitor's daughter shoveling and scraping the sidewalk in front of our apartment building. Snow or no snow, the candy store was a refuge from my claustrophobic apartment. Before I left, I stepped forward for Ma's mandatory critique. In winter, I knew I couldn't leave our apartment until I passed her pneumonia inspection.

"Who goes out in a storm like this?"

"OK, OK, Ma. I'm eighteen years old. Don't you think I know how to dress for a snowstorm?"

"Your ears are sticking out of your hat. You're not wearing a scarf. The gloves I bought you at Neuberg's—where are they? And button your fly."

Everything was in order by the time I opened the door to leave.

Fortunately, Refugee Jack, the candy store mogul, lived in a small apartment at the rear of the store. So, neither snow nor rain nor heat nor gloom of night closed the store.

The candy store filled up with bodies, but not a coin passed over the counter. Jack was becoming irritable. "There's no room in here for a customer. Buy something or get out!"

Lenny Blum came charging in with good tidings, "The city is hiring shovelers at $5 an hour. Let's go to the Department of Sanitation!"

"For $5 an hour? My father didn't earn half of that even during the early war years. Let's go!"

We dashed out of the candy store. Struggling through the mounds of snow, we charged toward the Department of Sanitation substation, a storefront adjacent to Litroff's Bakery. A nasty foreman, annoyed at having to leave his warm store, stepped outside. He lowered the earflaps on his olive drab hat, put on his black leather gloves, and then glared at us. "Don't think we're giving you shovels! You guys need ID photos and shovels if you want to work!"

We plowed our way home through knee-deep snow. Most of us had a string of four photos we'd taken at a booth in Kresge's for a quarter, but where would we get a shovel? I knew where, but I had to bypass the vicious German shepherd owned by Mr. Tekula, our janitor, who lived in the basement. Although the dog was chained to a hasp on a door, I stood paralyzed when he growled his eagerness to taste my flesh. The motivation of $5 an hour made me a hero: I stood my ground. The noise brought Mrs. Tekula to the doorway.

"Could I borrow a shovel? I need it to shovel snow."

She went to the furnace room and brought out a large coal shovel.

"This is for coal," I said.

"This is a shovel," she replied.

Without an alternative, I lugged the shovel to the Department of Sanitation. A long line of frozen applicants was stretched around the corner, passing Litroff's Bakery and heading toward Charlotte Street. The foreman passed out blank ID cards. Upon completing the forms, we gave him our photos, which he stapled to a square space on the cards. Soon after he passed me, I heard, "What the hell is this?"

"It's me! Who else?" shouted Artie Koeningsberg. He had handed the foreman a miniature of his studio bar mitzvah photo. There he was, wrapped in a large prayer shawl and topped with a skullcap the size of a chef's hat.

"There's no way you could be identified with this religious picture. Go home!"

Great! One competitor eliminated from the bonanza.

We were organized in groups of seven. One of the shovelers was arbitrarily appointed the group foreman. Mutt, the tallest of us, was designated our foreman.

"OK, you guys, follow me to our work area and get your shovels going."

Rock's temperament was riled by the wind, the cold, and the snow. "Screw you, Mutt. Who do you think you are, bossing us around?"

"I'm the foreman. You have to listen to what I say."

"Listen to *you?* You haven't said anything intelligent in years!"

"I'm going to report you, Rock."

"I can't believe this. You're a fink."

We moved on, and the squabbling continued until we had reached the area where we were about to violate freshly fallen virgin snow.

The regular employees of the Department of Sanitation were designated as roaming supervisors, going from group to group to see that the shoveling was being done.

At $5 an hour we had every intention of carrying out our assignments, but the combination of the wind and the unrelenting snowfall chased us into the hall of Julie's apartment house. Since we had scratched some furrows in the snow near the building, Julie suggested that we recover in his apartment. This was an offer we could not refuse. Our foreman, Mutt, thought it was a great idea.

Krebs was designated our fifteen-minute lookout. The rest of us relaxed in Julie's apartment. Jackets were removed, cards were shuffled, and cigarettes were lit. Within a few minutes the apartment resembled an opium den. We could hardly see the door through the smoke, when it was rattled by rapid knocking. It was Krebs.

"The foreman is coming! The foreman is coming!"

We raced down the three flights of stairs, pulling on our hats and slipping into our jackets. The shovels were waiting for us in the vestibule. Like the infantry with fixed bayonets, we charged onto the street wielding our weapons.

The foreman approached as we were going through the motions of shoveling. He turned out to be Mr. Oriole, plodding his way toward his candy store at the top of the hill on Boston Road—not a Sanitation foreman after all.

Jerry relieved Krebs, who joined us on our return to Julie's apartment. The chill soon left us, and our blood started to circulate again, but the dense smoke tested our respiratory systems. As the cards were being dealt, there was hard knocking on the door. It was Jerry.

"This time it's the foreman, and there's two guys with him!"

Again there was a mad dash down the stairs. Gathering our shovels without missing a step, we rushed into the street and over a snow-covered path that brought us to the previous work area. The foreman and his adjutants approached to the sound of shovels burrowing into newly fallen snow. He looked at the pitiful patch we had dug. Perhaps he was cold; perhaps he was sympathetic to our pathetic appearance; he simply asked if we could work a little faster and then left quickly with his boys.

We shoveled a small area and then concluded once again that our winter clothing was no match for the combination of bitter cold and harassing snow. The wise thing to do was to return to the candy store.

Jack was delighted when we treated ourselves to hot chocolate and a candy bar, contemplating fat checks for our shoveling efforts.

A young man we didn't know, who had been unwilling to face the cold and snow to earn an honest day's wages for an honest day's work, was eavesdropping on our conversation. He questioned our ethics. "Why aren't you outside shoveling, if you're being paid to do it?"

"*You're* in here," Jerry replied. "Would you go out there in the wind, cold, and snow?"

"You thieves!" he charged. "You're defrauding the city government!"

We thieves received a very nice paycheck within a few weeks for confronting and outmaneuvering the elements.

From Racks to Tracks

I met my high school guidance counselor for the first time in my senior year. "You're passing all your subjects," he said, and congratulated me for having varsity football on my permanent record card. Without knowledge or foresight, I did not ask whether I qualified for any of the city colleges. As for input from my parents about my future, they were as green as the day they had trotted down the gangplank and into the New World. They were happy that I hadn't failed any subjects and that I was going to get a high school diploma.

The year was 1948. World War II veterans were also looking for work. There weren't many opportunities for a high school graduate with an academic diploma and no employable skills. Employment agencies demanded the first week's pay for a job that began and ended as a messenger boy. I pictured myself at the age of fifty running with message in hand to a young lady at a reception desk and then standing pathetically waiting for a reply. The employment agencies should have been called unemployment agencies.

I had no rich uncle. It was demoralizing to conscientiously seek employment only to find I wasn't needed. What was I going to do? Live with my parents for the rest of my life? A job counselor at the New York State Employment Agency reviewed my underwhelming credentials and my brother's oversized sport jacket. He sent me to the Loma Dress Corporation as a billing clerk for 75 cents an hour. Loma Dress was a cog in the same industry that my father slaved in and that I swore would never employ me. But at this point I was desperate.

The firm occupied the sixth and seventh floors of 501 Seventh Avenue, fronting on Broadway and 37th Street in Manhattan. The girl at the switchboard directed me to the office of the personnel manager, Mr. Friedman. Below a mass of wavy pearl-white hair, his bushy jet-black eyebrows were a

*My high school graduation photo, 1948. I received an academic diploma,
and Harvard wanted me, but I opted for the garment district.*

threatening sight. Between his thick curly lips skidded a cigar the size of my mother's rolling pin. He shot questions at me:

"Name?"

"Address?"

"Phone?"

"Social Security number?"

After the last answer, he growled, "OK, follow me."

Leaving the office I chased a trail of dense cigar smoke through two glass doors and into the blue-collar area. Through his exhaled smog I saw countless racks of dresses waiting to be picked up and delivered by truckers. The floor area was the size of five to seven James Monroe High School gymnasiums but was paved in gray concrete, not wood.

By now I was able to taste the cigar Mr. Friedman was sucking on. He led me to the Patricia Fair department, one of four Loma Dress Corporation departments. With the charm he had exhibited during my inquisition, he approached the head of the department.

"Here's your new man. Put him to work."

Mr. Margolis, who appeared to be a contemporary of Mr. Friedman's, greeted me with a number 2 pencil and then showed me how to bill a customer for the dresses he had ordered. First, he picked the dresses from inventory and placed them on a rack. When the rack was full, he rolled it to me. He had looped a card onto a dress hanger, identifying the buyer, the style number, the number of dresses, and their destination. I then billed the customer from a cost sheet next to my billing machine. Once the bill was completed, I sent the rack to the packers.

Frequent visits by the female office personnel broke the tedium of the job. One aggressive female asked me, "What are you doing this Sunday?"

Totally unaware that she was fishing for a date, I replied, "I'm playing softball."

"What are you doing after softball?"

I was about to answer when Mr. Margolis's bulging, red-veined eyeball accelerated my pencil to atone for the lost time.

Leering at the half-dressed models rushing from the showroom to their changing room behind me was my meager compensation for a paltry salary of 75 cents an hour. Four months into my job I thought it was time for a raise. I entered Mr. Friedman's office. The rumor that this man was an ex-member of a mob did not bolster my confidence. With trepidation, I said, "Mr. Friedman, I think I deserve a raise."

"It's the middle of the season," he snarled. "You'll get your raise at the end of the season."

I left wondering what the season was and when it ended. Meanwhile, I was getting an unwanted education. I learned to distinguish between the various dress styles and their fabrics. Faille, tissue faille, moiré, organdy, and satin composed the dating or party wear. Peplum and Dolman sleeves left my vocabulary as soon as they entered it. Cotton was an informal summer fabric, rayon an artificial fabric. The dresses were manufactured somewhere in Pennsylvania and brought first to our examining room, where they were inspected for poor workmanship or other defects. The floor was swarming with incoming and outgoing racks of hanging dresses.

After six months on the job, I had an appendectomy. Following a few weeks of recuperation, I returned to Loma Dress. The old chipped gray cement floor had been painted a shiny battleship gray. It was easier on the eyes but I knew that walking on it all day would still send me home with aching feet. I tried wearing sneakers once, but Mr. Friedman threatened to fire me if I wore them again.

Then I was assigned to the comptroller, who had temporary work for me. He brought me to a small, isolated room on the floor above my old space. It was furnished with a billing machine, a comfortable chair, and billing ledgers from the present year. Blank bills, numbered to correspond to the numbers in the year's ledgers, were stacked alongside them. My job was to duplicate the original bill on a blank bill with the same number, except that the prices of the dresses were different: they varied from $2 to $4 less per dress than on the original bill, according to a price code I was given. Ultimately, my work would indicate a smaller gross income for the year. Consequently, Loma Dress would show a smaller profit resulting in a smaller tax debt.

No longer did I receive visits from the female office personnel, no longer were the models trotting by partially dressed, but there was no job pressure on me. For the first time since I began work at Loma Dress, I sat on a comfortable chair and relaxed as I worked. The false receipts saved the company tens of thousands of dollars, while I was still waiting for "the end of the season." After three months, my job as head chef of the books expired.

Carol Craig Fashions, another Loma department, needed an all-around utility man. Dan Stein, the department head greeted me. "This is a completely different operation," he said. "It functions like the Book-of-the-Month-Club. We have salesmen calling on dress shops in small southern and midwestern towns. They offer the proprietor a plan that sends them a minimum of nine dresses per month in a variety of styles and sizes. You'll choose the dresses and bill the stores."

Dresses that sold well were reordered, unsuitable dresses were returned for credit. I chose the dresses based on the sense of style inculcated in me by my mother, whose concept of high fashion was a faded cotton housedress covered by a stained apron. In spite of this handicap, we had very few returns.

Saturday was open house. I was assigned to usher the owners of small stores who came in to select dresses from our reduced-price racks. It was not a day I looked forward to. The customers argued with me as if I had determined the style and price of the dresses. As a result of these skirmishes, I was offered a job as a traveling salesman for Carol Craig Fashions. Anticipating the same results that I had found in waiting for "the end of the season," I refused.

Essie Reid, a forty-year-old black woman, was the other billing clerk for the department. With her sense of humor she dissolved the dark shadows Mr. Friedman cast as he stalked the floor daily. Essie was a short mirror image of Hattie McDaniel, the maid in *Gone with the Wind*. On Mondays, she usually arrived late and exhausted but regaled me with a detailed recital of the sexual gymnastics she had engaged in over the weekend. Unaware that such antics existed, I was awed by every incredible detail. One Monday when she stepped in late as usual, I asked her why the left side of her hair bob was sticking up in the air as if it had just seen a ghost.

"That's the side I lay on when Lehman plays with me," she said.

"Plays? Plays what?" I asked innocently.

"I'd 'splain it to you, but I can see you have no 'sperience."

She called me a mouse, because I would bring a cheese sandwich every day. She would call out, "I'm bringing a trap to work so I can take you home."

I didn't know what the foul-smelling "chitlins" were that she brought for lunch. "What is that?" I asked. "It smells like someone just opened the door to an outhouse."

"The closest thing to your nose is your upper lip," she replied. "That's what you smell!"

One day, Amalee came floating into my blue-collar territory. She was an attractive and very well dressed new employee. "I'm going to be the new liaison between you and the front office."

Thank God, I thought, no more heel clicking and repulsive perfume. She was replacing Muriel, who had a rear like the trunk of a Buick convertible and a pair of breasts on the other side to balance her upright. I always knew that Muriel was coming as soon as she left the front office because I heard her heels drilling into the concrete floor. In contrast, Amalee's heels floated in the air. Always conscious of her weight, she had only a flimsy sandwich and black coffee for lunch at her desk.

One day, while I was munching my sandwich, she came running to me, flustered. "I just stained my new dress. It's from the coffee," she sobbed.

I looked at the stain at the epicenter of her left breast.

"Come with me to the examining room," I lustfully replied.

On a shelf in a closet, there were solvents that would eliminate any stain we might find on the dresses shipped by the contractors. She sat on a chair while my eager hands searched for a solvent. I returned with a white cotton rag soaked in a liquid and slowly began to rub. I couldn't believe she just sat there as I was fantasizing what was behind that stain and her damn bra. Happy, yet unhappy, to complete the task, I said, "Amalee, I think we got it." She cheerfully returned to her desk.

The following week I was invited to Amalee's birthday party at the office. I created a birthday card that I thought was extremely clever. I wrote: "To a girl who doesn't know where her mouth is/But certainly knows where her personality is," and I put the word *personality* in a drawing of a breast.

It flew right over her head and breast.

Murray, one of the Loma Dress packers, was a pathetic weasel. His beady eyes certainly classified him as a rodent. He was nominally a packer, but he eavesdropped on all conversations and ran to Mr. Friedman with any news concerning the possible formation of a union. Everyone was wise to him.

Mrs. Rubin, about seventy-five years old, was the matriarch of the royal family. Her sons ran the business. She visited Loma Dress every Friday, accompanied by her latest acquisition: a jewel, a fur, a pocketbook, or a hat. Sporting her bauble, pelt, or chapeau, she would first come to the office to parade before the girls who were earning no more than 90 cents an hour. Then she ambled into Blue Collar Land, where she would lurk behind the hanging dresses to spy on the employees. I asked the girl at the switchboard to call me whenever she arrived.

"Danny, Mrs. Rubin just came in."

When I saw her approaching, I stood arms akimbo at my billing machine and stared out of the window.

"Look et heem stendink dere *mitt* hisz hendz on hisz heeps doink nahtink!" she stage-whispered from her blind.

She knew that, at 75 cents per hour, I could stand there all year, and the company would still turn a huge profit. With a tug on my sleeve she emerged from her cover and asked, "Say, no vun tuld you vatt to do?"

I told her I was thinking. She immediately ran to Mr. Friedman to report my behavior. No response from Mr. Friedman.

The end of my career at Loma came on a beautiful Saturday autumn day. The sunlight greeted me as I reluctantly crawled up the subway steps. Upon reaching the street, instead of going toward Loma, I turned onto Broadway, where my favorite singer, Billy Eckstein, was on stage at the Paramount Theater. His rendition of *Roses* brought ear-splitting applause. When the movie ended, doormen opened all the exit doors leading to Broadway. Of all the seven million people living in New York City, Dan Stein, the head of Carol Craig Fashions, appeared, walking directly toward me. I couldn't avoid him. We confronted one another. Was it serendipity or just good luck?

"Why aren't you at work?" he asked.

"It's a nice day. I didn't feel like coming in."

Without saying a word, he continued to wherever he was going.

The following Monday, my time card was not in the rack. I asked Jack, the supervisor at the door, whether he had seen my time card.

"Friedman told me to put it over there, at the end of the rack. He said you're not to punch in."

When I went to get my time card, a trucker (delivery worker) passed through, pushing a rack of dresses with his fly wide open. Jack told him, "Button your fly. There are women working here."

"What the hell," the trucker answered. "I work like a horse. I might as well look like one."

The omnipresent Mrs. Rubin was somewhere among the dresses and heard this. "Dat's terrible," I heard from the other side of the dress rack.

After a chuckle, I grabbed my card and punched in. Dan Stein didn't say a word as I passed him on my way to pick orders, but I saw him slink out to the Patricia Fair department and use the phone.

Within a few minutes, the stench of cigar smoke told me that A. E. Friedman was in the area. He stopped, looked at Dan, and then looked at me.

"What's he doing here?" he roared. Dan didn't answer.

"All he does is fuck around with the girls in the office," Friedman continued.

I was furious. For my pathetic salary I could have "fucked around" with the girls all day (if I'd had the strength), and not a single cigar would have been lost from the box at the top of his desk.

"If I fuck around with the girls in the office, you know what you could do about it," I replied.

He knew.

"Get the hell out of here!" was his response.

Thus ended an unwanted but memorable career in the garment district.

I applied for unemployment checks, claiming that I had been fired. Within a week I received a letter stating that my employer had challenged my claim, and a hearing was necessary before I could receive payment. When I related my story, the referee said that my reply to Friedman had left him with no alternative but to fire me. He ruled that I was not to receive unemployment checks for a month.

Where does a guy get a job around here? Within a few weeks, my friend Al told me that the New York Central Railroad was hiring switch tenders and brakemen, no experience necessary, for $25 dollars a day! This salary was higher than my father's after he had slaved for thirty years in the garment district.

A letter directed us to report for a physical to an office in Grand Central Station. We met at the East 174th Street station for a subway ride to prosperity. Upon entering Grand Central Station, we made our way to the top of wide marble steps and turned left to a room where an aging Dr. Stevens was to give us the required physical.

Between rasping inhales and hacking coughs, Dr. Stevens, who appeared to be a fragile senior citizen, told Alvin to strip.

"You sit here," he said to me. "You," he rasped at Alvin, "Get up on the table."

Al, completely naked, stood up on the table, like *Manneken Pis,* the famous statue of a peeing boy, in Brussels.

"What are you doing up there?" growled the doctor.

"You told me to get up on the table," replied Alvin.

"Not like that, goddamn it! Get down, and sit on your ass!"

I could hardly contain my laughter, but this incident was merely a preview of things to come.

We left Dr. Stevens and followed an employee to a darkened room. There, a mole in slightly human shape sat behind a large table awaiting the next applicant. From a leather satchel resembling a doctor's medical bag, he proceeded to throw woolen yarn dolls of various colors into a spotlighted area on the table. We were to tell him the color of the doll. Aside from the physical exam, this was our most challenging task in qualifying for the job.

An oral reading of the *Book of Rules*, published by the New York Central Railroad, was our final exam. We were directed to a room occupied by a large conference table with matching chairs and a gold-stamped *Book of Rules* at each place. Seated around the table was a cast of characters—our competitors—who looked as if they had just recovered from sipping

Thunderbird throughout the night. Their complexions were scrubbed pale green, and their eyes seemed eager to hide behind their lids. My suspicions about their scholarship abilities were confirmed once the recitation was under way. We were each to read paragraphs from the *Book of Rules*.

As one candidate read, I was transported to third grade, where Ernie Gitlitz, a poor reader, held a yellow slip under each line he butchered. Another candidate had difficulty locating the sentence he had just completed reading. In preparation for my performance, I noted that I was to read a rule that extended through two pages while the others had read a short paragraph. I started to read and then looked up to find Alvin staring directly at me. We burst into laughter. The class was dismissed. We went home thinking that we had let pass a great opportunity.

In two weeks, we each received a letter telling us to report to the 72nd Street freight yard on the Hudson River. This was the site of a "shape-up": the names of employees were called from a list. If an employee didn't respond, the yardmaster continued down the list until he had a full crew. Ten to twelve men were called for each shift.

On the first day of work, we arrived at the 72nd Street freight yard at 8:00 pm. Through the darkness, I could see a large red neon Ripley Clothes sign behind me and, across the Hudson, the Palisades Amusement Park, a green neon Spry sign, and a red Alcoa Aluminum sign.

Yardmaster Brophy introduced us to our co-workers. I wondered how I was going to get along working with these men. This was not a profession that required a three-piece suit, but being well groomed was not in their repertoire. Their bloodshot eyes danced everywhere but toward my face, and they didn't offer a handshake in welcome. But the pay was good, and I was not there to find new friends—I had my own. I was ready to earn my salary.

There were three means of generating power for the freight yard engine: diesel fuel, a battery in the engine, and electricity from a third rail. The week before, one of the workers told us, a brakeman carrying a kerosene lantern in a tunnel had brushed it against the third rail. "He fried like a frankfurter," the man said. "When his shoes and socks were removed, you could see an outline on the soles of his feet where the nails of his boots were. By the way, if no one told you, wear bicycle clips at night. Frightened rats have run up a leg a few times."

At the end of our shift, Alvin and I each bought a pair of bicycle clips. I always made sure to keep my distance from those seemingly harmless wood-covered third rails.

In general, we worked four or five days a week. At times our names came up twice on the shape-up when some of the men did not report. This resulted in a double shift that added substantially to our paychecks.

Tending switches was easy. Each track had a name or a number. We sat in a seven-foot-square, spare wooden shack plastered with nudes, until a phone call came from yardmaster Brophy. "A train is approaching the yard," he would say and then tell us which switch to throw.

Braking, on the other hand, was a dangerous operation. Up to this point none of the shape-up men were assigned to braking. There were few braking assignments in the yard because the regular brakemen were dependable. Since we had no experience, we thought that braking a freight car wouldn't be assigned to us. Then one day I was assigned to fill in for an absent brakeman. Without training and only verbal instruction, I should have quit on the spot.

Empty freight cars were dispatched to eighteen different tracks spread like a delta at the south end of the yard. Each track held automobile cars, utility cars, and so on. Usually coal trains were exclusively coal cars and cattle trains only cattle cars.

An engine pushed a line of connected empty freight cars to the top of the Hill, an area that provided a slope so that a released freight car would roll down the rail and be switched onto the track where a departing train was being assembled. It was my turn. I climbed to the top of a freight car with a bat in my hand. The freight yard, the Hudson River, the New Jersey Palisades, the familiar signs, the entire landscape went in and out of focus. I held tightly to the braking wheel and my club. Am I really going to speed down the Hill on this metal monster and brake it? I asked myself.

The engine pushed my car forward. When it reached the slope, yardmaster Brophy released the car. It went slowly at first down the Hill, then gained momentum, and rolled toward the track of its eventual destination.

Get hold of yourself, I thought. There is no way you're going to get down the track in this state. Sawicz was at the switch that shunted my car to track eight. I forced a smile and nodded to him, hoping that he hadn't seen the panic on my face. I gripped the brake wheel as tightly as I could: it and I were one as the ride continued. A few deep inhales helped calm me down. I turned the brake wheel to slow the car down and then placed the club between two spokes of the wheel to pull the brake tighter for further deceleration. As my car approached the connected cars, I pulled as hard as I could on the club. The car slowed down, and I jumped off.

"Back foot first when you jump off," Brophy had told us, "or else you'll fall on your ugly face!"

The knuckle at the end of my car joined the knuckle on the waiting car with a thud. I was safe, both feet on the ground! At that moment, with a surge of relief, I swore I would never do it again. Fortunately, that was my first and last assignment as a brakeman.

The club used for slowing the freight car had a dual use. In the evening, gray-brown rats the size of cats would creep into the switch tenders' shack. At night, whenever I sat outside the shack or in the tunnel, I kept bicycle clips fastened at the bottoms of my dungarees. In the shack, I sat club in hand, waiting for one of these visitors to arrive. I couldn't concentrate on anything but those ugly rodents. When one came in, my bat went flying toward it. No matter how determined I was, no matter how I tried, I never scored a hit, but fortunately they scooted out of the shack.

One day Pat Riley was my partner at a group of very active switches. We'd had a pleasant evening reminiscing about our families and their struggles during the Great Depression.

"Maybe we'll work together tomorrow, Danny."

"I won't be in tomorrow. It's Yom Kippur."

Startled, he drew back, as if I had just returned from the hardware store with hammer and nails to impale his savior.

"You're not a Jewish lad, are you?"

"Yes, I am," I replied.

A few days later, Pat's son accompanied him to the freight yard to celebrate his first pint. Introductions, laughs, and handshakes were exchanged, but Alvin and I were passed by. These were not people who could accept a differing point of view lightly. Their tolerance ebbed and flowed with the amount of alcohol diluted in their plasma. We tried to avoid any controversy.

Alvin did get into a continuing argument with an old-timer named South. Alvin, who was varsity catcher for the James Monroe High School baseball team, correctly claimed that a catcher attempting to throw out a runner stealing second had to throw the ball to the right side of second base, so that the baseman could quickly swoop down and tag the runner. South insisted that the ball would hit the base runner and he'd be safe.

"The throw must be to the left of the base," insisted South.

"This gives an extra step to the base runner," replied Alvin.

"Ah, you don't know your head from your ass."

"Your head is up your ass," replied Alvin.

The show continued to the day we left.

In February 1951, my episode as a brakeman convinced me that I did not have the skill to maneuver a freight car running wild. I came to the end of the line and quit. A counselor at the unemployment insurance office tried to shunt me back to the garment district. I convinced her that I was not acceptable by telling her of my experience in Hades (Loma Dress Company). Employers showed no interest in hiring anyone who had no practical skills and was of draft age. Unemployment insurance checks paid for my few meager indulgences.

The Cold War, warming in the late 1940s, ignited and blazed into the Korean War on June 25, 1950. On September 27, 1951, I was ordered to report for induction into the army. On that day, I left my parents, my friends, and the characters, smells, sounds, and sidewalks of my neighborhood Camelot for an indelible two years of fun, grief, and hell.

978-0-595-44043-6
0-595-44043-6

Lightning Source UK Ltd.
Milton Keynes UK
UKOW051105311011

181225UK00002B/101/A